NAFTA and the NAALC
Twenty Years of North American Trade-Labour Linkage

NAFTA and the NAALC Twenty Years of North American Trade-Labour Linkage

Lance Compa
Tequila Brooks

This book was originally published as a monograph in the International Encyclopaedia of Laws/Labour Law and Industrial Relations.

General Editors: Roger Blanpain, Frank Hendrickx

Wolters Kluwer
Law & Business

Published by:
Kluwer Law International
PO Box 316
2400 AH Alphen aan den Rijn
The Netherlands
Website: www.kluwerlaw.com

Sold and distributed in North, Central and South America by:
Aspen Publishers, Inc.
7201 McKinney Circle
Frederick, MD 21704
United States of America
Email: customer.service@aspenpublishers.com

Sold and distributed in all other countries by:
Turpin Distribution Services Ltd.
Stratton Business Park
Pegasus Drive, Biggleswade
Bedfordshire SG18 8TQ
United Kingdom
Email: kluwerlaw@turpin-distribution.com

ISBN 97-890-411-6010-2

This title is available on www.kluwerlawonline.com

The Authors

Lance Compa is a Senior Lecturer at Cornell University's School of Industrial and Labor Relations in Ithaca, New York, where he teaches US labor law and international labor rights.

Before joining the Cornell faculty in 1997, Compa directed labor law research at the NAFTA Commission for Labor Cooperation. Prior to his 1995 appointment to the commission, Compa taught labor law, employment law, and international labor rights as a Visiting Lecturer at Yale Law School and the Yale School of Management. He also practiced international labor law for unions and human rights organizations in Washington, DC.

Compa has written widely on trade unions, international labor rights, and other topics for a variety of law reviews and journals of general interest, magazines and newspapers. His most recent book project (with co-authors) is *International Labor Law: Cases and Materials on Workers' Rights in the Global Economy* (West Law Group, 2008), a 1000-page textbook for use in law schools and social science graduate programs. Other recent publications include 'From Chile to Vietnam: International Labour Law and Workers' Rights in International Trade,' a chapter in *Critical Legal Perspectives on Global Governance: Liber Amicorum David M. Trubek,* Gráinne de Búrca, Claire Kilpatrick and Joanne Scott, eds. (Hart Publishing 2014), 'A Glass Half Full: The NAFTA Labor Agreement and Cross-Border Labor Action' in George J. Andreopoulos, ed., *Concepts and Strategies in International Human Rights* (New York, Peter Lance Publishing, 2002) and 'NAFTA's Labor Side Agreement and International Labor Solidarity,' in Peter Waterman and Jane Wills, eds., *Place, Space and the New Labour Internationalisms* (Blackwell Publishers, 2001). Compa wrote the 2005 Human Rights Watch report *Blood, Sweat, and Fear: Workers' Rights in US Meat and Poultry Plants*, and is also author of the 2000 HRW report *Unfair Advantage: Workers' Freedom of Association in the United States under International Human Rights Standards* (republished by Cornell University Press in August 2004 with a new introduction and conclusion). In addition to his studies of workers' rights in the United States, Professor Compa has conducted workers' rights investigations and reports on Cambodia, Chile, China, Haiti, Guatemala, Mexico, Sri Lanka and other developing countries.

After law school and before turning to international labor law practice and teaching, Compa worked for many years as a trade union organizer and negotiator; first for the United Electrical Workers (UE), and then for the Newspaper Guild. While on the UE staff, he was involved in organizing and collective bargaining negotiations in multinational firms like General Electric and Westinghouse, and at many medium and small-sized firms throughout the United States. At the Newspaper Guild, he represented editorial, business, and production employees at the *Washington Post,* the *Baltimore Sun,* Agence France-Presse, and other news organizations.

Compa is a 1969 graduate of Fordham University, a 1973 graduate of Yale Law School, and a member of the Massachusetts Bar. He also undertook studies abroad at the Institut d'Études Politiques in Paris, France (1967–1968) and at the Universidad de Chile in Santiago, Chile (1972–1973).

Tequila Brooks is an attorney and international employment policy specialist living and working in the Washington, DC area. She is a member of the ILO's Research Network on Improving workers' rights in globalizing economies, serves as an expert advisor on gender and workplace issues for the ABA-UNDP International Legal Resource Center, is a frequent contributor to the American Bar Association International Employment Lawyer and serves as a lecturer on international labor and trade matters. Her publications include 'An Introduction to Mexican Workers' Compensation Law for the US Workers' Compensation Practitioner' (*IAIABC Journal*, fall 2003) and 'Cross-Border Workers' Compensation and Social Security Policy in North America: An Analysis of the NAFTA Trucking Dispute through the eyes of a Workers' Compensation Practitioner' (*IAIABC Journal*, spring 2005).

Ms Brooks served as Labor Law Advisor with the North American Commission for Labor Cooperation Secretariat for five and a half years. While with the North American CLC, Ms Brooks co-authored a study comparing the laws impacting migrant agricultural workers in Canada, Mexico and the United States (2003) and was primary author and project coordinator of a tri-national clear language guide to labor and employment laws for migrant workers in North America (2004). She also conducted and supervised research in the areas of employment discrimination, equal pay and employment equity law and policy and workers' compensation and occupational safety and health laws in North America, and was responsible for spearheading specialized focus groups and meetings on migrant worker issues, comparative workplace discrimination and equal pay law, women workers' issues and special issues involving women workers and long-term disabilities.

Prior to joining the CLC, Ms Brooks represented low income workers in workers' compensation and unemployment cases in the state of New Mexico. Ms Brooks received her JD and MA in Latin American Studies from the University of New Mexico in Albuquerque, New Mexico in 1997 and her BA from St John's College in Annapolis, Maryland in 1991. She has an LL.M. in International and Comparative Law from the George Washington University School of Law (2010) in Washington, DC, an LL.M. in International and European Labour Law from Tilburg University Law School in Tilburg, Netherlands (2012) and a Certificate in International Human Rights Law from Oxford University (2007).

Table of Contents

The Authors 3

List of Abbreviations 11

The NAFTA/NAALC from 2009 to 2013 – the First Half of the Obama Era and the NAALC at 20 15

Chapter 1. Background 20

§1. Negotiating NAFTA 20

§2. Negotiating the Side Agreements 21

§3. The Battle over NAFTA 21

§4. The NAFTA Framework 23

§5. Introducing the NAALC 24

§6. National Contexts 26

Chapter 2. Norms, Institutions, and Operations of the NAALC 30

§1. Preamble and Objectives 30

§2. Labor Principles 30

§3. NAALC Obligations 32

§4. Institutional Structure and Procedures 35

I. The Commission for Labor Cooperation: Ministerial Council and Secretariat 35

II. National Administrative Offices (NAOs) 37

III. Cooperative Consultations 43

IV. Evaluation Committees of Experts 44
V. Arbitral Panels 46

§5. Special Provisions for Canada 48

§6. NAALC Cooperative Activities 49

§7. Secretariat Research Reports 50

Chapter 3. NAALC Submissions and Cases 53

§1. Overview 53

§2. Cases Involving Alleged Workers' Rights Violations in Mexico 57
I. *Honeywell and General Electric* (US NAO cases nos. 940001 and 940002) 57
II. *Sony* (US NAO case no. 940003) 59
III. *Pesca Union* (US case no. 9601) 60
IV. *Maxi-Switch* (US NAO case no. 9602) 61
V. *Pregnancy Testing in the Maquiladora* (US NAO case no. 9701) 61
VI. *Han Young* (US NAO case no. 9702) 63
VII. *Echlin/ITAPSA* (US NAO case no. 9703; Canada NAO case no. 98-1) 64
VIII. *Aerovías de Mexico Flight Attendants* (US NAO case no. 9801) 65
IX. *TAESA* (US NAO case no. 9901) 66
X. *Autotrim/Breed Technologies* (US NAO case no. 2000-01) 67
XI. *North American OSH Working Group* 70
XII. *Duro Bag* (US NAO case no. 2001-01) 71
XIII. *Puebla (Tarrant and Matamoros Garment)* (US NAO case no. 2003-01 and Canada NAO case no. 2003-1) 72
XIV. *Yucatan-Markey Tex and Coco Tex* (US NAO case no. 2004-01) 76
XV. *Mexican Labor Law Reform* (US NAO case no. 2005-01) 78
XVI. *Mexican Pilots – ASPA* (US NAO case no. 2005-02, Canada NAO case no. 2005-1) 80
XVII. *Hidalgo – Child Labor at Rubie's de Mexico* (US NAO case no. 2005-03) 80
XVIII. *USW – Coahuila Pasta de Conchos Copper Mine Disaster Case* (US NAO case no. 2006-01) 83
XIX. *Sindicato Mexicano de Electricistas – SME* (US NAO case no. 2011-01) 86

§3. Cases Involving Alleged Workers' Rights Violations in the United States 89

I. *Sprint* (Mexico NAO case no. 9501) 89
II. *Solec, Inc.* (Mexico NAO case no. 9801) 91
III. *Washington State Apple Industry* (Mexico NAO case no. 9802) 91
IV. *DeCoster Egg Farm* (Mexico NAO case no. 9803) 92
V. *Yale Labor Department–INS Memorandum of Understanding* (Mexico NAO case no. 9804; Canada NAO case no. 98-2) 93
VI. *Labor Policy Association and Section 8(a)(2) of the NLRA* (Canada NAO case no. 99-1) 94
VII. *New York Workers' Compensation* (Mexican NAO Submission 2001-1) 97
VIII. *North Carolina H-2A Workers* (Mexican NAO Submission 2003-1) 98
IX. *Hoffman Plastics and the Inter-American Court of Human Rights Advisory Opinion on the Rights of Undocumented Workers* (Inter-American Court of Human Rights Advisory Opinion OC-18/03) 100
X. *H-2B Visa Workers* (Mexico NAO Submission 2005-1) 102
XI. *North Carolina Public Service Workers* (Mexican NAO case no. 2006-2) 105
XII. *H-2B Carnival and Fair Workers* (Mexican NAO case no. 2011-1) 107
XIII. *Alabama Anti-Immigration Law HB 56* (Mexican NAO case no. 2012-1) 111
XIV. *Porteadores del Noroeste SA de CV* v. *The Industrial Commission of Arizona* (Arizona Court of Appeals 2014) 113

§4. Cases Involving Alleged Workers' Rights Violations in Canada 115
I. *McDonald's* (US NAO case no. 9803) 115
II. *Canadian Rural Letter Carriers* (US NAO case no. 9804) 116

Chapter 4. The NAALC and ILO Standards 117

Chapter 5. Evaluating the NAALC 119

§1. Contrasting Views of the NAALC 119

§2. Trade Union Views 120

§3. Employer Views 123

§4. Independent Review Committee's Views 125

§5. Academic Views 127

Chapter 6. Continuing Controversy over NAFTA and the NAALC 129

Chapter 7. The NAALC and International Labor Solidarity 136

§1. Cross-border Collaboration 136

§2. Inside an NAALC Case 137

§3. Coalition Building 139

§4. Cross-border Bargaining 141

§5. Prospects for Convergence 143

§6. Key Criticisms and Responses 144

§7. Impact of the NAALC 146

§8. Is the NAALC a 'Model'? 147

Chapter 8. The OECD Guidelines: An Alternative to the NAALC and the Labor Provisions of Free Trade Agreements 151

§1. Background on the OECD Guidelines 151

§2. Complaint Procedure under the OECD Guidelines 152

§3. Recent North American Complaints Filed under the OECD Guidelines 154
I. Mexico: the *Continental (Euzkadi)* case (2002–2005) 155
II. Mexico: the *Michelin/Uniroyal* case (2004–?) 155
III. Mexico: the *Grupo Modelo* case (2008–2010) 156
IV. Mexico: the *América Móvil* case (2011–2012) 156
V. Mexico: the *Excellon La Platosa* mine case (2012–2013) 156
VI. Mexico: the *PKC Group* case (2012–2013) 159
VII. Canada: the *UPM Kymmene* case (2004–2005) 160
VIII. Canada: the *Accor* case (2010-2012) 160
IX. United States: the *Trico Marine Services* case (2001–2002) 160

Chapter 9. Labor Provisions of Post-NAFTA Free Trade Agreements in North America 162

§1. Background on Post-NAALC Labor Provisions in North American FTAs 162
I. Canadian Labor Cooperation Agreements 162
II. US Free Trade Agreement Labor Chapters 162
III. Mexican Free Trade Agreements 163

§2. ILO Standards and Labor Provisions in Post-NAALC North American FTAs 164

§3. Cooperation and Aid under Labor Provisions of Post-NAALC North American FTAs 165

§4. Complaint Procedures under the Labor Provisions of Post-NAALC North American FTAs 166

§5. Complaints Filed under Post-NAALC North American FTA Labor Provisions 167
I. CAFTA-DR: Guatemala (US OTLA 2008–01) 167
II. Peru: the *SINAUT* case (US OTLA 2010–2013) 168
III. Bahrain: the *Pearl Roundabout* case (US OTLA 2011–01) 169
IV. CAFTA-DR: Dominican Republic – the *Haitian Sugarcane Workers* case (US OTLA 2011–03) 170
V. CAFTA-DR: Honduras (US OTLA 2012–01) 172

Selected Publications 175

Selected Websites 183

Index 185

Table of Contents

List of Abbreviations

Frequently used abbreviations; others are explained in the text.

AFA	Association of Flight Attendants (US)
AFL-CIO	American Federation of Labor and Congress of Industrial Organizations
ANAD	*Asociación Nacional de Abogados Democráticos* – National Democratic Lawyers Association (Mexico)
ASSA	*Asociación Sindical de Sobrecargos de Aviación* – Flight Attendants Union (Mexico)
CAB	Conciliation and Arbitration Board (Mexico)
CAFTA-DR	Dominican Republic-Central American Free Trade Agreement
CANACAR	*Cámara Nacional del Autotransporte de Carga* – National Chamber of Cargo Transporters (Mexico)
CAW	Canadian Auto Workers
CDM	*Centro de Derechos de Mujeres* (Honduras)
CDM	*Centro de los Derechos del Migrante* (US)
COLSIBA	Coalition of Latin American Banana Unions
CONAPRED	*Consejo Nacional para Prevenir la Discriminación* – National Council to Prevent Discrimination (Mexico)
CPP	Consular Partnership Program (US and Mexico)
CTM	*Confederación de Trabajadores de México* – Mexican Workers Confederation
CWA	Communications Workers of America (US)
ECE	Evaluation Committee of Experts
EU	European Union

List of Abbreviations

FAT	*Frente Auténtico del Trabajo* – Authentic Labor Front
FCPA	Foreign Corrupt Practices Act (US)
FJF	Farmworker Justice Fund (US)
FLL	Federal Labor Law (Mexico)
FLOC	Farm Labor Organizing Committee (US)
FMCSA	Federal Motor Carrier Safety Administration (US)
FTA	Free Trade Agreement
FTAA	Free Trade Agreement of the Americas
ILO	International Labor Organization
ILRF	International Labor Rights Fund
LCA	Labor Cooperation Agreement (Canada)
LFPED	*Ley Federal para Prevenir y Eliminar la Discriminación* - Federal Law on the Prevention and Elimination of Discrimination (Mexico)
LPA	Labor Policy Association
NAAEC	North American Agreement on Environmental Cooperation
NAALC	North American Agreement on Labor Cooperation
NAFTA	North American Free Trade Agreement
NAO	National Administrative Office
NCP	National Contact Point
NGO	Non-governmental organization
NLRA	National Labor Relations Act (US)
NLRB	National Labor Relations Board (US)
OTLA	Office of Trade and Labor Affairs
PRI	*Partido Revolucionario Institucional* – Institutional Revolutionary Party
ProDESC	*Proyecto de Derechos Económicos Sociales y Culturales* – Economic, Social and Cultural Rights Project (Mexico)
SAWP	Seasonal Agricultural Worker Program – Canada

SNTMMSRM	*Sindicato Nacional de Trabajadores Mineros, Metalúrgicos, Siderúrgicos y Similares de la República Mexicana* – National Union of Mining, Metalurgical, Iron and Steel Workers of the Mexican Republic
STRM	*Sindicato de Telefonistas de la República Mexicana* – Mexican Telephone Union
TPP	Trans-Pacific Partnership
UAW	United Auto Workers (US)
UNT	*Unión Nacional de Trabajadores* – National Union of Workers (Mexico)
US CIB	US Council for International Business

List of Abbreviations

The NAFTA/NAALC from 2009 to 2013 – the First Half of the Obama Era and the NAALC at 20

Institutionally, it could be argued that the NAALC ended its 20th anniversary on a low point. On August 20, 2010, the North American Commission for Labor Cooperation Secretariat closed temporarily. As of the end of April 2014, the office had not reopened and the North American Council of Labor Ministers had not met since 2010, although the Presidents of Mexico, Canada and the US held trilateral summits in Washington, DC in April 2012 and in Toluca, Mexico in February 2014. The three labor ministers and their international labor designees encounter one another frequently in regional and international fora such as the G20 Labor Ministers Summits and the annual ILO conference. The CLC Secretariat produced what may be its final report (on migrant workers' rights) after the office closed, in late 2010.

Although the election of the progressive administration of Barack Obama in the US in November 2008 and the start of his administration in January 2009 hearkened a new era of potential for labor petitions under the NAALC, only one NAALC complaint was filed with the US Office of Trade and Labor Affairs (OTLA – the new designee for the National Administrative Office) regarding labor law enforcement in Mexico. The complaint was dual filed with the Canadian NAO. As of the end of April 2014, neither the Canadian NAO nor the US OTLA had issued a report on the complaint. The aftermath of the 2003 Puebla complaint had not been positive. In September 2012, the Worker Rights Center in Puebla closed its doors and its Executive Director was forced to flee to Canada and ultimately settle outside Puebla as a result of threats of violence and death. Violence against women and female human and labor rights activists in Puebla and the rest of Mexico continued unabated.

Despite these less than auspicious developments under the NAALC during President Obama's first term, on September 18, 2012, outgoing US Secretary of State Hillary Clinton and her Mexican counterpart Patricia Espinosa entered into a wide-ranging Memorandum of Understanding for the Promotion of Gender Equality, the Empowerment of Women and Women's Human Rights. Migrant labor activists in the US continued to file complaints with the Mexican NAO regarding treatment of immigrant and agricultural workers in the United States as part of national and international campaigns to effect changes in US law. Two such complaints were filed with the Mexican NAO during Barack Obama's first term of office – the 2011 Migrant Carnival and Fair Workers petition and the 2012 Alabama Anti-Immigrant

Law (HB 56) petition. At the end of the six-year presidential administration of Mexican President Felipe Calderón in 2012, the Mexican NAO issued a highly diplomatic, but also critical, report on petitions filed about treatment of migrant workers in the US over the previous decade. The Mexican NAO also issued a report on the North Carolina Public Workers complaint filed in 2006 at the same time. On April 3, 2014, US Secretary of Labor Thomas E. Perez and Mexican Secretary of Labor and Social Welfare Jesús Alfonso Navarrete Prida entered into a Joint Declaration concerning NAALC complaints filed with the Mexican NAO about treatment of migrant workers in the US in 2003, 2005 and 2011. Migrant activists in the US continued to file multiple regional and international petitions with the Mexican NAO, the Inter-American Commission on Human Rights (IACHR) and the International Labor Organization (ILO), utilizing such petitions with regional institutions to support human rights campaigns to improve the lives of migrant workers in the US. In February 2014, a coalition of migrant advocates from Canada, Mexico, the US, Guatemala and El Salvador requested a hearing before the IACHR to address human and labor rights violations encountered by migrant workers in the Canadian Seasonal Agricultural Worker Program (SAWP) and US H-2A and H-2B migrant worker visa programs.

Turning away from the NAALC process, Mexican trade unions pursued a strategy of filing complaints under the OECD Guidelines for Multinational Enterprises rather than the NAALC to address labor conditions at the Mexican operations of Canadian, international and Mexican-owned multinational companies. Two important complaints were filed with the Canadian and Mexican NCPs in 2012 relating to the Mexican operations of the Canadian mining company Excellon and of the Finnish auto parts company PKC. These were preceded by complaints filed under the OECD Guidelines with the Mexican NCP regarding failure to comply with labor and employment standards by the Mexican multinational beer conglomerate Grupo Modelo at Mexican operations and against the Mexican telecom company América Móvil regarding its operations in Central America. While it is rare for complaints under the OECD Guidelines to result in written reports like those produced under the NAALC, the 2012 Excellon complaint filed with the Canadian and Mexican National Contact Points (NCPs) under the OECD Guidelines touched on a wide range of issues involved in mining operations, including not only labor issues but economic development, land use, community relations, human rights, financial reporting and environmental issues. These complaints show the fundamental weakness of international dispute resolution processes that focus solely on a single issue (such as labor) to the exclusion of interconnected issues in complex situations.

With the highly contested and partial implementation of the NAFTA trucking provisions by the US in 2007 and 2011, Mexican trucking companies began operating more widely in US territory with concomitant jurisdictional issues arising when Mexican truck drivers suffered work-related injuries while operating in US territory. In January 2014, the Arizona Court of Appeals issued an important decision addressing the issues of whether a Mexican employer is required to obtain Arizona workers' compensation insurance while operating in the State of Arizona and whether a Mexican worker who is injured in the US is entitled to compensation for medical treatment of work-related injuries not covered under Mexican laws governing compensation for work-related injuries. This case, entitled *Porteadores del*

Noroeste SA de CV v. *Industrial Commission of Arizona/Valenzuela* (Arizona Court of Appeals, 14 January 2014), is included in this monograph although it does not relate to a NAALC complaint because the employer attempted (unsuccessfully) to argue that the NAFTA and NAALC pre-empted State of Arizona jurisdiction over a Mexican trucking employer in a case involving compensation for work-related injuries to a Mexican employee incurred in Arizona. This case shows that the lack of effective institutions and policy making at the North American level can have an impact on individual workers' lives, as the injured worker involved was required to wait close to four years for full compensation for medical treatment for his work-related injuries.

Books published in 2013 about the North American Region discussing issues related to labor, employment and migrant labor market issues had titles like *North American Integration: An Institutional Void in Migration, Security and Development* (Genna and Mayer-Foulkes 2013), showing just how little the promise of regional institutions to improve the lives of ordinary people had progressed during the first two decades of the NAFTA era. Similarly, much of the dialogue about the NAFTA/NAALC and the number of jobs lost or gained had changed little over a two decade period, with entrenched interests making the same arguments they had made before the NAFTA and NAALC went into effect in January 1994. President Obama's campaign promise to 'renegotiate the NAFTA' never materialized. In fact, the failure of NAALC institutions to protect the rights of workers in Mexico to organize and collectively bargain may have been a factor in the persistent 8-1 wage differential between the US and Mexico. Persistent obstacles to the exercise of the right to associate and collectively bargain as well as the continuance of the protection contract system in Mexico kept wages low and may have contributed to ongoing Mexico-US migration and entry of Mexican workers into the drug trade as a way to improve their wages and living standards.

While it might be argued that the NAALC closed 2013 on a low note institutionally, after 20 years the controversial NAFTA labor side agreement's positive impact on the incorporation of labor in trade agreements cannot be denied. Each of the three NAFTA partners continued to negotiate bilateral and multilateral free trade agreements. By the end of 2013, Mexico had implemented 12 trade agreements with 44 nations, the US had implemented 13 agreements with 19 nations and Canada had implemented 9 agreements with 13 nations. After 1994, almost no trade agreement negotiated by the US or Canada was without a labor provision. In the United States, at least one complaint filed under the labor chapter of an FTA (the Dominican Republic-Central American Free Trade Agreement – or CAFTA-DR) almost reached the arbitration stage, and a number of other petitions resulted in promising reports and follow-up actions that greatly expanded on and improved the area of FTA labor jurisprudence initiated by NAALC reports in the 1990s and 2000s. Since the reports issued in response to complaints filed under post-NAALC labor provisions of US and Canadian FTAs form part of the jurisprudence and practice that may be considered and applied in subsequent NAALC reports, the 2014 update to this monograph introduces a new chapter discussing these labor provisions, complaints and reports.

In addition to the incorporation of labor provisions in Canadian and US FTAs, the NAALC ushered in an era in which the idea that labor must be included as an integral component in international trade and financial policy discussions is no longer contested in many international policy and legal circles. The world of international trade and labor policy has been almost completely transformed in the 20 years since the NAALC went into effect. While the World Trade Organization (WTO) for the most part did not incorporate labor standards into its legal framework, relations between the ILO and Bretton Woods Institutions such as the World Bank, International Monetary Fund (IMF) and International Financial Corporation (IFC) thawed somewhat. Since 2008, G20 Labor Ministers have been meeting with G20 Finance Ministers together and separately to tackle employment and financial issues in the wake of the 2008 financial crash and subsequent global financial crisis. The ILO has been a prominent presence in these meetings. Since 2009, the IFC and the ILO have partnered on an international program called Better Work with the aim of improving labor compliance and competitiveness in global supply chains. Better Work operates in Cambodia, Haiti, Indonesia, Jordan, Lesotho, Nicaragua and Vietnam. In early 2014, Better Work was on the cusp of becoming operational in Bangladesh, after a series of horrific factory disasters in that country in 2012 and 2013. The issue of youth unemployment, which was recognized as a major international crisis after the 2008 economic crash and subsequent Arab Spring, became a factor in deepening the relationship between the ILO and other international organizations as the international community strives to create jobs for unemployed youth the world over. In June 2012, the ILO, OECD, IMF and the World Bank issued a joint report entitled *Boosting Jobs and Living Standards in G20 countries*, demonstrating just how different global financial policy making is in 2014 as compared to the pre-NAALC era.

The era of retrospective literature about the NAALC began, with authors like Tamara Kay in her 2011 book *NAFTA and the Politics of Labor Transnationalism* demonstrating that trade unionists in Canada, the US and Mexico were able to overcome national, economic, cultural and racial differences to create a truly transnational labor movement. Even in the pessimistically titled tome *An Institutional Void*, essayists pointed to civil society actors in Canada, Mexico and the US crossing racial, national and cultural divides to improve health care and human rights of immigrants. While many of the same systemic labor problems that existed in the pre-NAALC era continued to plague workers in North America – such as protection labor contracts in Mexico and unequal treatment of migrant workers in the US and Canada – the first 20 years of the NAALC ended with a conference in late 2013 that had a shimmer of hope for improvement of worker rights and social dialogue in the North American region. The shimmer of hope was the participation of the Mexican *Unión Nacional de Trabajadores* (National Workers' Union or UNT), an independent union federation, in a labor conference co-organized by the ILO in Mexico City in October 2013 at which Mexico's recently elected President Enrique Peña Nieto spoke. At the beginning of 2014, relations between progressive administrations in Mexico and the US continued to thaw in the area of diplomacy on labor matters, with hints at the February 2014 US National Advisory Committee for Labor Provisions of US Free Trade Agreements that several technical cooperation projects were in the works, including one on protection of women from workplace discrimination in Mexico. Between September 2009 and February 2014, the US Government funded an initiative to eliminate child labor in agriculture in Mexico.

The economic and labor market effects of the NAFTA were as contested and controversial as they were when the free trade agreement was being negotiated over 20 years prior.

Finally, the end of the NAALC's first 20 years and the beginning of the first half of the Obama era hearkened the new era of the Trans-Pacific Partnership (TPP), a free trade agreement with its genesis in the southern hemisphere which expanded to include all three North American partners by fall of 2012 had entered negotiations to be members of the TPP. The other trade partners in the TPP were Australia, Brunei, Chile, Japan, Malaysia, New Zealand, Peru, Singapore and Vietnam. At the end of April 2014, the TPP was still under negotiation. Civil society actors and both parties in the US Congress criticized the TPP negotiation process as being completely non-transparent. The final labor provisions of the TPP will likely have an impact on the implementation and application of the NAALC in coming years.

Chapter 1. Background

§1. Negotiating NAFTA

1. The North American Free Trade Agreement (NAFTA) was negotiated in 1990–1992 during the administrations of US President George Bush, Mexican President Carlos Salinas, and Canadian Prime Minister Brian Mulroney. Each had a mix of economic and political motives for moving toward a continental trade treaty.

2. President Bush was a Republican whose party is committed to a free market ideology. He drew much of his political support and campaign contributions from American business interests eager to make permanent, by means of a trade agreement, neoliberal economic reforms already undertaken by President Salinas. The Mexican president had begun a program of reducing tariffs, opening up sectors of the economy to foreign investors, privatizing state enterprises like *Teléfonos de México*, and other economic reforms.

3. US corporate and banking circles were concerned about the close 1988 election almost won by social democratic candidate Cuauhtemoc Cárdenas. According to many analysts, Cárdenas really won the election, but Salinas prevailed through vote fraud. 'Locking in' Mexico's neoliberal economic reforms with a trade treaty was seen as a guarantee that any future president would not reverse them.

4. Prime Minister Mulroney's conservative government in Canada also adhered to free market ideology. Although Canada and the United States had signed their own free trade agreement in 1988 and most of Canada's trade was with the United States, Canada did not want to be left out of a hemispheric trade accord. Any potential advantage to trade with Mexico might slip to the United States if Canada did not join NAFTA. For his part, President Salinas declared his intention to propel Mexico into the 'First World' with a trade agreement that would promote new foreign investments, mainly from the United States, in business in Mexico.

5. These three heads of state signed the NAFTA in August 1992. NAFTA was ratified in short order by the Mexican Congress, and in May 1993 by Canada's parliament. But it took more than one year for the US Congress to act. The delay was attributable to a sharp struggle in the United States not just over NAFTA itself, but also over NAFTA's social dimension, the North American Agreement on Labor Cooperation (NAALC). Congress finally approved NAFTA in November, 1993, and the trade agreement – along with 'side agreements' on labor and environmental matters – went into effect on 1 January 1994.

6. The NAFTA text contained only a passing reference in its preamble to advancing labor rights in North America. The Bush–Salinas–Mulroney negotiators reached a Memorandum of Understanding on labor rights and labor standards at the same time they agreed on NAFTA, but this MOU spoke only of cooperative programs and technical assistance, with no effort to set out norms and obligations to which the countries committed themselves.

§2. Negotiating the Side Agreements

7. The three leaders announced agreement on NAFTA just as the 1992 US presidential race was heating up. Labor, environmental and human rights organizations pressured Democratic party candidate Bill Clinton to repudiate NAFTA in his campaign for the presidency. They charged that the agreement favored multinational corporations and investors at the expense of workers and the environment, and they dismissed the labor MOU as meaningless. At the same time, however, Clinton's candidacy relied on support from important elements of the corporate and investment banking communities who supported NAFTA.

8. Responding to both pro- and anti-NAFTA forces, Clinton opted to support NAFTA if side agreements dealing with labor and the environment were added to the package sent to Congress for approval. After winning the November 1992 election and taking office in January 1993, the new Clinton Administration began negotiations on labor and environmental side agreements with Mexico and Canada. Negotiations commenced in March 1993. The United States first proposed a far-reaching labor accord with a strong, independent commission and broad availability of trade sanctions to enforce labor standards. Canada and Mexico rejected this approach, calling instead for a small administrative secretariat with a modest research agenda, and no economic sanctions under any circumstances, and complete preservation of national sovereignty over labor matters.

9. The parties concluded negotiations with final agreements in August, 1993 on the NAALC and a companion environmental accord, the North American Agreement on Environmental Cooperation (NAAEC). The labor accord reflected a compromise of the countries' initial positions. It created a secretariat with a modest degree of independence, but subject to oversight by the labor ministers. It set forth eleven labor principles that defined the subject matter of the NAALC, and created a complaint mechanism for private parties to initiate cases under the agreement. The use of trade sanctions was included in the NAALC, but only in very narrowly defined circumstances. Sovereignty was maintained over the substance of each country's labor laws and labor law enforcement system, but the countries opened themselves up to a process of review, evaluation and dispute resolution on the effectiveness of their enforcement. The NAALC was now part of the NAFTA package sent to the US Congress for a final vote.

§3. The Battle over NAFTA

10. In Canada, trade unions in the Canadian Labour Congress and allied civil society groups in a coalition called Common Frontiers led an effort to stop NAFTA's approval. They cited losses of manufacturing jobs under the US–Canada Free Trade Agreement, threats to Canadian cultural identity (notwithstanding the exclusion of cultural sectors from the trade agreement), and pressures on Canada's social programs as likely effects of NAFTA. They pointed in particular to the dangers of a US style marketized health care system, and the threat of importing such a system in place of Canada's socialized health insurance plan. However, the Mulroney government enjoyed a majority in the Canadian parliament, and easily passed legislation approving NAFTA.

11. In Mexico, the ruling Institutional Revolutionary Party (PRI) controlled the levers of government and had the support of the largest business and labor federations linked to the PRI in a longstanding corporatist labor relations system. The only voices of dissent over NAFTA came from small opposition groups such as the independent *Frente Auténtico del Trabajo* labor organization and grass roots NGOs like *Equipo Pueblo*, a research and advocacy group led by worker and community activists. These and other organizations came together in the *Red Mexicana ante el Libre Comercio* (RMALC), or Mexican Network before Free Trade (many Americans mistakenly thought the name of the group meant 'anti-free trade,' not appreciating the difference in Spanish between *anti* and *ante*).

12. RMALC voiced concerns about effects on Mexican workers and farmers by a sudden unleashing of US corporate and agribusiness power in Mexico. However, the PRI and the dominant labor federations dismissed RMALC's criticisms as the work of fringe groups supported by US protectionist forces. The FAT, Equipo Pueblo, and other NGOs in the RMALC coalition never actually opposed NAFTA. They offered trenchant critiques and asked for social reforms in Mexico to accompany economic reforms. However, the PRI apparatus ignored these calls and approved NAFTA overwhelmingly in the Mexican congress.

13. On a slogan of 'Not This NAFTA!' and a charge that the labor side agreement was 'toothless,' the American labor movement and labor allies tried to defeat the trade agreement, even with the NAALC attached to it. Jobs and wages were the key issues in US labor opposition to NAFTA. Unions argued that the trade agreement would impel US firms to relocate manufacturing operations to Mexico, lured by low wages and unenforced labor standards. Some NAFTA opponents argued that more than one million US jobs would be lost if NAFTA was approved by Congress.

14. Trade unionists and their allies said that the NAALC created no new, higher labor standards to which countries must adhere and no plan for upward harmonization of labor standards. By emphasizing enforcement of existing law, rather than improvement, the NAALC 'locked in' low labor standards. Critics pointed mainly at low minimum wage, child labor, and occupational safety and health laws in Mexico, compared with standards in the United States and Canada. While they recognized that Mexico could not immediately achieve labor standards equal to those of its trading partners, these critics argued that the NAALC should promote a process of upward harmonization to raise standards in Mexico and that it failed to do so.

15. Criticism of the NAALC during the battle over NAFTA's congressional approval also focused on the lack of a strong enforcement mechanism like that protecting investors and intellectual property holders. Bureaucracy, procedural timetables that would inevitably produce delays, and other elements of the NAALC also were targets of criticism. Those pointing to the NAALC as another reason for Congress to reject NAFTA cited another idiosyncratic feature of the labor accord, the division of the NAALC's 11 'labor principles' into three tiers with unequal treatment under its review, evaluation and dispute resolution mechanisms.

16. The trade union view clashed sharply with assurances of great gains for most workers by the Bush and Clinton administrations, by the business community, by mainstream academic economists including an array of Nobel Prize winners, and by analysts, commentators, and editorialists in the mass media. Countering claims of NAFTA opponents, these forces pointed to econometric studies finding variously that tens of thousands, hundreds of thousands, or millions of American jobs depended on NAFTA's passage.

17. NAFTA supporters prevailed in the November 1993 vote, with the House of Representatives voting 233–200 in favor of NAFTA. The US Senate, conceded from the start by NAFTA opponents, voted by a large margin in favor of the Agreement a few days later. NAFTA and the NAALC went into effect on 1 January 1994.

§4. The NAFTA Framework

18. Before analyzing the NAALC, a review of trade aspects of the NAFTA sets a comparative framework. Much of the criticism aimed at the NAALC laments what critics see as weak rights, feeble enforcement powers, and non-existent remedies for workers compared with the rights, enforcement powers and remedies available to employers, investors, executives, bankers and other key actors in the new trade regime.

19. The NAFTA trade agreement contains 22 chapters in more than one thousand pages of text, with a number of annexes. Many deal with the normal subjects of most trade agreements, such as tariffs, treatment of goods as they enter a country, 'national treatment' of foreign investors (i.e. treating foreign investors the same as national investors), transparency in applying tariff laws, etc. Annexes deal with special issues in auto and textile sectors, requiring a high percentage of North American content for goods to receive favorable NAFTA tariff treatment. The three countries sought to avoid having one of them (Mexico was the chief concern) serve as a 'platform' for other countries outside NAFTA (Japan was most often mentioned) to send products for final-stage, low value-added assembly and then reap the benefits of low-NAFTA tariffs.

20. But NAFTA goes far beyond the usual subjects of trade agreements. It takes up services, agriculture, investment, financial services, intellectual property and other matters treated only partially, or not at all, in venues such as the World Trade Organization, the European Union, or Mercosur. The NAFTA's investment chapter permits suits by corporations against governments for financial losses due to a country's application of law or policy in a manner seen to discriminate against the investor – a provision the international community could not agree upon in failed talks over the Multilateral Agreement on Investment (MAI) at the Organization for Economic Cooperation and Development (OECD).

21. In the view of many critics, this 'investor-state' provision in NAFTA gives private companies rights and protections above those of governments and the citizens who elect them. Similar criticism is aimed at NAFTA's intellectual property provisions, which provide for swift, strong sanctions against violators of intellectual property rights. A correspondingly strong enforcement regime for workers' rights violations is lacking.

22. In negotiating the trade agreement, each country put forth matters that it insisted must remain within the sphere of national sovereignty without being altered by NAFTA. For Mexico, the energy sector, and more specifically public ownership and control of petroleum and natural gas, was off-limits to NAFTA. The nationalization of the Rockefeller-owned oil industry in the 1930s is still a touch-stone of Mexicans' national identity that even political leaders otherwise disposed to promote trade liberalization and privatization are loath to change. While Mexico agreed to open some energy-related services to foreign investment, basic ownership and control remained public. In December 2013 the Mexican Congress and administration of Enrique Peña Nieto passed a series of reforms to Mexico's energy sector.

23. Canada was chiefly concerned about cultural issues and resisted liberalization in areas such as arts, film, publishing, radio and television. With most of its population grouped along the border with the United States and already having wide access to US mass media, Canadian political leaders are especially sensitive to potential domination by their giant neighbor and possible dissolution of Canadian national identity and culture.

24. For the United States, migrant labor was the issue to keep off the table in NAFTA negotiations, despite proposals from Mexico to take up the matter. With a two thousand mile border between the two countries and evidence of continued unauthorized migration to the United States by tens of thousands of Mexican workers each year, US leaders feared a political backlash if they moved to 'open the gates' for Mexican workers. In contrast to the European Union, which provides for free movement within the EU by citizens of member countries, the NAFTA leaves all national border immigration controls in place. However, NAFTA countries did establish a number of new provisions making it easier for corporate executives, investors, lawyers, accountants and other professionals to move from country to country.

§5. Introducing the NAALC

25. The North American Agreement on Labor Cooperation is the first international labor agreement directly connected to a trade pact. Some critics have assailed the NAALC as a 'side agreement' that marginalizes workers' rights, compared with integral chapters within the NAFTA trade pact dealing with investors' rights.

Although the 'side' nature of the NAALC does suggest lower priority, it is an agreement nonetheless, signed by three sovereign governments, setting forth norms and obligations to be fulfilled under its terms.

26. One starting point for understanding the NAALC is to see three things it does *not* do:

- It does not set new common standards to which countries must adjust their laws and regulations. Instead, the NAALC stresses sovereignty in each country's internal labor affairs, recognizing 'the right of each Party to establish its own domestic labor standards.'
- The NAALC does not create a supranational administrative tribunal to take evidence and decide guilt or innocence in labor disputes or to order remedies against violators. This is left to national authorities applying national law.
- The NAALC does not create a supranational labor judicial body to take appeals from decisions of national tribunals and overrule decisions that arguably fail to 'enforce' the NAALC. Decisions by national courts are undisturbed by the NAALC.

27. Instead of an international enforcement system supplanting national systems, the NAALC countries have created an oversight, review and dispute resolution system designed to hold each other accountable for their performance in eleven defined areas of labor law. Oversight is conducted first by a review body in *another* government. Then, depending on the subject area, evaluation and arbitration can be had by independent, non-governmental committees or panels.

28. The NAALC repudiates the idea of common standards or harmonization of standards. But at the same time that sovereignty is strictly observed, the NAALC commits the parties to certain common 'principles' and 'obligations' to effectively enforce their national labor laws, with an oversight mechanism meant to deter commercial competition on the basis of lower labor standards.

29. The NAALC contains a broad, as opposed to a 'core,' elaboration of norms. The NAALC's 11 labor principles include core standards as defined in the ILO's 1998 Declaration of Fundamental Principles and Rights at Work. But the NAALC goes farther, embracing social and economic matters related to wages, hours, and working conditions including minimum wage, occupational safety and health, compensation for workplace injuries and illnesses, and treatment of migrant workers.

30. The NAALC provides relatively easy access to both its cooperative activities agenda and to its complaint mechanism not only for trade unions and employer organizations but also for NGOs, workers, students, and other citizens. There are no citizenship requirements for filing a complaint, or 'submission' in NAALC terminology. Any citizen of any country or organization based in any country may submit a complaint. In practice, a wide range of trade unions, human rights organizations, labor lawyers associations, student groups and other NGOs have presented complaints.

31. Most notably, the NAALC is the first international labor agreement directly connected to a trade agreement with potential for trade sanctions as a means of enforcing labor rights. A fine of up to 0.007 per cent of the volume of trade between two disputing countries can be levied against a government if it fails to adopt an 'action plan' recommended by an arbitral panel after the panel finds a persistent pattern of failure to effectively enforce its laws related to one of three labor principles susceptible to dispute resolution (covering child labor, minimum wage standards, and workplace health and safety). This fine was approximately $20 million when the NAALC took effect. It is now over $6 billion with the increase in the volume of trade among the three NAFTA partners.

32. The fine must be expended at the direction of the NAALC ministerial council to improve enforcement in the subject area of the arbitration. If the country complained against fails to pay the fine, the other countries may suspend NAFTA tariff benefits in an amount and for a time necessary to collect the fine. Such suspension of beneficial tariff treatment normally would apply to the 'same sector or sectors' where violations of workers' rights occurred.

33. It should be noted at the outset that no NAALC case has reached this stage. Practically speaking, it is unlikely that a case would reach this point because NAALC procedures include ample opportunity for a cooperative solution to disputes before reaching a point of sanctions. While it will be seen that the 'linkage' of trade and labor rights by means of trade disciplines is extremely limited, one may still conclude that the NAALC contains the essential elements of the much-debated 'social clause' in international trade.

§6. National Contexts

34. Fashioning a labor rights agreement in North America posed significant challenges to negotiators coming from countries with disparate political and institutional backgrounds. For example, Mexico's Constitution explicitly affirms the right to organize a union and the right to strike. The Mexican Constitution also specifies basic conditions of labor regarding minimum wages, hours of work and work shifts, overtime pay, child labor, maternity leave, vacation and overtime pay, profit-sharing, housing, training, safety and health, just cause for dismissal, equal pay for equal work, seniority in promotions, and other labor standards.

35. In contrast, the Canadian and American charters are silent on labor rights. Instead, they contain general civil rights and civil liberties provisions that have given rise to labor protections. Section 2(d) of Canada's Charter of Rights and Freedoms guarantees freedom of association and the right of peaceful assembly. The Canadian Supreme Court has ruled that these guarantees protect the right to form and join trade unions, but not the right to bargain collectively or the right to strike. However, the federal and provincial governments are empowered to legislate in these areas

36. The US Constitution's first amendment protects freedom of assembly, free speech, and the right to petition the government of redress of grievances. These constitutional protections have been applied to many aspects of workers' rights such as forming unions, picketing, leafleting, boycotting, and engaging in political action. The commerce clause of the Constitution, empowering Congress to regulate interstate commerce, is the basis for federal labor legislation setting protections for workers' rights and labor standards.

37. All three NAALC countries are federal states composed of national and subnational governments. Labor laws are enacted at national and at state or provincial levels. Enforcement of labor laws and resolution of disputes are allocated to both federal and state authorities. The countries' labor law jurisdictional systems range from a fundamentally national system in the United States, to a mixed federal– state system in Mexico, to a fundamentally provincial system in Canada.

38. In the United States, federal labor laws cover most workers except state and local public employees and employees of very small enterprises. Federal administrative authorities and courts enforce the laws throughout the country. Even for workers covered under state laws, state standards are often similar to federal norms or guidelines, though states are often innovators in improving work place standards.

39. Mexico maintains exclusively federal labor legislation in force throughout the country. However, enforcement power is delegated to the 31 state governments and the Federal District, where Mexico City is located. The federal government retains enforcement authority over twenty-two specified industrial sectors of national scope and enterprises operating in more than a single state.

40. Canada has eleven separate and distinct labor law systems governing labor relations: one for the federal sector (including territories) and one for each of the ten provinces. Only 10 per cent of Canadian workers are covered by federal labor laws; the rest come under provincial law coverage. Fully two-thirds of Canadian workers are covered by the laws of the three largest provinces, Ontario, Quebec, and British Columbia.

41. Trade union density varies in the three NAALC countries, too. In the United States, 12–14 per cent of the total workforce is unionized; 10 per cent in the private sector. These levels follow a decline from 35 per cent overall, and 40 per cent in the private sector, in the 1950s. In contrast, Canada has maintained a higher level of union density, still close to 30 per cent but also reflecting a decline from earlier years.

42. Mexico's union density rate is difficult to calculate, with no systematic surveys having been conducted in many years. Most companies with more than fifty employees are unionized, but many of these, particularly in Northern Mexico industrial areas where thousands of *maquiladora* plants have been established in recent decades, are considered to have 'white' or 'ghost' unions and 'protection contracts' that impede independent workers' organizations.

43. The more traditional trade unions in the Mexico City area and other parts of the country were historically part of a corporatist system, tightly linked to the Institutional Revolutionary Party (PRI) which dominated Mexico's political system for seven decades until national elections in 2000 ousted the PRI from power.

44. In 2000, politics in both Mexico and the United States took a turn toward to the right when Mexicans elected the popular and charismatic rancher and former Coca Cola executive Vicente Fox Quesada of the conservative National Action Party (PAN) in July and George Walker Bush barely won a hotly contested election in the United States after the intervention of the US Supreme Court several weeks after the November election. Although Canada elected liberal Prime Minister Paul Martin to replace Jean Chrétien in 2003, Canada also took a turn toward the right when it elected conservative Stephen Harper to be its Prime Minister in 2006.

45. The election of Vicente Fox did not have the transformative effect on labor politics in Mexico that many observers expected. Despite Fox's initiatives to improve government administrative process and reduce corruption, labor law administration at the state level did not change much during his six-year presidency. Nor did conservative PANistas and employer groups in Mexico succeed in their efforts to 'flexibilize' Mexico's labor law despite renewed efforts and the introduction of conservative labor reform legislation in Mexico's Congress in 2002. These proposed reforms were the subject of a 2005 NAALC complaint which was rejected by the US and Canadian NAOs. The political opening in Mexico and growing strength of Mexico's independent union movement and the PRD, however, did more to protect Mexico's Federal Labor Law from reform than NAALC processes. Congressional PRIistas opposed Fox's proposed reform because of the almost mythical status of the Federal Labor Law in Mexico and because of what the reforms would do to the PRIista power base. Congressional PRDistas opposed Fox's proposed reforms because they did nothing to improve the administration and implementation of Mexico's labor protections and were seen as reducing worker protections. Although the PAN and Mexico's progressive party, the Revolutionary Democratic Party (PRD), gained in-roads in state politics and in the Mexico's capital Federal District in 2000 and later, the PRI maintained governorships and control of power structures in many Mexican states – including in local labor boards. In the 2006 election, however, the PRI presidential candidate was a distant third to PANista candidate Felipe Calderón Hinojosa and PRDista Andrés Manuel López Obrador (AMLO). In an echo of the 2000 US election, conservative Calderón barely prevailed over López Obrador amidst claims of electoral fraud. Mexico passed a controversial labor reform in December 2012.

46. Because of close personal ties between Fox and Bush, who had been governor of Texas for 1½ terms (six years) before becoming President of the United States, many observers were optimistic about the possibility of a bilateral US–Mexico solution to the problem of undocumented migration of workers from Mexico to the United States. Secret inter-governmental discussion and negotiations occurred until the first week of September 2001. Everything changed, however, as a result of the 11 September attacks on the twin towers in New York and the Pentagon in Washington, DC. Many of the laws passed by the US Congress during the period just after 11 September had negative implications for undocumented immigrants working in the United States – including the increase of workplace raids of factories and plants suspected of employing undocumented immigrants. Federal prosecutors began using laws designed to protect consumers from identity theft and to protect Americans from terrorist attacks to prosecute undocumented workers, resulting in deportation and imprisonment for many undocumented workers. One such prosecution, which began after an undocumented worker filed a claim for benefits after suffering an on-the-job injury in a meatpacking plant, became the subject of a human rights advisory opinion issued by the Inter-American Court on Human Rights in 2004. Political relations between the US and its North American partners became strained when Mexican and Canadian politicians expressed their opposition to the US invasion of Iraq in 2003.

47. In November 2008, the US elected its first African American President Barack Obama, a Democrat. Obama handily won election for a second term in November 2012. In July 2012, Mexico elected Enrique Peña Nieto, the first successful PRI presidential candidate since 1994. Conservative Stephen Harper, first elected in 2006, continued as the Prime Minister of Canada in 2014.

Chapter 2. Norms, Institutions, and Operations of the NAALC

§1. Preamble and Objectives

48. Preamble: the NAALC begins with a preamble stating the Parties' intent to improve working conditions and living standards and to protect, enhance and enforce workers' basic rights as a complement to the economic opportunities created by NAFTA. The Parties affirm their respect for each other's constitution and laws and their desire to strengthen their cooperation on labor matters. The three countries resolve to promote, in accordance with their respective laws, high-skill, high-productivity economic development in North America by:

- investing in continuing human resource development;
- promoting employment security and career opportunities;
- strengthening labor–management cooperation;
- promoting higher living standards as productivity increases;
- encouraging tripartite consultation and dialogue;
- fostering investment with due regard for the importance of labor laws and principles; and
- encouraging compliance with labor laws.

49. Objectives: Article 1 of the NAALC sets forth the agreement's objectives of improving working conditions and living standards in each country, promoting the labor principles of Annex 1, encouraging cooperation, encouraging publication and exchange of information to enhance mutual understanding of labor laws and institutions in each country, pursuing cooperative activities, promoting compliance with and effective enforcement by each Party of its labor laws, and fostering transparency in the administration of labor law.

§2. Labor Principles

50. Under the NAALC's Annex 1, the United States, Mexico and Canada 'are committed to promote' the following labor principles, but they do not establish common minimum standards for their domestic law:

(1) Freedom of association and protection of the right to organize – 'The right of workers exercised freely and without impediment to establish and join organizations of their own choosing to further and defend their interests.'
(2) The right to bargain collectively – 'The protection of the right of organized workers to freely engage in collective bargaining on matters concerning the terms and conditions of employment.'
(3) The right to strike – 'The protection of the right of workers to strike in order to defend their collective interests.'

(4) Prohibition of forced labor – 'The prohibition and suppression of all forms of forced or compulsory labor, except for types of compulsory work generally considered acceptable by the Parties, such as compulsory military service, certain civic obligations, prison labor not for private purposes and work exacted in cases of emergency.'
(5) Labor protection for children and young persons – 'The establishment of restrictions on the employment of children and young persons that may vary taking into consideration relevant factors likely to jeopardize the full physical, mental and moral development of young persons, including schooling and safety requirements.'
(6) Minimum employment standards – 'The establishment of minimum employment standards, such as minimum wages and overtime pay, for wage earners, including those not covered by collective agreements.'
(7) Elimination of employment discrimination – 'Elimination of employment discrimination on such grounds as race, religion, age, sex, or other grounds, subject to certain reasonable exceptions, such as, where applicable, bona fide occupational requirements or qualifications and established practices or rules governing retirement ages, and special measures of protection or assistance for particular groups designed to take into account the effects of discrimination.'
(8) Equal pay for women and men – 'Equal wages for women and men by applying the principle of equal pay for equal work in the same establishment.'
(9) Prevention of occupational injuries and illnesses – 'Prescribing and implementing standards to minimize the causes of occupational injuries and illnesses.'
(10) Compensation in cases of occupational injuries and illnesses – 'The establishment of a system providing benefits and compensation to workers or their dependents in cases of occupational injuries, accidents or fatalities arising out of, linked with or occurring in the course of employment.'
(11) Protection of migrant workers – 'Providing migrant workers in a Party's territory with the same legal protection as the Party's nationals in respect of working conditions.'

51. NAALC negotiators took obvious pains to insist that the 11 labor principles do not amount to new international norms to which they must conform their labor law and practice. The agreement recognizes 'the right of each Party to establish its own domestic labor standards.' It declares that 'nothing in this agreement shall be construed to empower a Party's authorities to undertake law enforcement activities in the territory of another Party.'

52. The introduction to the labor principles insists that the countries 'do not establish common minimum standards for their domestic law.' At the same time, NAALC negotiators made the perhaps overconfident assertion that they are 'areas of concern ... where the Parties have developed, each in its own way, laws, regulations, procedures and practices that protect the rights and interests of their respective workforces.' In other words, they implicitly stated that they comply with these 11 principles, and thereby established *de facto* a supranational normative framework for North American workers' rights, even if they stopped short of creating new enforceable standards.

§3. NAALC OBLIGATIONS

53. After declaring the 11 labor principles, the three countries adopt six 'obligations' whose fulfillment should give effect to the labor principles. These obligations are included here in full because, together with the labor principles, they are the heart of the NAALC, comprising solemn commitments by international agreement among nations:

> *Article 2: Levels of Protection*
>
> Affirming full respect for each Party's constitution, and recognizing the right of each Party to establish its own domestic labor standards, and to adopt or modify accordingly its labor laws and regulations, each Party shall ensure that its labor laws and regulations provide for high labor standards, consistent with high quality and productivity workplaces, and shall continue to strive to improve those standards in that light.
>
> *Article 3: Government Enforcement Action*
>
> 1. Each Party shall promote compliance with and effectively enforce its labor law through appropriate government action, subject to Article 42, such as:
>   a. appointing and training inspectors;
>   b. monitoring compliance and investigating suspected violations, including through on-site inspections;
>   c. seeking assurances of voluntary compliance;
>   d. requiring record keeping and reporting;
>   e. encouraging the establishment of worker-management committees to address labor regulation of the workplace;
>   f. providing or encouraging mediation, conciliation and arbitration services; or
>   g. initiating, in a timely manner, proceedings to seek appropriate sanctions or remedies for violations of its labor law.
> 2. Each Party shall ensure that its competent authorities give due consideration in accordance with its law to any request by an employer, employee or their representatives, or other interested person, for an investigation of an alleged violation of the Party's labor law.
>
> *Article 4: Private Action*
>
> 1. Each Party shall ensure that persons with a legally recognized interest under its law in a particular matter have appropriate access to administrative,

quasi-judicial, judicial or labor tribunals for the enforcement of the Party's labor law.

2. Each Party's law shall ensure that such persons may have recourse to, as appropriate, procedures by which rights arising under:
   a. its labor law, including in respect of occupational safety and health, employment standards, industrial relations and migrant workers, and
   b. collective agreements, can be enforced.

Article 5: Procedural Guarantees

1. Each Party shall ensure that its administrative, quasi-judicial, judicial and labor tribunal proceedings for the enforcement of its labor law are fair, equitable and transparent and, to this end, each Party shall provide that:
   a. such proceedings comply with due process of law;
   b. any hearings in such proceedings are open to the public, except where the administration of justice otherwise requires;
   c. the parties to such proceedings are entitled to support or defend their respective positions and to present information or evidence; and
   d. such proceedings are not unnecessarily complicated and do not entail unreasonable charges or time limits or unwarranted delays.
2. Each Party shall provide that final decisions on the merits of the case in such proceedings are:
   a. in writing and preferably state the reasons on which the decisions are based;
   b. made available without undue delay to the parties to the proceedings and, consistent with its law, to the public; and
   c. based on information or evidence in respect of which the parties were offered the opportunity to be heard.
3. Each Party shall provide, as appropriate, that parties to such proceedings have the right, in accordance with its law, to seek review and, where warranted, correction of final decisions issued in such proceedings.
4. Each Party shall ensure that tribunals that conduct or review such proceedings are impartial and independent and do not have any substantial interest in the outcome of the matter.
5. Each Party shall provide that the parties to administrative, quasi-judicial, judicial or labor tribunal proceedings may seek remedies to ensure the enforcement of their labor rights. Such remedies may include, as appropriate, orders, compliance agreements, fines, penalties, imprisonment, injunctions or emergency workplace closures.
6. Each Party may, as appropriate, adopt or maintain labor defense offices to represent or advise workers or their organizations.
7. Nothing in this Article shall be construed to require a Party to establish, or to prevent a Party from establishing, a judicial system for the enforcement of its labor law distinct from its system for the enforcement of laws in general.
8. For greater certainty, decisions by each Party's administrative, quasi-judicial, judicial or labor tribunals, or pending decisions, as well as related proceedings shall not be subject to revision or reopened under the provisions of this Agreement.

Article 6: Publication

1. Each Party shall ensure that its laws, regulations, procedures and administrative rulings of general application respecting any matter covered by this Agreement are promptly published or otherwise made available in such a manner as to enable interested persons and Parties to become acquainted with them.
2. When so established by its law, each Party shall:
   a. publish in advance any such measure that it proposes to adopt; and
   b. provide interested persons a reasonable opportunity to comment on such proposed measures.

Article 7: Public Information and Awareness

Each Party shall promote public awareness of its labor law, including by:

a. ensuring that public information is available related to its labor law and enforcement and compliance procedures; and
b. promoting public education regarding its labor law.

54. It is important to note that effective labor law enforcement is the subject of just one of the NAALC's six obligations. Other obligations are equally important. The first, in Article 2, is a general duty clause creating an obligation to provide high standards and to try to improve those standards, in light of quality and productivity considerations. Implicit in their agreement on this obligation was an understanding among negotiators for each of the countries that each already provided high standards, since the need to change any of their laws was not acknowledged.

55. While the general thrust of the NAALC stresses effective enforcement of existing law and the right of each country to adopt or change its labor laws, the existence of this general duty clause in Article 2 has served as foundation for elements of several NAALC complaints arguing that certain laws themselves, even if they are 'effectively enforced,' fail to provide high standards and that, indeed, their effective enforcement violates workers' rights. In one such case, for example, workers challenged Mexico's public sector labor law mandating a single, monopoly, government-approved union for public employees. It was Mexico's law and it was being effectively enforced, but it arguably violated the obligation to provide high labor standards evinced in labor principle 1 on freedom of association.

56. Similarly, the obligation to provide access to legal recourse can be invoked to bring certain laws under the scrutiny of a NAALC review. In the United States, for example, agricultural workers are excluded from coverage by laws meant to protect the right to organize trade unions. Farm workers can be dismissed for attempts to form a union, and they have no legal recourse – there is no labor board or other agency they can turn to for assistance. Failing to provide access to legal recourse has been the basis of NAALC complaints on behalf of migrant farmworkers, even though it does not involve any 'failure to effectively enforce' any law.

57. Likewise, the obligation to provide 'remedies to ensure the enforcement' of labor rights is also grounds for a NAALC complaint, as labor rights advocates have carefully documented the weakness and lack of force in many remedies in national labor law systems even when the law is otherwise being enforced. The obligation to provide a system without 'unwarranted delays' hardly needs elaboration. Enervating delays plague the labor law systems of all three countries and have been elements of several NAALC complaints. In sum, while effective enforcement of national law rather than compliance with new supranational standards is a fundamental obligation and the one most often cited in commentary about the NAALC, it is not the only obligation taken on by the three countries. Failure to fulfill any of the obligations can be the subject of a complaint.

§4. Institutional Structure and Procedures

I. The Commission for Labor Cooperation: Ministerial Council and Secretariat

58. The NAALC creates a Commission for Labor Cooperation that includes a cabinet-level Ministerial Council and a permanent staff Secretariat. The three labor ministers of each country make up the Council, the highest authority of the Commission. The Council must meet at least once a year in regular session, and may meet in special session at the request of any country, although in practice the Council has gone for several years without meeting. All decisions and recommendations of the Council are made by consensus, except where the NAALC provides for a two-thirds vote.

59. The Council oversees the implementation of the NAALC and directs the work and activities of the Secretariat. The Council sets priorities, approves an annual plan of activities and budget, approves reports and studies for publication, facilitates consultation among the Parties, promotes the collection and publication of comparable data on labor law enforcement, standards, and labor markets, and addresses any questions and differences that may arise between Parties regarding the interpretation or application of the NAALC. The Council also promotes cooperative activities on a variety of labor law subjects through seminars, workshops, conferences, joint research projects, and technical assistance. The Secretariat was closed temporarily in August 2010 and had not reopened as of March 2014 and the Council of Ministers had not held an official meeting since August 2010. In a 2011 report on the effectiveness of its international trade and labor grants system, Human Resources Skills and Development Canada (HRSDC) found that program stakeholders expressed dissatisfaction with the way the NAALC Secretariat was meeting its mandate and expressed concerns about the efficiency, leadership and organization of the organization.

60. The Secretariat of the Commission for Labor Cooperation is to be headed by an Executive Director chosen by the Council for a three-year term. The Executive Director's term may be extended for an additional three years. This position must rotate consecutively between nationals of each Party. As a matter of practice since the Secretariat opened in 1995 until it closed in 2010, the Executive was supported by a Director of Research and a Director of Administration/Cooperative Consultations. These positions rotated between nationals of the other two countries. More often than not, these Directors are proposed by and generally appointed at the behest of the member governments' labor ministries.

61. The first Executive Director, Canadian John S. McKennirey, served from 1995–1999. During McKennirey's term, Americans Lance Compa (1995–1997) and Sandra Polaski (1997–1999) served in the position of Director of Research and Mexicans Maria Elena Alcaraz (1995–1996) and Leoncio Lara (1996–1999) served as Director of Administration/Cooperative Consultations. Michael McDermott, also a Canadian, served as Interim Executive Director from June 1999 to December 1999. Alfonso Oñate Laborde of Mexico served from January 2000 to December 2003. Canadian Anthony Giles, Research Director from June 2001 to December 2003, served as Interim Executive Director from January 2004 to June 2004. American Mark S. Knouse served as Executive Director from August 2004 until September 2006, the remainder of his term being served by Interim Executive Director Peter Accolla until the end of September 2007. Canadian Daniel Bernier was appointed as Executive Director in March 2008 and served until the end of 2009. Mexican Gabriel Jimenez served as Administrative Director and there was no Research Director during that period. In April 2008 the US Department of Labor Office of the Inspector General (OIG) published a report addressing internal governance issues in the CLC for the period August 2004 to August 2006.

62. As outlined in the NAALC, the Executive Director appoints the staff of the Secretariat under general standards set by the Council, taking into account lists of candidates prepared by the Parties. The number of staff members is set at fifteen, subject to later change by the Council. The Council may reject by a two-thirds vote, in confidence, an appointment that does not meet the general standards. The agreement emphasizes the importance, but does not require, recruitment of an equitable proportion of the professional staff from among the nationals of each Party. In addition to the Directors of Research and Administration/Cooperative Consultations, the Executive Director has appointed a professional staff generally evenly divided between nationals of each of the three countries. The Executive Director also appointed a small locally recruited staff consisting of finance and administrative personnel to support the Secretariat's activities.

63. The Secretariat staff included labor lawyers, economists, and other professionals experienced in labor affairs in their countries. They worked in the three languages of North America, Spanish, French, and English. They had the status of international civil servants with an obligation not to accept instructions from any government or any other authority external to the Council. Correspondingly, each Party must respect the international character of the responsibilities of the Executive Director and the staff, and must not seek to influence them in the discharge of their duties.

64. The Commission's Secretariat was first based in Dallas, Texas where it began operations in September 1995. A counterpart secretariat for the environment was placed in Montreal, Canada. Some confusion accompanied the announcement that the Secretariat would open in Dallas. City leaders and economic development officials envisioned a large staff of high-paid international civil servants ('Brussels West,' as some called it) moving to Dallas and buying homes, sending their children to private schools, and generally boosting the local economy. With a glut of office space on the market at the time, city officials offered an empty 40-story downtown office building rent-free for the Secretariat's use. A palpable sense of disappointment overtook these visions when the Secretariat's small, 12-person staff trickled into Dallas as they extricated themselves from jobs in their home countries.

65. In 2000 the Secretariat relocated to Washington, DC. The move was made on two main grounds: (1) the difficulty of recruiting to Dallas experienced labor experts, most of whom are based in capital cities in their countries, and (2) the absence of any international labor milieu with access to international institutions, national and international trade union and employer groups, research institutes and university centers with an international labor rights focus, and the like, all of which are present in the Washington DC area. An early signal of potential problems came when a prominent Dallas businessman told Secretariat staffers at a welcoming reception in 1995 that the city of Dallas and the state of Texas were proud to be 'union-free,' and that he hoped the Secretariat would help spread the gospel of non-unionism throughout North America.

66. The NAALC Secretariat is to serve as the staff support organization for the Council. It proposes a plan of activities and budget for carrying out three principal functions. The first is a research agenda under which the Secretariat publishes comparative reports on labor laws and labor markets of the three countries, and special reports as directed by the Council. Second, the Secretariat is to provide research and staff support to *ad hoc* Evaluation Committees of Experts and Arbitral Panels (see below). Finally, it is to serve as the general administrative arm of the Commission – organizing ministerial and subministerial meetings, retaining records, offering public information through a web site and a library open to the public, etc.

II. National Administrative Offices (NAOs)

67. The NAALC also sets up three National Administrative Offices (NAOs), one in the labor ministry of each country. This feature distinguishes the NAALC from its companion environmental side agreement, which does not have such domestic offices in each country's environmental ministry. Labor concerns are sensitive and complicated in each country. Relations with peak labor organizations like the AFL–CIO in the United States, the Canadian Labour Congress in Canada, and the CTM in Mexico has more profound political implications than with a decentralized environmental movement with hundreds of organizations. The three countries wanted to keep one agency that each fully controls among the new institutions created by the NAALC.

68. Under the NAALC, each government must designate a Secretary who is responsible for administering and managing of the NAO, and each country provides the financial support it deems necessary to support the work of its NAO. This is distinct from the budget of the Secretariat, which is funded in equal proportion by each of the countries.

69. In addition to the secretary, each of the three national NAOs has created a professional and administrative staff of 5–10 persons to carry out its work. Professional staff include labor lawyers, labor economists, and public policy experts. Each NAO may convene a tripartite national advisory committee, as well as an advisory committee of government officials from other federal agencies or from states or provinces, to advise it on the implementation and further elaboration of the NAALC.

70. Each NAO serves as a point of contact with each other, with other agencies in each of their own governments, and with the Secretariat. Upon request, the NAO must provide publicly available information to each other, to the Secretariat, and to an Evaluation Committee of Experts (see below). As Canada and the US negotiated post-NAALC FTAs with labor provisions beginning in 2000, the Canadian and US NAOs served as the point of contact for labor affairs under those FTAs as well.

71. The key mandate of the NAO's is found in Article 16(3) of the NAALC, presented here in full because of its importance:

> Each NAO shall provide for the submission and receipt, and periodically publish a list, of public communications on labor law matters arising in the territory of another Party. Each NAO shall review such matters, as appropriate, in accordance with domestic procedures.

72. The 'public communications' noted here are complaints from any person or organization about workers' rights violations related to 'labor law matters issues arising in the territory of *another* Party' (emphasis added). This is an unusual but critical feature of the NAALC: workers, unions and allied NGOs, employers, or other persons or organizations filing a complaint must submit it to an NAO in *another* country, not in the country where events giving rise to the submission occurred, to start the review process.

73. Each NAO has established domestic procedures for receiving and reviewing complaints about labor law matters in other countries. In general, they provide first for a threshold consideration to ensure that a complaint meets minimum requirements for acceptance for review. Once a case is accepted for review, usually within sixty days of submission, the NAO is to begin a 4–6 month process of conducting a review and writing a report. In practice, the review process for complaints filed under the NAALC and labor chapters of other FTAs can take a year or more.

74. An important characteristic of the NAALC is the relative openness of the complaint process. Aside from normal requirements that complainants (or 'submitters,' as they are often called) identify themselves, provide a return address, and specify the labor law matters complained of, there are no 'standing' requirements such as injury or harm, financial interest or other personal stake in events equivalent to standing requirements for administrative claims or lawsuits in national legal systems. Furthermore, the scope of issues that can be subjects of complaints is extremely broad. The term 'labor law matters' encompasses any of the 11 labor principles contained in Annex 1, leaving practically all potential workers' rights violations within the subject matter jurisdiction of the NAALC.

75. Until around 2004, when they accepted a complaint for review, the NAOs of the United States and Canada normally held public hearings on the matter where any interested person or group may present views. Hearings tend to be held in the country of the NAO undertaking the review, not in the country where the events giving rise to the complaint took place. The US NAO has held public hearings in Washington, DC and in several cities closer to Mexico, such as San Diego, California, Tucson, Arizona, and San Antonio, Texas, to make it easier for Mexican workers to participate. Rather than public hearings, the Mexican NAO holds private 'informative sessions' for comments by workers, unions, NGOs, employers, and other actors, including those from the United States or Canada. After changes in US regulations governing the NAALC and FTA labor chapter complaint processes in 2004 and 2006, the US NAO adopted more of an investigatory procedure like that of the Mexican NAO rather than holding public hearings. This procedure was applied in response to complaints filed under the NAALC and labor chapters under CAFTA-DR and FTAs between the US and Peru and Bahrain. In practice, the Canadian NAO also did not conduct a hearing on the one FTA labor chapter complaint filed under a Canadian FTA labor chapter between 2003 and 2011.

76. NAO hearings can be an important part of a public review process. They are not judicial proceedings. NAOs do not have powers of compulsory process, such as serving a subpoena on any person or organization ordering them to appear at a public hearing or to produce documents or other evidence. Hearings are not adversarial proceedings with examination and cross-examination of witnesses where rules of evidence apply.

77. In general, NAO hearings have involved trade union leaders, workers, and their allies providing information to the NAO secretary conducting the hearing (usually accompanied by staff members) and responding to questions. Most employers whose alleged workers' rights violations gave rise to the complaint have chosen not to participate in NAO hearings, although some have, and in recent years more have done so.

78. On 17 December 2004, the US Department of Labor renamed its NAO the Office of Trade Agreement Implementation (OTAI), issuing a notice in the federal register on 23 December 2004. The OTAI continued to be responsible for administering the NAALC as well as the labor chapters of other free trade agreements, including the US–Chile Free Trade Agreement which was signed on 6 June 2003 and the US–Singapore Free Trade Agreement, signed on 6 May 2003. Both agreements went into effect on 1 January 2004 and contained labor chapters that required signatory nations to designate an office in their labor ministries to operate as a contact point for the submission, receipt and consideration of public communications. The original public communication submission guidelines for the US did not change. The US–Jordan Free Trade Agreement, signed on 24 October 2000 and implemented on 7 December 2001, is excluded because it has a different structure and is not subject to labor department administration. The first complaint filed under a non-NAALC FTA labor chapter was filed about labor rights abuses in Guatemala by the AFL–CIO in April 2008. This complaint as well as four other complaints filed under non-NAALC FTA labor chapters will be discussed in Chapter 9, paragraphs 513 *et seq.*

79. On 14 December 2006, the US Department of Labor reassigned the duties of its NAO/OTAI to the Office of Trade and Labor Affairs (OTLA), a newly established division of the recently reorganized Bureau of International Labor Affairs (ILAB). The OTLA is divided into three sub-divisions, which are the Trade Policy and Negotiations Division; the Economic and Labor Research Division; and the Trade Agreement Administration and Technical Cooperation Division. Like the OTAI, the OTLA serves as the contact point/NAO for the NAALC and the labor chapters of the Central America–Dominican Republic (CAFTA–DR), US–Chile, US–Singapore, US–Bahrain, US–Morocco, US-Oman, US–Australia, US-Peru, US-Panama, US-Colombia and US-South Korea FTAs. It also serves as the contact point for the labor chapters of the labor chapter of any other FTA to which the US becomes a party. The US–Jordan FTA is not included under OTLA administration for the same reason it was excluded from OTAI administration, although in early 2014 the US and Jordan entered into a side letter for cooperative programs which will be administered by the OTLA. The Director of the OTLA is designated and functions as the NAO Secretary under the NAALC.

80. Unlike the 2004 changes to the NAO, the 2006 changes resulted in an amended public communication procedure. The three key changes to the 2006 US OTLA/NAO Guidelines were to change the time frames for US OTLA/NAO action on public communications, to add an additional pleading requirement for public communications and to increase the number of issues the US OTLA/NAO shall consider in determining whether to accept the submission for review.

81. While the time frame between the filing of a public communication and the US OTLA/NAO determination whether or not to accept the public communication for review is still 60 days, under the new guidelines the US OTLA/NAO now has discretion to determine that it may grant itself an extension to decide whether or not to accept the public communication. The guidelines do not contain an outside limit on how long the US OTLA/NAO may take to determine whether or not to accept the public communication. Similarly, the Guidelines call for a 180-day time frame for the US OTLA/NAO to issue a public report of its review of the submission but now grant the US OTLA/NAO discretion to extend that time frame based on circumstances it determines. Under the original guidelines, the US OTLA/NAO had 120 days with the possibility of a 60-day extension to issue a public report. These regulations were not changed after Barack Obama became US President in January 2009. By the end of the first year of Obama's second four-year term, the US OTLA had issued four important public reports under non-NAALC FTA labor chapters, but in every case the OTLA issued itself an extension to draft the report leading to average waiting times of at least a year or over two years for reports on petitions. While petitioners and other stakeholders were generally kept appraised of the progress of the investigatory process during the Obama era, the OTLA was frequently criticized for the long time it took to issue reports on complaints – especially when workers often risked their lives and livelihoods to file FTA labor chapter complaints and suffered retaliation from their employers for speaking with OTLA officials.

82. In addition to allowing the US OTLA/NAO discretion to extend the time frames indefinitely for determining whether or not to accept a public communication for review and to issue a public report on its review, the revised US OTLA/NAO Guidelines require submitters to address in the initial public communication whether the matters referenced affect trade between the parties. This was not a requirement in the original guidelines. In its response to comments made by the AFL–CIO objecting to the addition of this pleading requirement, the Secretary of Labor noted that it was not the US Department of Labor's intent to limit the acceptance of public communications and the addition of the new 'factor' would not necessarily be determinative of whether or not the public communication would be accepted. While this regulation was not changed during the Obama administration, it appears as though the trade-related pleading guideline has not been applied after 2008, as exemplified by the 2010 labor complaint filed under the US-Peru FTA (see paragraphs 531 *et seq.*).

83. Under the original guidelines, the NAO Secretary could decline to accept a submission for review if it lacked basic pleading information, contained facts that would not constitute a failure to comply with a country's NAALC (or FTA labor chapter) obligations, showed that appropriate in-country relief had not been sought or if the submission was substantially similar to a recently-filed submission. Current guidelines require that in making its decision to accept or decline a public submission, the US OTLA/NAO consider whether the submission raises matters arising under the NAALC (or FTA labor chapter) and whether a review would further the objectives of the NAALC (or FTA labor chapter), in addition to the requirements set forth in the original guidelines. Beginning in 2009, the US OTLA made a number of changes to the methods it utilized in addressing public complaints under the NAALC and other FTA labor chapters. Rather than utilizing a more formal pleading and hearing process, the OTLA began applying more of an independent investigatory process. This method was most apparent in the OTLA's treatment of the 2011 CAFTA-DR labor complaint regarding child and forced labor and mistreatment of Haitian sugarcane workers in the Dominican sugar industry. The complaint was sparsely pleaded by a Catholic social services priest using publicly available reports. Rather than place additional burdens on the petitioner to plead more facts, the OTLA conducted an independent investigation of the allegations.

84. The 2006 US OTLA/NAO guidelines also contain a subtle change regarding whether or not the US OTLA/NAO will hold a public hearing regarding a public communication. While the original guidelines required the NAO Secretary to conduct a public hearing unless the Secretary determined that a hearing would not be suitable, the new guidelines require the OTLA to provide a process for the public to submit relevant information to the review 'which may include holding a public hearing.' The requirement to publish notice of the hearing in the Federal Register 30 days in advance of the hearing remains the same. The Secretary of Labor's response to comments made by the US Chamber of Commerce indicate that the Department of Labor responded in part but not in whole to that organization's proposal that there be a presumption against holding a public hearing, 'and the guidelines will retain the flexibility for the OTLA to hold public hearings in appropriate cases.' The practice of not holding public hearings regarding complaints filed under the NAALC and other FTA labor chapters continued in both the Bush II and Obama administrations after 2006. There was some criticism of the lack of public hearings to air issues raised in complaints filed under the NAALC and other FTA labor chapters, but at the end of 2013 it was unclear what the ultimate impact of not utilizing public hearings in the OTLA process will be. Some of the downsides of the NAO public hearing process were the expense incurred by complainants and their allies to participate in hearings in Washington, DC (expense that increases the further away the trade partner is – for example, Bahrain, Peru or Singapore) and the heightened danger of retaliation that might be faced by workers who brought notoriety to themselves by participating in public hearings. On the other hand, public hearings are still part of the US generalized system of preferences (GSP) process where, for example, numerous grievances have been raised and aired publicly about frequent fires and factory collapses in the garment manufacturing industry in Bangladesh. Such public hearings call government officials and employers to account in the public eye and may give complainants more leverage in achieving their goals.

85. In addition to changes to the public communication process, the 2006 US OTLA/NAO guidelines contain some changes regarding the office's cooperative activity function. One subtle change is the use of the term 'national contact point,' which is language from the Organization for Economic Cooperation and Development (OECD) Guidelines for Multi-National Enterprises (OECD Guidelines) for an NAO-like complaint mechanism. The new guidelines require the US OTLA/NAO to 'endeavor to the maximum extent possible to resolve matters through consultation and cooperation' in dealing with the contact point of another party 'and all persons.' In proposing cooperative activities, the US OTLA/NAO is now required to receive and consider views from worker and employer representatives and from 'other members of civil society' rather than from 'any person' as set in the original guidelines. One significant change to the US OTLA/NAO's role is that the office is now required to consult with the Office of United States Trade Representative (USTR), the Department of State and other appropriate entities in the US government in carrying out its responsibilities under the NAALC and FTA labor chapters.

While at first it seemed as though such consultations outside the OTLA might breach the integrity of the due process afforded during the complaint process under the NAALC and FTA labor chapters, in fact multi-agency cooperation may allow for more coordination between US government ministries in addressing issues raised by petitioners. Such cooperation yielded positive results with regard to the 2008 Guatemala complaint filed under the CAFTA-DR in which pressure was placed on the government of Guatemala by USTR to encourage cooperation between Guatemalan Ministries of Commerce and Labor to deny customs licenses to employers that do not comply with workplace-related court and administrative orders. See paragraphs 527 *et seq*.

III. Cooperative Consultations

86. Cooperative consultations between or among NAALC countries is a key feature of the agreement. Countries are constrained to 'endeavor to agree on the interpretation and application of this Agreement' and to 'make every attempt through cooperation and consultations to resolve any matters that might affect its operations.'

87. The first level of cooperation takes place among NAOs. Any one may request consultations with a counterpart over the latter's labor law, labor law administration, or labor market conditions. The responding NAO must provide publicly available data or information on these subjects, along with clarifications or explanations related to them. The third NAO must be afforded, upon request, the opportunity to participate in NAO cooperative consultations.

88. Above the level of the NAOs, members of the Council – the cabinet ministers responsible for labor – may request consultations with a counterpart labor minister 'regarding any matter within the scope of this Agreement.' As with the subject matter jurisdiction for NAO complaints, matters subject to ministerial consultation include all 11 labor principles, and may also include procedural matters arising out of the agreement's application.

89. In practice, although they have the authority to initiate ministerial consultations without any complaint on any matter having been filed, the NAALC labor ministers have only requested consultations in cases involving complaints. In concluding a review of a submission regarding any of the 11 labor principles, an NAO can recommend cabinet-level consultations among labor secretaries. Several cases have gone forward to ministerial consultations, which are seen as open-ended efforts to resolve a dispute before it enlarges. They have generally led to further hearings, special research reports, seminars and conferences, worker education programs, meetings of labor ministry staff from different countries, and the like. Cooperative consultations are also a primary means of addressing complaints under post-NAALC Canadian and US labor provisions.

IV. Evaluation Committees of Experts

90. If a matter has not been resolved through ministerial consultations, one country can obtain creation of an independent Evaluation Committee of Experts (ECE) to examine matters treated in the consultation. The ECE is a three-person *ad hoc* body of independent experts, one from each NAALC country, drawn from a list of labor law and labor economics experts developed by each party to the agreement.

91. As of 1 May 2014, no ECE had yet been formed under the NAALC. Several NAALC cases appeared to be close to moving to this stage at the beginning of 2001, but by April 2014 it was apparent that not even the best-strategized NAALC complaint would reach the ECE stage. Moreover, as the NAALC Secretariat has closed, it is unclear what entity would support the ECE if one were to be convened. A thorough understanding of the ECE process is vital for understanding what the NAALC countries sought to accomplish with their agreement.

92. An ECE is charged with analyzing, 'in light of the objectives of this Agreement and in a non-adversarial manner' each country's labor law enforcement effectiveness in the area chosen for study. However, certain subject matters are *not* subject to movement beyond ministerial consultations to the ECE level. Labor principles 1, 2 and 3 on freedom of association, collective bargaining, and the right to strike cannot be taken up by an ECE. Issues of union organizing, collective bargaining, and the right to strike are so bound to the balance of power between workers and employers (or imbalance, as the case may be) that none of the NAFTA parties wanted to yield domestic control. Attention should be called to the analogous situation in the European Union, where matters of pay, right of association, and the right to strike are insulated against regulation by EU Directives. Beginning with the US–Jordan FTA, the United States abandoned the tiered approach to addressing labor right issues in FTAs. Some of the subsequent US free trade agreements included trade sanctions as a potential remedy but others did not.

93. ECEs are empowered to evaluate the countries' record in one or more of the following eight labor law matters:

- forced labor;
- child labor;
- minimum employment standards;
- employment discrimination;
- equal pay for women and men;
- occupational safety and health;
- workers' compensation for occupational injuries and illnesses;
- migrant workers' protection.

94. A matter giving rise to formation of an ECE must be 'trade-related' and must be 'covered by mutually recognized labor laws.' Trade-relatedness is defined in the NAALC as 'related to a situation involving workplaces, firms, companies or sectors that produce goods or services (a) traded between the territories of the Parties; or (b) that compete, in the territory of the Party whose labor law was the subject of ministerial consultations ... with goods or services produced or provided by persons of another Party.'

95. The 'mutually recognized labor laws' requirement for establishing an ECE means that both countries – the one whose labor minister requests formation of the ECE, and the one who responded to the earlier request for ministerial consultations – must have laws 'that address the same general subject matter in a manner that provides enforceable rights, protections or standards.' Thus, for example, since the United States does not have any law requiring profit-sharing by firms with employees, a case involving effective enforcement of such laws in Mexico may not be susceptible to an ECE requested by the United States, even where the trade-relatedness prong is satisfied.

96. The sole mention of the ILO in the NAALC appears in connection with formation of an ECE. The NAALC Council is required to consult with the ILO in developing a roster of experts from which the chair of an ECE shall be selected. The chair and other ECE members must have expertise of experience in labor matters, be chosen strictly on the basis of objectivity, reliability and sound judgment, be independent of any government, and comply with a code of conduct established by the Council.

97. In 1999 the Council adopted Rules of Procedure for ECEs calling for appointment of ECE members within 21 days of a minister's request, unless there is an intervening request for an interpretive ruling regarding the requirement of trade-relatedness or mutually recognized labor laws. The ECE rules of procedure call for a permanent roster of 15 international trade experts from which one shall be selected to arbitrate a dispute over trade-relatedness, and 15 labor law experts from which one shall be selected to arbitrate a dispute over mutually recognized labor laws. If either rules that the matter is not trade related or not covered by mutually recognized labor laws, an ECE may not be convened.

98. Where an ECE is to be convened, a roster of 12 experts is created in consultation with the ILO, from which one may be selected to serve as chair of an ECE. A larger roster of 45 experts is established from which the other two ECE members shall be selected. If the Council cannot agree on one or more individual selections for chair and members of the ECE, they shall be selected by lot, with the requirement that the final three members of an ECE must be of different nationality.

99. Any interested person may make a written submission to an ECE. In addition, the ECE is empowered to hold 'information forums' to 'gather information from the Parties or the public.' The ECE shall present a confidential draft report to the Council within 120 days after it is established, containing a comparative assessment of the matter under consideration, the ECE's conclusions, and 'practical recommendations that may assist the Parties in respect of the matter.' The countries then have 14 days to respond to the ECE, which then proceeds to prepare a final report within 60 days after presentation of the draft report. The final report is published within 30 days after its presentation to the Council.

V. Arbitral Panels

100. Of the eight principles susceptible to an ECE, five cannot advance beyond the stage of treatment by an ECE. If a country is concerned that another is still failing to effectively enforce law laws in one or more of three areas – child labor, minimum wage, or occupational safety and health – it may request an emergency consultation. Countries must then 'make every attempt to arrive at a mutually satisfactory resolution of the matter through consultations.' These consultations can include calling on technical advisors or creating working groups or expert groups, recourse to conciliation or mediation, or development of recommendations that might assist the consulting countries to resolve the dispute.

101. If such consultations fail, two out of three countries can demand an independent Arbitral Panel if they believe there is still a 'persistent pattern of failure' by the third country to effectively enforce national labor laws on one, two, or all three of the labor law matters subject to this stage of treatment – child labor, minimum wage, or occupational safety and health. As of 1 January 2001, no arbitral panel had yet taken shape under the NAALC. Nonetheless, the importance of this final stage of the NAALC complaint process cannot be gainsaid, as it contains the 'teeth' of economic sanctions for workers' rights violations.

102. As with ECE's, any matter taken up by an arbitral panel must be trade-related and covered by mutually recognized labor laws. The arbitral panel is a five-person *ad hoc* body composed of independent experts from the three NAALC countries. Panel members must have expertise in relevant areas of the law, and are chosen from a roster of 45 persons. Two panel members are citizens of each of the two countries originally involved in the dispute, with the fifth panel member coming from the third country. The arbitral panel is charged with examining 'whether there has been a persistent pattern of failure by the Party complained against to effectively enforce its occupational safety and health, child labor, or minimum wage' laws and to make related findings, determinations, and recommendations.

103. An important condition for determining whether a country has failed to effectively enforce its laws is expressed in the NAALC's definitions clause, which states that a country has *not* failed to effectively enforce its health and safety, child labor or minimum wage laws 'where the action or inaction by agencies or officials of that Party: (a) reflects a reasonable exercise of discretion … with respect to investigatory, prosecutorial, regulatory or compliance matters, or (b) results from *bona fide* decisions to allocate resources to enforcement in respect of other labor matters determined to have higher priorities.'

104. The NAALC calls for adoption of Model Rules of Procedure for arbitral panels, but as of 1 January 2001 such procedures had not yet been promulgated.

They must provide a right to at least one hearing before the panel, with opportunity to make initial and rebuttal written submissions. If one country is not a disputing party, it is entitled, upon request or at the initiative of the panel, to make written and oral submissions to the panel and to receive written submissions of the disputing parties. The arbitral panel may turn to information and technical advice 'from any person or body that it deems appropriate,' subject to agreement by disputing parties.

105. Within 180 days after its establishment, the arbitral panel must present an initial report to the Council containing findings of fact and a determination as to whether there has been a persistent pattern of failure by the party complained against to effectively enforce its laws in matters of safety and health, minimum wage, or child labor. If such determination is affirmative, the panel must offer recommendations for resolution of the dispute.

106. Panel recommendations take the form of an 'action plan' for the country under scrutiny to adopt and implement 'sufficient to remedy the pattern of non-enforcement.' Countries have 30 days to comment on the panel's initial report. Thirty days after that, the panel must present a final report. If the final report reaffirms a persistent pattern of failure to effectively enforce labor laws, the countries in dispute may agree on an action plan based on the recommendations of the panel.

107. The countries have 60 days to agree on an action plan. If no agreement is reached, or if afterwards the countries cannot agree that the action plan is being implemented, one country can trigger reconvening of the arbitral panel. In the case of no agreement, the panel can impose an action plan, either by adopting the plan proposed by the country complained against, or by fashioning and adopting its own plan.

108. If the government refuses or fails to implement the final action plan, the arbitral panel can impose a fine (a) 'monetary enforcement assessment,' in the words of the NAALC) in an amount up to 0.007 per cent of the total value of trade in goods and services between the disputing countries. At the end of 2008, this amount surpassed $6 billion in the case of disputes between the United States and Mexico.

109. In setting the amount of the fine, the Arbitral Panel must consider:

(a) the pervasiveness and persistence of the country's persistent pattern of failure to effectively enforce its laws;
(b) the level of enforcement that could reasonably be expected given a country's resource constraints;
(c) the reasons offered for no fully implementing an action plan;
(d) efforts to begin remedying the pattern of non-enforcement; and
(e) any other relevant factors.

110. Any such fine is paid into a fund established by the Commission for Labor Cooperation and expended at the direction of the Council to improve or enhance labor law enforcement in the country complained against.

111. Finally the NAALC arrives at the much-debated 'teeth' of trade sanctions to punish workers' rights violations under a trade agreement. If the United States or Mexico fails to pay a fine required by a final order of an arbitral panel, any complaining country may suspend application of NAFTA tariff benefits in an amount sufficient to collect the fine. In suspending NAFTA tariffs, the collecting country may impose on those goods targeted for sanctions the lesser of (a) tariff rates in effect prior to the date of entry into force of NAFTA, or (b) Most-Favored-Nation (MFN) tariff rates in effect on the date of suspension.

112. In considering what tariffs to suspend under the sanctions clause, a country must first seek to apply the sanctions to the same sector or sectors where violations occurred and the government failed to effectively enforce its laws. If it 'is not practicable or effective' to target the offending sector, sanctions may be applied to other sectors to collect an amount in higher tariffs equal to the unpaid fine.

113. The NAALC exempts Canada from the trade sanctions discipline. Instead, Canada opted to guarantee payment of any fine. It accomplished this by adopting procedures to make any final determination by an NAALC Arbitral Panel a judicial order under Canadian law, enforceable by summary proceedings in the courts.

§5. Special Provisions for Canada

114. The federal structure of Canada's governmental system required several other special provisions in the NAALC to take into account the fact that labor law and labor law enforcement are primarily provincial responsibilities, not responsibilities of the federal government. Canada has eleven separate labor law regimes, that of the federal government (which also governs three federal territories) and those of each of the ten provinces. Except where federal constitutional issues might arise to call into question a provincial law or act of enforcement, or where a matter of criminal law is implicated (criminal law is within federal jurisdiction), each province is fully sovereign in labor law matters.

115. Federal labor law jurisdiction in Canada extends to employees of the federal government and in sectors specified as having national, international, or interprovincial importance. These include broadcasting, banking, transportation, shipping, telecommunications and key national industries such as grain handling and uranium mining. Approximately 10 per cent of the Canadian labor force is comprised of workers covered by federal labor law jurisdiction.

116. The Canadian federal government negotiated and signed the NAALC on behalf of Canada, but at that point it bound only the federal government and covered labor law matters in federal jurisdiction. Canada's labor minister held a seat on the Council. Canada could participate in NAALC cooperative activities. The Canadian NAO could receive complaints on labor law matters in another country, conduct reviews, and issue reports. It could also respond to complaints filed in another country's NAO over matters in federal jurisdiction. But Canada was blocked from initiating ministerial consultations, ECE formations, or dispute resolution in any matter unless a sufficient number of provinces ratified the NAALC.

117. Canada committed itself to 'use its best efforts to make the Agreement applicable to as many of its provinces as possible' by soliciting provincial ratifications. For the agreement to be fully implemented, ratification was required among a threshold level of any number of provinces whose total labor force, added to the 10 per cent of the labor force within federal jurisdiction, amounted to 35 per cent of Canada's total labor force, Then, only those provinces which ratified the NAALC would be bound by it. Furthermore, for any matter concerning a specific industry or sector, at least 55 per cent of the workers involved in that industry or sector must be employed in jurisdictions having ratified the NAALC.

118. The province of Alberta ratified the NAALC in 1995. Manitoba and Quebec followed in 1997, and Prince Edward Island in 1998. Being the second most populous province after Ontario, Quebec's ratification brought Canada beyond the 35 per cent threshold. As of 1 January 2009, the two other largest provinces, Ontario and British Columbia, had not ratified the NAALC. Motivations for ratification and non-ratification are mixed. Alberta was governed by a conservative party committed to free trade ideology which saw the NAALC as an element of NAFTA, which it supported. Quebec was governed by a nationalist, social-democratic government also committed to free trade, which Quebec's economy thrives on. It saw the NAALC as a valuable social dimension in the new trade regime.

119. Ontario was also governed by a conservative, pro-free trade prime minister, but protests by employer groups that the NAALC was being used by unions to attack companies turned Ontario away from ratification. British Columbia was governed by social democrats, but the BC labor movement was so strongly opposed to NAFTA in general that it also opposed any instrument or institution associated with NAFTA, including the NAALC. Any further ratifications of the NAALC among Canadian provinces will likely have to await changes in provincial government or changes in the positions of organized employer and organized labor groups.

§6. NAALC Cooperative Activities

120. The NAALC is filled with references to cooperation among the parties and an emphasis on the non-adversarial nature of most NAALC functions. As shall be shown below, the more contentious complaint mechanism has generated more comment, analysis, and action. However, the three NAALC countries have undertaken an extensive program of cooperative activities.

121. The NAALC specifies a broad range of subjects that can be taken up in cooperative activities. In addition to the labor principles set forth in Annex 1 of the NAALC, the following topics are included in cooperative activities programs:

- human resources development;
- labor statistics;
- work benefits;
- social programs for workers and their families;
- programs, methodologies and experiences regarding productivity improvements;
- forms of cooperation among workers, management and government;
- technical assistance from one country to another.

122. Cooperative activity programs have included meetings among labor ministry officials of the parties; joint sponsorship of public conferences and seminars with participation of unions, employer organizations and NGOs; and agreements for technical assistance and training. More than 40 specific activities have been held in more than a dozen cities in the three countries, including a annual, simultaneous 'North American Occupational Safety and Health Week' in each country. Written reports on most cooperative activities are available from the NAOs.

123. NAO-sponsored cooperative activities are government-to-government initiatives. The Secretariat also sponsors cooperative activities oriented toward private actors. A major Secretariat undertaking is a large-scale annual 'incomes and productivity' seminar examining the critical issue of whether productivity gains translate into rising living standards or whether, on the contrary, they flow to the benefit of owners, investors, and high-paid employees and contribute to greater income inequality. In fact, the Secretariat's reports from these seminars have provided compelling evidence of disproportionate benefits from productivity gains going to owners and investors, contributing to income inequality in the 3 NAALC countries. The Secretariat has also convened smaller-scale seminars, workshops, and 'focus groups' for private actors, such as one in early 2001 for migrant labor advocates from the three countries to assist the Secretariat in preparing a 'know your rights' handbook for migrant workers.

§7. Secretariat Research Reports

124. The NAALC Secretariat produced several valuable research reports between the time it opened operations in 1995 and closed in August 2010. All are available at the Secretariat's web site, naalc.org. It began with a *Preliminary Report to the Ministerial Council on Comparative Labor Law* highlighting similarities and differences among the three countries in areas of labor law dealing with the right to organize, the right to bargain collectively, and the right to strike.

125. The Secretariat followed with the comprehensive *North American Labor Markets: A Comparative Profile*. Making ample use of charts and graphs to accompany non-technical text, this report puts information on labor markets in each of the three countries into a continental framework. A second edition entitled *North American Labor Markets: Main Changes since NAFTA* was published in 2003. The third edition was published on the Secretariat's website in 2007.

126. Instructed by the Council to produce a special research report as part of a ministerial program related to the *Sprint* case (see below), the Secretariat published a 240-page book titled *Plant Closings and Labor Rights*. The report reviews the effects of workplace closures and threats of closures on the principle of freedom of association and protection of the right to organize in the three countries. It describes how each country's laws address workplace closures in the context of workers' organizing efforts, and reviews how those laws were administered and applied in the ten-year period prior to publication.

127. The Secretariat commissioned studies from several experts in the three countries and reviewed hundreds of labor board and court decisions in preparing its findings. The report concluded that the problem of anti-union closures and threats is especially acute in the United States, compared with Canada and Mexico.

128. After issuance of the workplace closures report, the Secretariat produced two smaller comparative studies, *The Employment of Women in North America*, and *Income Security Programs for Workers in North America*. Each provides timely, useful text and graphics, the first detailing the status of women workers in each country's labor market, the second detailing laws and regulations designed to protect migrant workers, and the third describing income support systems such as unemployment insurance, severance pay, and disability pay.

129. The NAALC Secretariat produced two major works in 2000. *'Standard' and 'Advanced' Practices in the North American Garment Industry* was the first full-scale comparative study of the structure and functioning of the garment manufacturing sector. This sector was chosen because it is a significant source of employment in all three countries and has been characterized by relatively labor-intensive techniques of production and low wages relative to other industries. The danger of 'sweatshop'-style production also motivated the study, since effective enforcement of national labor laws and labor standards – the heart of the NAALC obligation – is vitally important to avoiding wages and conditions that violate workers' rights. The report was based on extensive field research to identify strategies and practices that can promote protection of labor rights and labor standards.

130. The second major report by the Secretariat in 2000 was *Labor Relations Law in North America*, a 235-page book examining each country's laws, regulations, practices and institutions dealing with the first three labor principles on workers' organizing and bargaining rights and the right to strike. This volume was to be succeeded by new ones dealing with the remaining eight labor principles. *Labor Relations Law in North America* provides a detailed look at how each country seeks to meet its obligations under the NAALC. Woven into each section dealing with one of the countries are key comparisons with the other two, affording readers an accessible treatment of law and practice in all three countries. In 2002 and 2003 the Secretariat published two more comparative law studies, *The Protection of Migrant Agricultural Workers in North America* (2002) and *The Rights of Non-Standard Workers in North America: A Guide* (2003).

131. In 2000 the Ministerial Council instructed the Secretariat to produce a guide to labor and employment laws for migrant workers. The guide was part of the work program set forth in the May 2000 Ministerial Agreement arising out of public communications filed with the Mexican NAO about the treatment of migrant workers in the United States. The online version of the *Guide to Labor and Employment Laws for Migrant Workers* was published in June 2004. The hard copy version was published the following year. It was the first Secretariat publication to be conceived of and drafted in collaboration with the community for which it was written. In the fall of 2000, the Secretariat conducted surveys and gathered information from governmental and non-governmental organizations throughout North America seeking models of educational materials for migrant workers and to determine what kind of product it could craft that would be useful to migrant workers and their advocates. In March 2001 the Secretariat conducted a two-day tri-national focus group of 20 migrant worker advocates and educators from throughout North America, seeking their guidance on the format and substance of the *Migrant Guide*. In 2003, the draft text and samples of guide mock-ups were shared with focus groups of migrant agricultural workers in Leamington, Ontario and Baja California, Mexico, as well as with migrant educators and health workers in Houston, Texas to obtain their observations and an idea of how useful the *Migrant Guide* would be in the field. The result was a series of mini-guides written in question-and-answer style on 12–14 labor law subjects for each country, published in individual topic brochures, illustrated country guidebooks and a tri-national guide. The series of mini-guides was accompanied by a comprehensive directory of federal and state governmental and non-governmental offices dealing with a variety of labor issues in every state and province throughout North America.

132. The NAALC Secretariat's final publication was a comparative study of the legal treatment of migrant workers in each NAFTA country, published on the organization's website in 2010.

Chapter 3. NAALC Submissions and Cases

§1. Overview

133. As of 1 May 2014, 39 complaints had been filed under the NAALC. Some observers have called this number distressingly low considering the volume of workers' rights violations in North America, but it must be emphasized that the NAALC is not intended as a mechanism for resolving specific complaints and implementing remedies like orders to reinstatement workers unjustly discharged and related orders for back pay to victimized workers, orders to recognize and bargain with trade unions, orders to remove children from unlawful labor, orders to adjust pay for women to equal that of men, orders to install air filters to reduce health hazards, orders to provide compensation to injured workers, and other remedies associated with labor law enforcement. These matters are left to 'hard law' under national legislation and national enforcement mechanisms. Nevertheless, during the period between January 2009 and April 2014, the US OTLA/NAO issued four reports under non-NAALC FTAs indicating that while the FTA labor chapter review process is not intended to be an appellate process, international negotiations can place pressure on government authorities in trade partners to effect positive administrative outcomes for complainants. For example, in its 2013 report in response to a complaint filed under the US–Bahrain FTA labor chapter (see paragraphs 534 *et seq.*), the US NAO/OTLA noted that many public employees fired for participating in anti-government protests were in fact reinstated in part as a result of pressure from US government and the ILO.

134. The NAALC is intended as a review mechanism by which member countries open themselves up to investigation, reports, evaluations, recommendations and other 'soft law' measures so that over time such enhanced oversight and scrutiny will generate more effective labor law enforcement. In January 2001 it appeared to observers that to the extent legislative responses could be fashioned within national systems, rather than imposed by a supranational power, oversight under the NAALC could also change the climate for labor law reform in each country to achieve greater adherence to NAALC principles and obligations. This principle was to be tested in 2005 when a coalition of labor rights organizations challenged a labor law reform proposal being considered by the Mexican Congress, but both the US and Canadian NAOs rejected the resulting NAALC complaint.

135. The universe of NAALC cases is small enough to examine each briefly in detail, so that readers of the *Encyclopaedia* might appreciate how the NAALC is used by complaining parties, how other social actors as well as governments respond and participate in the process, and the range of outcomes. Before turning to such a case-by-case analysis, however, an overview provides orientation.

136. Between 1995 and 2000, the rate of NAALC complaints increased, and the pattern of complaint targets and subjects shifted. Most early cases such as those involving General Electric, Honeywell, Sony, employees of the Fisheries Ministry,

Maxi-Switch, Han Young and ITAPSA dealt exclusively with violations of workers' organizing and bargaining rights in Mexico. One case addressed a similar matter in the United States where Sprint Corp., the US telecommunications giant, closed a workplace while workers were attempting to form a union.

137. By the end of 1997, nine of the first ten NAALC complaints targeted Mexico for allowing workers' rights violations to occur without effective labor law enforcement to remedy or deter such violations. Only one case – the *Sprint* case – targeted the United States, and no complaints involving Canada had been filed. The Mexican government questioned whether the NAALC was becoming a 'Mexico-bashing' tool rather than a balanced agreement meant to enhance workers' rights in all three countries. Some Mexican critics charged that the NAALC had been captured by protectionist groups in the United States whose real goal was to halt foreign investment in Mexico by harassing multinational companies there, thereby keeping jobs in the United States.

138. An inherent limitation afflicted the early cases. Dealing solely with the NAALC's 'industrial relations' principles – freedom of association and protection of the right to organize, the right to bargain collectively, and the right to strike – they were not susceptible to treatment beyond the NAO review stage. An NAO review could be followed by ministerial consultations, but there was no recourse to an ECE or to an arbitral panel. Thus, there was no prospect of enforcement by means of economic sanctions against a government for failing to enforce labor law, or against companies or sectors where violations occurred.

139. Moreover, specific remedies such as reinstatement of workers unjustly dismissed for union activity or an order to bargain with an independent union not affiliated with the dominant central labor body were not forthcoming under the NAALC. Some workers rights advocates became discouraged and escalated criticisms of the NAALC as 'toothless.' However, others saw the longer-term potential for using the NAALC as a 'climate-changing' mechanism, especially through the availability of public hearings and public accountability by government officials. They persevered with new complaints raising new subjects, including more cases arising in the United States and Canada.

140. The years 1998 and 1999 saw new cases addressing labor rights violations in the United States and the first cases dealing with Canadian labor law matters. These years also brought the first case filed by Mexico's official CTM union federation, which earlier had effectively boycotted the NAALC as an infringement of Mexican sovereignty. For the first time, too, an employer organization sought to use the NAALC to its advantage. At the turn of the millennium, these developments suggested that NAFTA's labor side agreement was gaining traction as a tool to address worker rights issues in North America. Observers thought that the NAALC would develop into a sustained forum for labor rights advocacy.

141. After the change of the millennium, the number of NAALC complaints dwindled to one to three a year. In 2002 and 2007, not a single NAALC complaint was filed. No NAALC complaints were filed with the US NAO between 2006 and 2011 and no NAALC complaints were filed with the Canadian NAO between 2008 and 2011. During President Barack Obama's first presidential term, only one complaint was filed under the NAALC regarding a labor law matter arising in Mexico. This complaint was filed with both the Canadian and US NAOs in October and November 2011 and was still pending with no report issued at the end of April 2014. Two petitions were filed with the Mexican NAO regarding the treatment of migrant workers in the United States. The decrease in the number of NAALC complaints can be attributed to at least three factors. During the early part of the 21st century, cross-border and international labor and human rights movements and organizations matured and became more sophisticated in the kinds of tools and advocacy methods they use to bring international attention to labor rights issues. Some of these tools include independent monitoring and reporting by non-profit organizations such as the Worker Rights Consortium (WRC) and neutral organizations like Verité. Corporate codes of conduct proliferated, with some corporations turning to business auditors and accounting firms such as Ernst & Young and Price Waterhouse & Coopers to ensure that offshore manufacturers in the supply chain complied with international labor standards. As an alternative to corporate codes of conduct, global trade union federations such as the International Confederation of Free Trade Unions (ICFTU) and International Union of Food Workers (IUF) began negotiating International Framework Agreements (IFAs) with multi-national enterprises (MNEs) that cover MNE operations in a number of countries and in a variety of industries. An example is the IFA between the IUF, the Coalition of Latin American Banana Unions (COLSIBA) and the Chiquita banana conglomerate, which was negotiated and went into effect in 2001. In April 2012, the Ford Motor Company signed an IFA with the International Metalworkers Foundation (IMF). By the end of 2008, approximately 32 IFAs had been negotiated between global union federations and MNEs and were in effect. This number had increased to 73 by the end of 2011. As US companies, Chiquita and Ford were exceptions to the trend in the first decade of the 21st century, when almost all IFAs negotiated between global trade union federations and MNEs involved European MNEs. An example of an IFA that applies to workers in Mexico is the IFA between the International Metalworkers' Federation and Volkswagen, a Germany company.

142. During the early 21st century, North American labor and human rights activists turned increasingly to inter-governmental structures and organizations other than the NAALC and other FTA-based labor clauses for redress of labor rights violations, such as the Organization for Economic Development and Cooperation (OECD) Guidelines for Multi-National Enterprises (the OECD Guidelines). Activists also began to turn to the Inter-American Convention on Human Rights (IACHR), filing complaints with the Inter-American Commission on Human Rights. It could be argued that the most significant development in North American Labor Law in the first decade of the 21st century was the 2003 Advisory Opinion of the Inter-American Court of Human Rights requested by the United Mexican States on the Juridical Condition and Rights of Undocumented Migrants.

143. Many trade unionists and activists, such as the United Electrical Workers Union (UE), became increasingly disillusioned with what they found to be the lack of transparency and inadequate outcomes of the NAALC process and the high cost of filing public communications. Other trade unions, such as the AFL–CIO, focused their efforts on applying the lessons learned through the NAFTA/NAALC negotiation process and the application of the NAALC to their trade and labor advocacy efforts in Congress and internationally. Surprisingly, this state of disillusionment with the NAALC did not change with the election of Barack Obama and the development of a very active, progressive and responsive US OTLA. In an interesting development, in the mid-2000s Mexican trade unions and worker advocates pursued a strategy of filing complaints under the OECD Guidelines about labor matters arising out of the Mexican operations of both international and Mexican multinational companies.

144. Despite many activists' and trade unionists' disappointment with and widespread skepticism of the NAALC public communication process, the complaints filed between 2001 and 2008 were some of the most creative and well-strategized filed under the NAALC, such as the 2001 New York Workers' Compensation complaint filed with the Mexican NAO and the 2003 Puebla Matamoros Garment/ Tarrant complaint filed with the US and Canadian NAOs. Increasingly, non-profit activist groups such as the United Students Against Sweatshops (USAS) and the Canadian-based Maquiladora Safety Network (MSN) filed public communications based on their own independent investigations and reports by organizations such as the Worker Rights Consortium (WRC).

145. Another post-millennium development in free trade and labor in North America was the negotiation by all three North American countries of bilateral and multilateral free trade agreements (FTAs) with countries outside North America. While Mexico has FTAs with a number of countries, most of those FTAs do not have labor and environmental provisions. The exception is the FTA Mexico entered into with the EU in 2000, which makes reference to women's rights and human rights. All of the post-NAFTA US and Canadian FTAs contain labor and environmental provisions. The Canadian and US NAOs administer the labor provisions of post-NAFTA FTAs, with the exception of the US–Jordan FTA. During the Bush II administration (2001-2008), the US DOL changed the regulations governing the NAO in 2004 and 2006 and changed the name of the office performing NAO functions to the Office of Trade Agreement Implementation (OTAI) in 2004 and the Office of Trade and Labor Affairs (OTLA) in 2006 – while increasing the mandate of the NAO/OTLA and reducing its stature, budget and staff. In 2008, the US NAO/ OTLA had a dedicated staff of three to four people with back-up from other ILAB staff and its mandate covered more than a dozen countries on five different continents. After the inauguration of US President Barack Obama in January 2009, the stature, staff and budget of the OTLA increased significantly, covering a mandate of numerous countries all over the world including 13 existing trading partners and several potential trading partners.

146. Before looking at the cases it is important to remember that any 'labor law matter' related to one or more of the 11 labor principles can be the subject of a complaint before an NAO. There is no requirement that the matter be trade-related, no requirement of a 'pattern of practice' on the matter, and no requirement that the matter involve 'effective enforcement' of national law. These requirements come into play at the creation of an ECE, and beyond that in formation of an arbitral panel. Also, as noted earlier, there are no 'standing' requirements for a person or group filing a submission to show personal interest or injury in the case, and no citizenship requirement for filing with a particular NAO. Any person, from any country, singly or in coalition, may file a complaint with any NAO, including the NAO of their own country or the NAO of another country. The only jurisdictional limitation is that a complaint filed with the NAO of one country must involve labor law matters in another country, not the country where the complaint is filed.

§2. Cases Involving Alleged Workers' Rights Violations in Mexico

I. *Honeywell and General Electric* (US NAO cases nos. 940001 and 940002)

147. In February 1994 two US unions, the International Brotherhood of Teamsters and the United Electrical Workers, filed separate complaints with the US NAO alleging discharge of workers attempting to form unions at Mexican *maquiladora* facilities of two major multinational corporations. Citing violations of labor principle 1 and the failure of Mexican labor law authorities to adequately protect the right to organize, the unions charged that several workers at an electronic controls plant of Honeywell Corp. and at an electric motor plant of the General Electric Co. in the state of Chihuahua were dismissed for union activity.

148. The US NAO accepted the submissions for review in April 1994, and held a public hearing in Washington, DC in September 1994. Workers from the Honeywell and GE factories in Mexico testified at the hearing, along with Mexican labor lawyers and US union representatives. Neither of the companies appeared at the hearing. They defended their actions in written statements to the US NAO, arguing that the dismissal were for lawful causes unrelated to union activity.

149. The US NAO noted that its review 'reveals disagreements about the events at each of the plants,' namely whether workers were fired because of union activity or for lawful reasons unrelated to union activity. The NAO made no finding on the reasons for the workers' discharge, but it noted that 'the timing of the dismissals appears to coincide with organizing drives by independent unions at both plants.' The US NAO cited 'other relevant issues' including 'difficulties in establishing unions in Mexico, the hurdles faced by independent unions in attaining legal recognition, company blacklisting of union activists … and government preference for and support of official unions.'

150. Despite this background, the US NAO declared itself 'not in a position to make a finding that the Government of Mexico failed to enforce the relevant labor laws.' The NAO noted that the dismissed workers' acceptance of severance pay as indemnization for relinquishing their legal claims were in keeping with Mexican labor law.

151. Significantly, the NAO report did not conclude with a recommendation for ministerial consultations. Instead it called for a series of cooperative activities coordinated by the NAOs of the three NAALC parties regarding freedom of association and protection of the right to organize. US unions sharply criticized this failure to advance the case to the consultation stage. The United Electrical Workers angrily withdrew another NAALC complaint it had filed charging General Electric Co. with intimidation of workers in a union organizing election at the same Juarez plant where the first case arose.

152. Despite disappointment that this first test of the NAALC did not lead to even the single modest follow-up of ministerial consultations, the case set several procedural precedents that served labor rights advocates well in future cases. For one, the US NAO made it clear that it would normally hold public hearings on a complaint. US corporations had urged that hearings only take place in extraordinary circumstances. The US NAO reversed this approach, saying it would only *not* hold hearings in extraordinary circumstances. This approach was reversed in 2006.

153. Business organizations also insisted that the NAO should not take up any case unless all domestic labor law proceedings on the same matter have been exhausted. The NAO rejected this policy, requiring only a showing that domestic procedures have been begun, not exhausted. In this case, dismissed workers had made claims for *indemnización* (severance pay) under Mexican law. An exhaustion requirement would mean that several years would go by before a complaint could be made under the NAALC. While the US Department of Labor rejected a renewed proposal by business interests in 2006 to add an exhaustion-of-remedies requirement to US OTLA/NAO guidelines, the US OTLA/NAO referred to such a principle in its discussion of the 2003 Matamoros Garment/Tarrant public communication.

154. Corporate representatives also urged the NAO to refuse to accept any complaint naming a specific company as an alleged workers' rights violator. Since the NAALC deals with government obligations, they argued, complaints should only mention government conduct, without calling into question any actions by a private company or even allowing its name to appear in a complaint or to be mentioned in a public hearing. The NAO rejected this argument, on grounds that effective labor law enforcement can only be measured in light of specific cases and that events in cases involving specific companies are relevant to the public review process. The US DOL rejected this argument again in its response to US Chamber of Commerce comments to the 2006 changes to US OTLA/NAO Guidelines, but only to point out that as a matter of practice the NAO had stopped referring to complaints by the name of the specific company as an alleged workers' rights violator.

155. Ease of access to the public review process was also reinforced in this first NAALC case. In addition to testimony by trade union leaders and workers from the GE and Honeywell plants in Juarez, the NAO also heard from US and Canadian trade union leaders, panels of Mexican and US labor lawyers and human rights activists, and academic commentators.

156. Demonstrating the power of the law of unintended consequences, even press accounts of the NAO's decision helped drive the US NAO to call more ministerial consultations in future cases. The then-US Secretary of Labor, Robert Reich, was speaking at a convention of the United Auto Workers union on the day that newspaper stories recounted the NAO's report that ended without recommending ministerial consultations. UAW members angrily waved newspapers with a headline saying 'Reich sides with Mexican government on rights violations' and demanded an explanation. Reich was furious, and instructed the NAO never to put him in a position like that again. Since that time, the US NAO has never conducted a review and written a report without recommending ministerial consultations in the case, nor has the Canadian or Mexican NAO.

II. *Sony* (US NAO case no. 940003)

157. In August 1994 a coalition of four NGOs in the US and Mexico filed a complaint alleging discharge of workers and discrimination against dissident unionists at a Sony Corp. factory that made magnetic tapes for video cassettes. The plant is located in a Mexican *maquiladora* industrial park in Nuevo Laredo, Tamaulipas, along the border with Texas. In their complaint the International Labor Rights Fund, the Coalition for Justice in the Maquiladoras, the American Friends Service Committee, and the *Asociación Nacional de Abogados Democráticos* (ANAD) of Mexico cited collusion by management, incumbent union leaders and local political officials to crush an attempt to elect new leadership. Dissident union leaders were fired, and police attacked a peaceful march of independent union members.

158. The US NAO accepted the submission in October 1994 and held a public hearing in San Antonio, Texas in February 1995. Mexican workers, their attorneys, and US supporters addressed the hearing. Sony management refused to appear at the hearing. Much of the testimony dealt with Mexico's Conciliation and Arbitration Boards (CABs), tripartite agencies with government, labor and management representatives that adjudicate all labor disputes.

159. Citing allegations of blacklisting against workers who supported the independent union leadership group, the 'plausible' argument that they were fired for union activity, evidence of police violence against workers, and 'irreparable harm' from delays in legal proceedings, the US NAO recommended the first Ministerial Consultations under the NAALC.

160. Ensuing consultations resulted in a program of activities including (1) trinational workshops and public conferences in Mexico and in the US on union registration and certification, (2) a special study by independent Mexican experts on labor law dealing with union registration and its implementation, and (3) a series of meetings by officials of the Mexican Department of Labor and Social Welfare with Sony workers, local labor authorities, and company representatives.

161. In December 1996 the US NAO delivered a follow-up report on the *Sony* case. The report discussed the current status of Sony workers, initiatives in Mexico to change the labor law, and decisions of the Mexican Supreme Court that appeared to provide greater rights for independent union organizers. It concluded that 'potentially significant developments' continued to take place in Mexico in a wide range of labor matters, including labor legislation, labor–management relations, labor–government relations, and within labor organizations themselves. Though the situation on the ground did not change, independent union advocates in Mexico maintain that the international attention sustained the independent Sony workers' movement, which is still active.

III. *Pesca Union* (US case no. 9601)

162. In June 1996 the International Labor Rights Fund, Human Rights Watch, and the Mexican lawyers group ANAD filed a complaint with the US NAO on behalf of the *Sindicato Unico de Trabajadores de la Secretaría de Pesca* (SUTSP or Pesca [fisheries] union), which had long represented employees of the Mexican fisheries ministry. The union lost its representation rights when the fisheries ministry merged with a larger ministry of environment and natural resources.

163. The submission alleged that the new ministry and the labor authorities improperly revoked the Pesca union's registration and granted recognition and favorable treatment to the larger, pro-government union at the environment and natural resources ministry. The submission raised issues concerning a federal labor law requirement prohibiting more than one union in a governmental entity. This was cited by complainants as a violation of ILO Convention 87, which under the Mexican Constitution is part of the country's domestic law, as well as a violation of Mexico's own constitutional guarantee of freedom of association. Complainants also charged that the participation in the tripartite *Junta de Conciliación y Arbitraje* (conciliation and arbitration board) by union representatives who might have a conflict of interest in ruling on disputes with another union violated the NAALC's requirement for impartial labor tribunals.

164. The US NAO accepted the petition for review in August 1996. It held a public hearing in Washington, DC in December 1996 with testimony from representatives of the submitting US and Mexican organizations, union representatives and counsel from the contending unions, interested public citizens, and from a representative of the Mexican labor department. As part of its review, the US NAO also commissioned special studies on labor law enforcement in the federal sector.

165. In January 1997 the US NAO issued a report that recommended ministerial consultations on relevant legal doctrines in Mexico, including the effects on Mexican labor law of constitutional provisions assuring freedom of association, 'for the purpose of examining the relationship between and the effect of international treaties, such as ILO Convention 87, and constitutional provisions on freedom of association on the national labor laws of Mexico.' This was the first case with an extensive discussion of ILO conventions and their applicability in the NAALC context.

166. Mexico agreed to engage in consultations in March 1997. The follow-up program centered on an international conference on the application of treaties on national labor law. On the ground, however, further action became unnecessary. A series of Mexican court decisions found in favor of the independent union. In related cases, the trade union monopoly in the public employee sector was found unconstitutional by the Supreme Court of Mexico. In the end, registration was restored to the *Pesca* union. It has continued to try to organize the merged ministry in competition with the bigger union. It has not been successful in this, but the union and its leaders still play a role in the independent labor movement in Mexico.

IV. *Maxi-Switch* (US NAO case no. 9602)

167. The Communications Workers of America (CWA) filed a complaint with the US NAO in October 1996 on behalf of the Mexican telephone workers' union, the STRM. The submission alleged that a workers' attempt to organize a union affiliated with the STRM at the Maxi-Switch facility in Cananea, Sonora was thwarted by a collusive 'protection contract' between the company and another union affiliated with the dominant union federation. The submission argued that the contract was made without employees' knowledge or consent, and that the local *Junta de Conciliación y Arbitraje* improperly denied registration to the STRM group.

168. In December 1996 the US NAO scheduled a public hearing in the matter in Tucson, Arizona on 18 April 1997. Testimony was to be received from Maxi-Switch workers and from representatives of the CWA and the STRM. However, on 15 April 1997 the CWA withdrew the submission at the request of the STRM because the labor authorities in Mexico took steps to resolve the matter to the satisfaction of the STRM. The public hearing was canceled.

V. *Pregnancy Testing in the Maquiladora* (US NAO case no. 9701)

169. Two US-based human rights groups, Human Rights Watch and the International Labor Rights Fund, along with the ANAD of Mexico, filed a complaint with the NAO of the United States in May 1997 alleging 'a pattern of widespread, state-tolerated sex discrimination against prospective and actual female workers in the *maquiladora* sector along the Mexico–US border.' The submission alleged a common practice of requiring pregnancy testing of all female job applicants and denying employment to those whose test results were positive. The submission also said that employers pressured employees who become pregnant to leave their jobs. Companies do this, the submission argued, to avoid the legal requirement of three months' fully paid maternity leave for workers who give birth.

170. The submitters argued that the practice by employers and the failure of the labor authorities to combat it – sometimes by omission, sometimes by overt support for the employers' discriminatory policy – violated Mexico's obligations under the NAALC. The complaint sought a US NAO review, public hearings in cities along the Mexico–US border, and the formation of an Evaluation Committee of Experts to report on employment practices related to pregnancy in Canada, Mexico, and the United States.

171. In January 1998 the US NAO issued a report confirming widespread pregnancy testing that discriminated against women workers. Citing workers' direct testimony, the NAO found that pregnancy testing affected both women who were applying for work and women already employed. On pre-hire pregnancy discrimination, the NAO met confusion, including among Mexican government officials and labor law experts, about whether non-discrimination rules in Mexican law applied to persons not yet employed, and whether employers thus were free to discriminate against women applicants if they were pregnant. Post-hire discrimination against women already working was conceded to be unlawful. The NAO found that some women obtained relief through labor law enforcement, but that many others were unaware of their rights, of available protections and of the means and procedures for seeking redress. Ministerial consultations were recommended.

172. Concluding ministerial consultations in October 1998, the labor secretaries of Canada, Mexico, and the United States issued a ministerial agreement in which they approved of a program of workshops for government enforcement officials, outreach to women workers, and an international conference on gender discrimination issues. Under this agreement the Secretariat was to produce a public report for the Ministers reflecting the issues considered in the workshops and conferences. In the meantime, some US companies in the *maquiladora* zones announced they would halt pregnancy testing, and the federal government has prohibited pregnancy testing of women applying for employment in federal ministries. Women legislators in the Mexican Congress introduced bills that would make clear the applicability of non-discrimination requirements in the pre-hire context for women applying for positions. In 2001, it was thought that the pregnancy testing case would give rise to the first ECE under the NAALC. By the end of 2008, however, the pregnancy testing case was considered to be open and the Secretariat report mandated by the October 1998 ministerial agreement was yet to be published over a decade later.

173. In April 2003 Mexico passed the Federal Law to Prevent and Eliminate Discrimination (*Ley Federal para Prevenir y Eliminar la Discriminación* – LFPED). The LFPED prohibits discrimination based on national or ethnic origin, sex, age, disability, economic or social condition, health condition, pregnancy, language, religion, opinion, sexual preference or civil status in Mexico. The National Council on the Prevention of Discrimination (CONAPRED – *Consejo Nacional para Prevenir la Discriminacion*) opened its doors to complaints that same year. The main proponent and author of the LFPED legislative initiative in the Mexican Congress was Gilberto Rincón Gallardo, a long-time politician and disability and human rights activist who ran for the presidency of Mexico on the Social Democratic party ticket in 2000. Rincón Gallardo is the President of CONAPRED.

174. The LFPED prohibits discrimination on the basis of sex or pregnancy, including in the hiring process. In November 2005, CONAPRED signed an agreement with CANACINTRA, an employer organization, to change employer culture and end illegal practices such as pregnancy testing and the firing of women because they are pregnant. In 2012, the LFT was amended to prohibit pre-employment pregnancy testing and discrimination based on sex or pregnancy.

VI. *Han Young* (US NAO case no. 9702)

175. In October 1997 a coalition of Mexican and US unions and NGOs filed an NAALC complaint about events at a Tijuana, Baja California factory named Han Young, a supplier to Hyundai. Workers thought they had no union and moved to register a new one, but management produced a union contract with a local, pro-government union federation that blocked any new organizing effort. Han Young workers had never heard of the union or seen the contract.

176. A cross-border solidarity movement including informational picketing at Hyundai dealerships in the United States resulted in an unprecedented reversal on the part of Mexican authorities. The independent union got its registration. However, management still resisted bargaining.

177. After a series of serious health and safety incidents in the plant resulting in burns, broken bones, respiratory illnesses, and hearing and vision loss, an expanded coalition now joined by Canadian unionists filed an amended submission in February 1998. They added health and safety issues under labor principle 9 of the NAALC, arguing that Mexican enforcement authorities did nothing to apply federal health and safety laws at Han Young. This became the first NAALC case susceptible to arbitration and possible fines against the government or trade sanctions against the company. Since health and safety is one of three matters, along with minimum wage and child labor violations, that can reach this stage of NAALC treatment.

178. The US NAO conducted a public hearing in San Diego, California on 18 February 1998. One day after the public hearing in San Diego on Han Young's health and safety hazards, the Mexican government fined the company $9,000. It was the largest fine against an employer for safety violations in Mexican history.

Later in 1998, the company moved to a new factory with improved safety conditions.

179. The US NAO's report in August 1998 found serious safety and health hazards and recommended ministerial consultations. The resulting program included public forums on workers' organizing rights and on workplace health and safety. While the matter proceeded through NAALC stages, Han Young workers kept up their independent organizing and now bargaining effort, with occasional strikes to back up their demands. The company and state government authorities, meanwhile, promoted the formerly 'ghost' union as their preferred bargaining agent.

180. US Secretary of Labor Alexis Herman and Mariano Palacios Alcocer, Secretary of Labor and Social Welfare in Mexico, signed an agreement on ministerial consultations for US NAO Submissions 9702 and 9703 in May of 2000. In this agreement, the Mexican Department of Labor committed to continue to promote a registry of collective bargaining contracts. The agreement set forth an action plan in which the labor ministries would hold a public seminars in Tijuana, Baja California and in the state of Mexico on freedom of association, the registration of trade unions and mechanisms for gaining and challenging the title to a collective bargaining contract as well as conduct a government-to-government session on occupational injuries and illnesses. Violence broke at the public seminar in Tijuana, Baja California held in June 2000 and the union that filed the public submission held a protest outside the hotel where the seminar was held. The situation remained unresolved, with continued organizational activity and occasional strikes by the independent union.

VII. *Echlin/ITAPSA* (US NAO case no. 9703; Canada NAO case no. 98-1)

181. A broad coalition of more than thirty US, Canadian and Mexican unions and human rights groups filed two separate NAALC complaints, one with the US NAO in late 1997 and one with the Canadian NAO in mid-1998. This was the first case to be filed in Canada, and the first case to be filed with two NAO's simultaneously. The submission involved efforts by the independent FAT-affiliated union in Mexico to supplant a pro-government CTM union at a Mexico City auto parts factory called ITAPSA owned by US-based Echlin corporation. The complaints also cited health and safety violations involving exposure to asbestos and other toxic substances without adequate personal protective equipment.

182. Concerned in part about health and safety hazards, a majority of ITAPSA workers sought to enlist the independent union STIMAHCS to represent them. The CTM launched a campaign of threats and violence against STIMAHCS supporters. Company management sided with the incumbent union, firing several independent unionists and hiring new employees sent by the CTM to break up the independent organizing drive. Events culminated on the day of an election between the two unions, which was held not by secret ballot but by an open declaration in front of company and CTM officials. On the day of the election dozens of men armed with sticks, chains, bars and metal rods from the CTM were given free run of plant premises, where they threatened to kill any workers who voted for STIMAHCS.

183. The election, like reinstatement appeals from fired workers, was conducted by a tripartite Conciliation and Arbitration Board (CAB) made up of government, employer, and labor representatives. The labor officials on the CAB handling the *Echlin* case were all from the CTM, creating an inherent conflict of interest.

184. Both the US and Canadian NAOs held public hearings in the two *Echlin* cases where workers recounted these events and supporters voiced outrage. In addition to filing the NAALC complaint, US unionists organized protests at Echlin stockholders' meetings. Unions were also instrumental in convincing the state legislature of Connecticut, Echlin's corporate home, not to pass legislation sought by Echlin management protecting Echlin against a hostile takeover. Such a take-over was accomplished by Dana Corp. the largest US auto parts manufacturer, and the union coalition entered negotiations with Dana to resolve the Echlin dispute. In the meantime, the US and Canadian NAOs issued hard-hitting reports in 1998 and 1999 on the apparent violations of workers' rights, and recommended ministerial consultations in the matter.

185. The labor ministers of the three NAALC countries crafted an extensive follow-up program that included a special seminar on the workings of labor boards in the three countries, a government-to-government meeting on techniques and policies to promote compliance with health and safety regulations, and a program to disseminate information resulting from these events. In addition to the public seminar held in Tijuana, Mexico on 23 June 2000 resulting from the ministerial declaration adopted to resolve both US NAO 9702 and 9703, the occupational safety and health issues raised in the Echlin/ITAPSA complaint were to be addressed by the North Occupational Safety and Health Working Group established in the 2002 Ministerial Declaration signed to address US NAO 2001-01, discussed below. The press reported a violent confrontation between CTM and independent trade unionists at the June 2000 public seminar.

VIII. *Aerovías de Mexico Flight Attendants* (US NAO case no. 9801)

186. In August 1998 the Association of Flight Attendants (AFA), the principal US union of flight attendants, filed a complaint with the US NAO on behalf of its Mexican union counterpart, the Flight Attendants Association (ASSA). The submission was filed in response to President Ernesto Zedillo's back-to-work order to end a strike that began 1 June 1998 by attendants at *Aerovías de México*, a recently privatized airline company. Zedillo used executive authority under laws permitting a *requisa*, a government takeover of an enterprise where national security, defined as military or economic, is at stake. The complaint argued that government intervention in the strike violated Mexico's constitutional protection of the right to strike.

187. Soon after the submission was filed, the Mexican flight attendants' union reached a contract agreement with the airline on terms that the union declared victorious. The strike settlement removed the US NAO from a position between a rock and a hard place. Trade unionists were pressuring the NAO to accept the case for review. However, the Mexican government insisted that emergency powers to end strikes affecting economic security lay at the heart of any country's sovereignty, and that acceptance of the case by the NAO could provoke a diplomatic crisis. The US NAO declined to accept the submission for review, stating that the issue was 'better left to appropriate domestic fora.'

188. Although it declined to accept the case for review, the NAO added that it would engage an outside consultant for further research on how all three countries reconcile the principle of the right to strike with national interests of safety, security, and the general welfare. Titled *Emergency Procedures for Resolving Labor-Management Disputes in the United States, Canada and Mexico*, the consultants' report was released in September 2000, and is available on the web site of the US NAO.

IX. *TAESA* (US NAO case no. 9901)

189. On 10 November 1999 the AFA and ASSA filed a new complaint on violations of freedom of association, minimum employment standards, and health and safety rules affecting flight attendants at TAESA, a low-cost airline that flies to a number of US cities including Oakland and Chicago. Some 100 flight attendants who supported ASSA were fired by the airline when they voted in favor of ASSA and against an incumbent, government-affiliated union. The vote was taken at company headquarters in a procedure where each worker had to declare support for ASSA or for the official, government and employer-sponsored union in the presence of company and union officials, who openly took notes on how workers voted. Reprisals were taken almost immediately against ASSA supporters. The complaint also cited the company's violations of overtime, pension and wage requirements, and health and safety violations affecting both flight attendants and the flying public.

190. In January 2000 the US NAO accepted the case for review and scheduled a public hearing in Washington, DC. At the March 2000 hearing, the presidents of the two unions, joined by dismissed flight attendants, labor lawyers, and the AFL–CIO's Mexico representative, testified on the election, minimum labor standards violations, and health and safety hazards. Witnesses presented compelling and disturbing testimony about threats and intimidation during the election, excessive overtime and lack of emergency training, unsafe passenger cabin conditions, and company failure to make timely and complete payments for workers' health insurance, pension and housing funds.

191. The US NAO issued its report in the case in May 2000, crediting workers' accounts of serious violations of freedom of association, minimum labor standards, and occupational health and safety. Ministerial consultations were recommended, concluding in June 2002 with a ministerial agreement purporting to resolve the TAESA complaint, the Yale/INS complaint (MEX 9804) and the Auto Trim/Breed Technologies complaint (2000-01, discussed below).

X. *Autotrim/Breed Technologies* (US NAO case no. 2000-01)

192. In July 2000 a coalition of more than twenty trade unions, NGOs and student organizations filed a complaint with the US NAO over events at the US-based corporation Breed Technologies' Autotrim plant in the Mexican state of Tamaulipas. Autotrim supplies wheel covers and gear shift covers for General Motors, Ford and Daimler-Chrysler. Petitioners included current and former workers at the plant, the Coalition for Justice in the Maquiladoras, Mexican labor, human rights and religious organizations, the AFL–CIO and several affiliated unions, a number of worker health and safety support groups, and students from human rights clinics at St Mary's Law School in San Antonio, Texas and Columbia University law school in New York.

193. The complaint focused on health and safety matters in the Autotrim plant in the Mexican state of Tamaulipas, citing widespread illnesses and injuries from exposure to toxic materials and muscular-skeletal disorders caused by poor ergonomics. Illnesses and injuries were under-reported and under-compensated, said the submitters. The complaint charged that the Mexican government failed to monitor compliance and investigate suspected violations, failed to require record-keeping and reporting, failed to seek appropriate sanctions or remedies, failed to guarantee access to tribunals for enforcement, and failed to ensure that all proceedings for the enforcement of labor law were fair, equitable, transparent, and are not unnecessarily complicated or involve unwarranted delays – all obligations stemming from the NAALC.

194. At a public hearing held by the US NAO in San Antonio, Texas on 12 December 2000, several Autotrim workers testified that they suffered injuries and were exposed to severe health hazards, including open containers of chemicals such as benzene, toluene, methyl chloroform, and other known carcinogens. Workers explained that they stretched, sewed, and glued leather using toxic glues and solvents onto steering wheels and gear shifts in close quarters with no ventilation and no personal protective equipment. Symptoms included chronic sore throats, respiratory problems, nausea, memory problems, and rashes. Injuries related to substandard ergonomic practices include chronic pain in the hand, wrist, arm, and back and diminished mobility and use of hands, wrists, and arms. Workers also reported an unusually high rate of birth defects in their children.

195. One worker employed at Autotrim from 1991 to 1994 testified that she and other employees never wore any personal protective equipment such as masks, gloves, or safety glasses. Another former worker testified that she often felt faint on the job and suffered headaches. Plant supervisors told her and other workers that the illnesses were 'normal and harmless reactions to the use of glues and chemicals.'

196. Another former employee testified that he did not receive any type of training or information about the hazards of exposure to glues and solvents or how to diminish risk. Plant managers frequently failed to refer workers to IMSS (the Mexican Institute of Social Security) when employees became sick or suffered injuries on the job, another former worker testified.

197. A Mexican toxicologist specializing in occupational health and safety charged Mexican government authorities with gross negligence and disregard of workers' health. He told the hearing that in spite of clear and precise regulations that mandated the health and safety of employees in the workplace, the plants and management had systematically violated Mexican laws. For example, authorities failed to address employee reports of the lack of proper ventilation systems at the plants and lack of proper gloves to prevent absorption of toxic substances into the workers' skin.

198. The US NAO issued its public report in the *Autotrim/Breed Technologies* submission on 6 April 2001. In its report, the US NAO found that while STPS and IMSS, the Mexican Social Security Institute, had conducted inspections of the Breed Trim and Auto Trim plants between 1991 and 2000, it questioned the efficacy of these inspections because workers were not allowed to speak with inspectors confidentially and inspectors did not actually test equipment during inspections. The report also found that some IMSS doctors with the duty to assess on-the-job injuries for purposes of treating and compensating workers also worked for private employers, creating an inherent conflict of interest. The US NAO found workers' testimony and statements to be credible on a number of points, such as the unsafe conditions in the factories, their lack of confidence in company and IMSS physicians to make fair determinations about on-the-job injuries and illnesses, STPS' failure to respond adequately to workers' complaints about OSH violations and workers' concerns that factory OSHA committees did not adequately investigate the causes of on-the-job accidents or propose measures to remedy unsafe working conditions. In particular, the US NAO expressed concern that the Government of Mexico failed to communicate to the workers about its efforts undertaken in response to their petitions, failed to maintain records on their 1999 petitions, and failed to respond to workers' inquiries about the petitions. It found the Government of Mexico's lack of action and communication to violate its obligations under Articles 3, 4, 5 and 7 of the NAALC. The US NAO recommended ministerial consultations between US Secretary of Labor Elaine Chao and Secretary Carlos Abascal Carranza of the STPS. These were formally requested on 25 June 2001 and accepted on 24 July 2001.

199. The *Autotrim/Breed Technologies* public communication was a first in a number of aspects of NAALC investigation and resolution. It was not the first public communication to be drafted by clinical law students under the direction of a law professor (that first was the *Yale/INS* public communication), but it was the first to focus entirely on the issues of occupational safety and health and compensation for on-the-job injuries. It was the first time an NAO investigation team visited the premises of a factory involved in a public communication. The delegation included OSH experts from the US Occupational Safety and Health Administration (OSHA) and National Institute of Occupational Safety and Health (NIOSH), also a first. The OSHA and NIOSH experts wrote a safety report of the factories which the US NAO used in writing its report – another first.

200. Many observers found the *Autotrim/Breed Technologies* public communication to be the best strategized to date and most likely to result in an Evaluation Committee of Experts (ECE) and sanctions against Mexico. The *Autotrim/Breed Technologies* public communication became the test case for the effectiveness and transparency of the NAALC, its outcome to determine the NAALC's credibility among safety and health experts, trade unionists and worker activists in North America. *Autotrim/Breed Technologies* was also the first public communication to result in a Ministerial Agreement that addressed public communications regarding NAALC violations in both the US and Mexico.

201. The Maquiladora Health and Safety Support Network (MHSSN) conducted a sustained public advocacy campaign in support of the *Autotrim/Breed Technologies* public communication, publishing its numerous letters to US Secretary of Labor Elaine Chao and others on its website. The MHSSN pressed the US Department of Labor to take action on the public communication, to initiate an ECE and to implement a number of practical solutions within the confines of the NAALC to address the issues raised in the public communication. One of the MHSSN's advocacy efforts resulted in a letter to Elaine Chao signed by 35 members of the US House of Representatives criticizing the lack of action on the *Autotrim/Breed Technologies* public communication. The US Department of Labor did not adopt any of the MHSSN's suggestions.

202. On 11 June 2002, Secretaries Chao and Abascal issued a ministerial agreement Joint Declaration, ostensibly resolving the *Autotrim/Breed Technologies* public communication as well as MEX NAO 9804 (*Labor Department-INS Memorandum of Understanding*) and US NAO 9901 (*TAESA*). In the ministerial agreement, Secretaries Chao and Abascal agreed to exchange information about types of unions in their respective countries in a public seminar to be held in Mexico and to establish a bilateral working group of government experts on occupational safety and health issues, including those issues raised in public communications. The US Labor Department also obligated itself to develop worker education materials in Spanish to be disseminated in areas with the highest concentration of migrant workers in the United States.

203. As of the end of 2007, the 11 June 2002 Joint Declaration was the last Ministerial Agreement to be published under the NAALC until April 2008. It is both the symbol and manifestation of a stalemate in North American labor politics under the NAALC, in which Mexico's failure to effectively enforce laws related to the freedom of association, gender equity and occupational safety and health was matched by the US failure to effectively enforce labor and employment laws as they applied to immigrant workers in its territory. Each country's failure becomes the other country's trump card in a negotiation process that increasingly involves the indulgence of a mutual desire to avoid addressing uncomfortable issues that can embarrass the governing administration politically. The next ministerial agreement was not signed until 2014, to address a series of NAALC complaints filed with Mexico about unequal treatment of migrant workers in the US from 2003 to 2013.

XI. *North American OSH Working Group*

204. The OSH Working Group resulting from the 11 June 2002 ministerial agreement became trinational when Canada joined in September 2002, forming the Tri-National Working Group of Government Experts on Workplace Safety and Health.

205. In one respect, the establishment of the North American OSH Working Group was a historic moment in the NAALC because it was the first time the three labor ministries utilized NAALC provisions to establish a sustained trinational working group related to a common problem in the three nations. On the other hand, the OSH Working Group reflected two trends that had been in place since before the NAALC was implemented. The occupational health and safety agencies of the three North American countries had an active relationship predating the implementation of the NAALC, reflected in the numerous North American OSH public cooperative activities organized over the years. Given this history, it was no surprise to NAALC observers that the first tri-national working group related to occupational safety and health. The other trend was a lack of transparency and public participation in the working group, reflected in comments and criticisms made by workplace safety advocates throughout North America, especially those involved in filing the *Auto Trim/Breed Technologies* public communication.

206. The OSH Working Group first met in Mexico City in July 2002, where it established four sub-groups, including Web Page, Handling Hazardous Substances, Voluntary Protection Systems and Training and Technical Systems. The members of these subgroups were governmental OSH administrators and experts. The Secretariat had no formal role in the Working Group though there was discussion over the years of involving the Secretariat more actively. Unions, grassroots organizations, non-profits and employer groups were not members of the OSH Working Group.

207. The OSH Working Group had its second meeting in conjunction with the Second Hispanic Forum on a Safe and Healthy Environment in San Diego, California in October 2002. The Hispanic Forum on a Safe and Healthy Environment was itself a historic initiative resulting from cooperation between the Pan-American Health Organization (PAHO), the US Environmental Protection Agency (EPA) and two non-governmental organizations: the National Safety Council (NSC's), a century-old US-based employer–union non-profit organization dedicated to improving occupational safety and health, and the grassroots organization Hispanic

Alliance for Hispanic Health. The Hispanic Forum was a dynamic partnership of governmental and non-governmental activists and experts dedicated to improving the lives of Hispanics and Latinos in the United States and throughout the Americas through study, education and creative initiatives in the areas of environmental, health and occupational safety and health policy. The Hispanic Forum consisted of public workshops and meetings as part of the NSC's annual convention.

208. In contrast to the Hispanic Forum, the North American OSH Working Group met behind closed doors during the NSC convention, resulting in protests and press conferences criticizing the North American OSH Working Group, its lack of transparency and its lack of responsiveness to the particular issues raised in the *Auto Trim/Breed Technologies* public communication.

209. During its most active period (2002–2005), the OSH Working Group set up a web page and organized a number of workshops and meetings throughout North America. One such workshop was held in Mexico City in August of 2003 on Best Practices in the Construction Industry. Construction unions and construction employer groups from all three countries participated in the workshop. Like the OSH Working Group itself, the workshop on Best Practices in the Construction Industry may have been a useful and positive activity but unresponsive to the issues raised in the *Auto Trim/Breed Technologies* public communication. By failing to address the issues raised in the public communication, the North American OSH Working Group had little credibility in the grassroots worker safety community.

XII. *Duro Bag* (US NAO case no. 2001-01)

210. The *Duro Bag* complaint was another test of the NAALC, though of a different kind. In June 2001 the AFL–CIO and the Paper, Allied-Industrial, Chemical & Energy Workers International Union (PACE International Union) based in Nashville, Tennessee filed a public communication with the US NAO arising out of workers' action to assume leadership of the union representing them at the Duro Bag plant in Rio Bravo, Tamaulipas, Mexico. The Duro Bag factory was owned by a private company based in Kentucky and manufactured gift bags for brands like Niemann Marcus and Hallmark. Dissatisfied with the lack of representation provided by the CTM affiliate with which Duro Bag had signed an agreement when it opened the factory, workers filed a petition with the local labor board to elect new union leadership that better represented their interests. As part of their petition, the workers requested a secret ballot election in a neutral site free from employer coercion. Although Mexico's Federal Labor Law (LFT) is silent on the issue of secret ballots in union elections, Mexico had agreed to promote secret ballot union elections in the Ministerial Agreement it signed with the US to resolve public communications 97-02 and 97-03 filed with the US NAO.

211. In the *Duro Bag* complaint the AFL–CIO and PACE argued that the Mexican government failed to comply with the obligation it assumed in the 2000 Ministerial Agreement to promote secret ballot union elections as well as with a number of NAALC obligations such as ensuring that its labor law and regulations provide for high labor standards; continuing to strive to improve those standards; promoting compliance with and effectively enforcing its labor laws; ensuring that its administrative, quasi-judicial, judicial and labor tribunal proceedings are fair, equitable and transparent; and providing parties effective access to administrative, quasi-judicial, judicial and labor tribunal proceedings.

212. The *Duro Bag* submission was the first in the history of the NAALC to seek to enforce a previously agreed-to Ministerial Agreement signed under the NAALC. The US NAO declined to accept the submission for review on 22 February 2002. In his letter to the submitters declining to accept the public communication for review, the Deputy Under-Secretary for International Labor Affairs wrote that the secret ballot in union elections was not required under Mexican labor law, so there was no violation of the NAALC.

XIII. *Puebla (Tarrant and Matamoros Garment)* (US NAO case no. 2003-01 and Canada NAO case no. 2003-1)

213. In September 2003 the United Students Against Sweatshops (USAS), the *Centro de Apoyo al Trabajador* (Worker Support Center or CAT), a grassroots non-profit worker solidarity support organization established in the state of Puebla, Mexico in 2000, and Canada-based Maquiladora Safety Network (MSN) filed a public communication with the US and Canadian NAOs alleging that the Mexican government failed to effectively enforce its labor laws in events arising from a worker rights campaign and union drive at the Matamoros Garment Factory in the state of Puebla, Mexico. In their complaint, USAS, CAT and MSN mentioned events that occurred at the Mexmode (formerly Kukdong) plant in the state of Puebla, Mexico, and reported that cross-border solidarity and use of corporate codes of conduct had not achieved their worker rights goals so they sought NAO intervention. In addition to filing public communications with both the Canadian and US NAOs, USAS, CAT and MSN simultaneously filed a complaint with the International Labor Organization's Committee on Freedom of Association – a first in the history of the NAALC.

214. Matamoros Garment Factory was a *maquiladora* that manufactured clothing for brand-name companies like Puma. It opened its doors in 1999 in Azúcar de Matamoros, Puebla. In 2000, 190 workers staged a work stoppage due to unpaid wages. Riot police were called in and workers were assaulted. Many of the workers were women in their late teens and early twenties, some of them single mothers. Shortly after the workers returned to their jobs, Matamoros Garment signed a protection contract with a CTM-affiliated union. Despite an on-site factory inspection by PUMA, the international sports clothing brand, pursuant to its Corporate Code of Conduct in 2002, workers continued to suffer violations of their rights under Mexican labor law, including unsafe working conditions, unpaid wages, failure to pay minimum wages, an unsanitary factory cafeteria, mandatory overtime, mandatory work on holidays and being locked in the factory to meet production quotas.

On 13 January 2003, 190 workers went on strike for 11 hours to protest working conditions in the factory. A week later, 162 Matamoros Garment employees petitioned the local state labor board for recognition of their union, the *Sindicato Independiente de Trabajadores de la Empresa Matamoros Garment* (Independent Union of the Workers of Matamoros Garment or SITEMAG). By the end of January 2003, PUMA canceled its production contracts with Matamoros Garment, stating that it was due to the factory's incapacity to complete orders and not due to the independent union drive at the factory. By the end of March 2003 Matamoros Garment Factory had closed. After the factory announced it would be closing, the Puebla labor board denied SITEMAG's union recognition petition on technical grounds. SITEMAG did not receive official written notice in time to file proper appeals.

215. In November 2003, USAS, CAT and MSN submitted an amendment to the original public communication with the US and Canadian NAOs adding facts about Mexico's failure to effectively enforce labor laws in regard to events at the Tarrant factory in Ajalpan, Puebla, Mexico. In June 2003 workers at Tarrant had conducted a three-day work stoppage to protest unsafe working conditions, failure to pay wages and verbal and sexual harassment. A month later, after unsuccessful negotiations between Tarrant and the workers' organizing committee, 400 of 1,100 workers formed the *Sindicato Único Independiente de Trabajadores de la Empresa Tarrant México* (Only Independent Union of Workers of Tarrant Mexico or SUITTAR). Over three-quarters of the workers who formed the union marched together to the local labor board to file a petition with the local labor board seeking recognition of their union. By the middle of July 2003, Tarrant fired the members of the union's executive board and had them forcibly removed from the factory, then fired 300 union members. In October 2003 the local labor board rejected SUITTAR's union recognition petition on technical grounds such as the misspelling of one of the 736 names on the petition. During this period some fired workers sought reinstatement through individual labor proceedings before the local labor board and others accepted individual severance pay.

216. The US NAO accepted the public communication on 5 February 2004 and the Canadian NAO accepted the public communication on 12 March 2004. The US NAO conducted a public hearing in Washington, DC on 1 April 2004 in which former Tarrant workers and representatives of CAT, USAS, MSN, the Worker Rights Consortium (WRC) and others provided testimony expanding on the allegations in their complaint.

217. At the US NAO hearing, workers explained that at the Tarrant factory workers were required to work overtime to meet production quotas and would be docked a day's work if they did not comply and that security guards blocked workers' exit from the factory if they tried to leave before quotas were filled. They were also required to clock out for bathroom breaks and stand in line to use inadequate and dirty toilet facilities. In addition to elaborating on the issues raised in the public communication and its amendments, witnesses testified that the Director of the Tehuacan Human and Labor Rights Commission had been assaulted and received death threats as a result of his work related to trade union movements in the state of

Puebla. Witnesses testified that workers involved in the Tarrant and other union movements in the state of Puebla were fired unlawfully, were forcibly removed from the work site, had difficulty obtaining new employment due to blacklisting and were unable to obtain redress from the local labor boards.

218. The US NAO published its report on 4 August 2004. The report and its treatment of facts reflect the heightened corporate involvement and NGO activism on the ground, referring to factual reports prepared by independent monitoring organizations like Verité, which conducted inspections pursuant to the Corporate Code of Conduct of one of the brands that sourced textile goods in the state of Puebla, as well as the non-profit Worker Rights Consortium, which prepared an independent report of the facts in Puebla. Brand name companies like PUMA and Levi's participated in the process by submitting information to the US NAO confirming or denying the workers' allegations (in the case of PUMA) or, in the case of Levi's, sending a letter to the US NAO expressing support for the public communication process and recommending ministerial consultations – a first in the history of the NAALC.

219. In addition to conducting interviews with workers who supported the trade union movements in Puebla, the US NAO met and interviewed with workers who did not support the trade union movements. The report tested the factual allegations in the public communication using all of these factual sources, using the additional information both to confirm the credibility of the workers and their statements and to question those statements. The report referred to numerous letters sent by USAS and CAT to Mexican government officials at the state and federal level to determine whether the Mexican government was aware of labor law violations raised in the submission to determine whether government officials took action.

220. The US NAO recommended ministerial consultations to explore a number of issues with the Mexican government. Throughout its report, the US NAO referred to the fact that the Mexican NAO and STPS would not facilitate or in some cases even allow the US NAO to interview state and federal labor officials and would not fully answer the US NAO's questions about the facts in the cases raised in the submission. Both the public communication and the report referred to prior US NAO reports filed under the NAALC. Tellingly, the US NAO wrote, 'In light of the recurring freedom of association issues raised in the current submission, it would appear that despite the passage of 10 years, the same enforcement deficiencies persist in Mexico.'

221. The report relied heavily on facts indicating that workers did not pursue legal remedies in the courts after union and individual claims were denied or discontinued appeals in exchange for receiving severance pay. The standard the US NAO applied almost reached an exhaustion of remedies standard, but not quite, granting less credibility to the workers' allegations about Mexico's failure to enforce its labor laws because they did not show that they attempted to utilize various domestic legal processes. Reflecting findings that were in the end rather ambiguous, the US NAO noted that the issue of workers being harassed and intimidated into accepting compensation was an area to be explored further in ministerial consultations with the Mexican government. The US NAO wrote, 'It is clear that the Government of Mexico was made aware on numerous occasions of the alleged worker rights violations taking place at the Matamoros Garment and Tarrant factories, through letters, local news reports, and face-to-face meetings with workers, worker rights groups, and Mexican and foreign private companies. The US NAO is awaiting response from the Government of Mexico as to what, if any, action resulted from the various requests for action.'

222. As part of its review process, the Canadian NAO conducted a public meeting in Toronto, Ontario on May 28, 2004. Like the US NAO, the Canadian NAO questioned the allegation that Mexico had failed to effectively enforce its labor laws when workers did not file complaints regarding the labor law violations raised in the public communication. The Canadian NAO tempered this observation by noting the passivity of the local labor boards, especially when presiding over conciliations between workers and employers where workers signed severance agreements in which they were paid far less than what they were untitled under Mexican labor law. The Canadian NAO's analysis of the local labor boards' denial of the union registration of SITEMAG and SUITTAR was clearer and stronger than that of the US NAO, stating plainly that according to its analysis, there was no basis in Mexico's Federal Labor Law (LFT) for the reasons given by the local labor board for rejecting the unions' registration. Unlike the US NAO, the Canadian NAO indicated that Mexico failed to comply with the NAALC obligation to have high labor standards by not having legal provisions protecting workers' right to have access to a copy of their union's collective bargaining agreement.

223. The *Puebla Tarrant /Matamoros Garment* complaint was the first in which there were joint trinational ministerial consultations between the Ministers of Labor of all three North American countries. On 24 April 2008 – almost 4½ years after the initial complaint was filed – the three labor ministers signed a joint declaration agreeing to undertake a number of activities to address raised in the Puebla complaint. The agreement mandated that the CLC Secretariat develop and prepare a background report and guide describing labor laws, regulations, procedures and best implementation practices for in three North American countries, with special emphasis on unjustified dismissal for organizing or joining a union, registering unions and access to collective bargaining agreements. The Joint Declaration instructs that the information be made available to be disseminated in all three countries after approval by the Ministerial Council. The Joint Declaration also mandates that the Mexican Labor Ministry STPS host a government-to-government session in Puebla with federal and state official for exchange of information to be followed by a seminar with 'other relevant stakeholders' to share and build upon information gathered in the government exchange. The NAOs of the three countries were to develop a work plan to implement these mandates within 90 days. On 2 December 2008 the three North American labor departments held an intergovernmental meeting in Mexico regarding Puebla complaint. On 3 December 2008, a public trinational conference was held in Puebla. The non-governmental submitters of the complaint – the Centro de Apoyo a Trabajadores Puebla (CAT Puebla), USAS and Maquiladora Support Network – boycotted the conference because they were denied access to the planning stages and were not invited to make presentations or participate meaningfully in the conference. In September 2012, the Worker Rights Center in Puebla closed its doors and its Executive Director was forced to flee to Canada and ultimately settle outside Puebla as a result of threats of violence and death. On September 18, 2012, outgoing US Secretary of State Hillary Clinton and her Mexican counterpart Patricia Espinosa entered into a wide-ranging Memorandum of Understanding for the Promotion of Gender Equality, the Empowerment of Women and Women's Human Rights.

XIV. *Yucatan-Markey Tex and Coco Tex* (US NAO case no. 2004-01)

224. In July 2004, UNITE-HERE, a 440,000 member US union that came into existence in early 2004 when the US leading apparel worker and hotel workers unions merged, and the Mexico-based *Centro de Apoyo a los Trabajadores de Yucatán* (Yucatan CAT – Yucatan Worker Rights Center) filed a public submission with the US NAO alleging worker rights violations at Markey Tex and Coco Tex, two clothing factories in the city of Mérida, Yucatán, Mexico. Although the submission was withdrawn by the submitters in late August 2004 and was never refiled, the *Yucatan-Markey Tex* and *Coco Tex* NAALC complaint marks a number of significant developments in NAALC practice and jurisprudence. Importantly, the *Yucatan-Markey Tex* and *Coco Tex* case was the first to be filed simultaneously under the NAALC and the OECD Guidelines for Multi-National Enterprises (OECD Guidelines). The complaint was also part of UNITE HERE's campaign to US organize workers at the Cintas Corporation, a uniform manufacturing and rental company based in Cincinnati, Ohio. Finally, reflecting the wage-and-hour enforcement practice of low-wage worker advocates in the United States, the *Yucatan-Markey Tex* and *Coco Tex* complaint was one of the first to include actual timesheets demonstrating that workers at these factories did not receive the legally-mandated minimum wage in the state of Yucatan, Mexico.

225. On 24 March 2004, UNITE HERE published a report linking issues faced by immigrant workers employed by Cintas Corporation contractors in Chicago with those faced by workers manufacturing uniforms for Cintas subcontractors in Mexico and Haiti. This report, entitled *Code of Conduct: Safeguarding standards or shielding abuses*, highlighted the common problems faced by Cintas workers in all three of these countries, including high quotas and low wages, lint- and dust-filled air, excess heat, and machines that lacked safety guards. It also used working conditions faced by workers to call into question the efficacy of Cintas' Code of Conduct. According to the report, Coco Tex and Markey Tex were two plants in the industrial park of Mérida, Mexico owned by a married couple and connected by a passageway that manufactured medical uniforms for Cintas. Shipping records and worker testimony shows that these two factories manufactured uniforms for Cintas throughout the fall of 2003 and first half of 2004.

226. The NAALC complaint alleged that the governments of Mexico and the state of Yucatan failed to effectively enforce minimum employment and occupational standards laws in these two plants. Markey Tex employed 150 workers and Coco Tex employed 300 workers. The complaint quoted workers saying that they were required to work during breaks and after hours to fix errors, were docked a full day's pay for attending a one-hour medical appointment, were not paid overtime overages, were coerced into working overtime although this is illegal under Mexican labor law and were often not able to take their legally mandated work breaks because the break bell malfunctioned. The complaint included copies of employee time sheets that showed workers received less than the weekly mandated minimum wage of 281 pesos (about $28.00) and noted that workers were often required to provide their own tools (scissors) and safety equipment (face masks) at their own expense. The UNITE HERE report on which the complaint was based cited a study showing that the minimum wage in Yucatan was one fourth of a sustainable wage required for a family of four in the state of Yucatan, Mexico. Factory safety violations included one or two functioning toilets for 150–300 women, poor ventilation and inadequate control of lint in the workspace, inadequate safety guards on sewing equipment resulting in frequent needle punctures and poorly placed and insufficient fire extinguishers.

227. As part of its discussion and proof, the complaint alleged that the government of Yucatan created a union-hostile environment through anti-union sentiments and pronouncements of labor officials and the Governor, and that this violated NAALC Article 5, Section 1 which obligates each NAALC signatory to ensure that its administrative, quasi-judicial, judicial and labor tribunal proceedings for enforcing its labor law are fair, equitable and transparent. The argument was that government pronouncements indicated bias on the part of state officials charged with enforcing labor law in the state of Yucatán and a failure to comply with the NAALC Article 7 requirement to ensure public information and awareness of workplace protections. It is not clear from the complaint whether workers at the Coco Tex and Markey Tex factories sought to organize a union or sought to enforce their rights in local labor boards. Had this been clear and had the complaint not been withdrawn, the Yucatán Markey Tex/Coco Tex complaint might have been poised jurisdictionally to proceed all the way to the final Arbitration and Sanctions phase of the NAALC submission process, as it dealt with the issues of Minimum Standards and Occupational Safety and Health.

228. UNITE HERE also filed a complaint about conditions at the Markey Tex and Coco Tex factories under the OECD Guidelines. The complaint was filed with the US, Canadian and Mexican National Contact Points (NCPs). The OECD Guidelines complaint focused on a subsidiary of Angelica Corporation, Life Uniform, that sourced medical scrubs from the Markey Tex and Coco Tex plants in Mexico. In August 2004, Angelica Corporation sold Life Uniform to Healthcare Uniform Co, an enterprise of Sun Capital Partners. At the end of 2007 it was not clear whether conditions at the Coco Tex and Markey Tex factories had improved or whether the plants are still open, but it appeared that a confidential agreement was reached between the union and the corporation as a result of the OECD Guidelines complaint.

229. In addition to the OECD Guidelines complaint filed regarding abuses at the Mexican plants in the state of Yucatan, UNITE HERE partnered with the Dutch union FNV Bondgenoten to file a separate OECD Guidelines complaint with the US and Dutch/Netherlands NCPs about Angelica Corporation's anti-union tactics at several plants in the United States as well as failure to provide training and a safe and healthy working environment for its employees. The Dutch/Netherlands NCP had jurisdiction because the Angelica Corporation sought financing for expansion from LaSalle Bank, a Chicago-based subsidiary of the Dutch bank ABN AMRO. The US NCP declined to address the complaint because it arose out of facts arising in the United States as a result of actions by a US corporation. Nevertheless, as a result of the OECD Guidelines complaint and letters that UNITE-HERE wrote to LaSalle Bank and ABN AMRO, UNITE HERE and Angelica Corporation came to an understanding that workers at non-unionized plants would be able to choose whether to be represented by the union.

XV. *Mexican Labor Law Reform* (US NAO case no. 2005-01)

230. In February 2005, the Washington Office on Latin America (WOLA) and a coalition of 22 unions and worker rights groups from Canada, Mexico and the United States filed a path breaking complaint with the US NAO/OTAI and Canadian NAO alleging that a series of proposed reforms to Mexico's Federal Labor Law (LFT) violated NAALC Article 1(1) and 1(2) objectives to improve working conditions and promote the 11 NAALC labor principles, the Article 2 obligation to ensure its labor laws and regulations provide for high labor standards, the Article 3 obligation to promote compliance with and effectively enforce its labor laws and the Article 4 obligation to ensure that persons with legally recognized interests under law in a particular matter have appropriate access to administrative, quasi-administrative, judicial and labor tribunals for labor law enforcement, as well as the Article 6 publication obligation.

231. The series of proposed reforms at issue were called 'Plan Abascal,' named for the Carlos Abascal Carranza, a former head of Mexico's major employer's organization COPARMEX, who served as Mexico's Secretary of Labor from 2001 (the beginning of Vicente Fox's administration) to 2005, when he was appointed as Secretary of State to replace Santiago Creel. The reforms were first submitted to the Mexican Congress in December 2002 and were scheduled to be voted on in the February 2005 session. Plan Abascal was designed to 'flexibilize' Mexico's labor law, making it easier for employers to hire and fire workers and have more control over workers' schedules. In addition to changes in individual employment relationships, Plan Abascal would tighten government control over union formation and collective bargaining without addressing problems raised in NAALC complaints about the transparency of union affairs. Reforms proposed by the independent National Union of Workers (UNT) and supported by the progressive party in

Mexico, the Democratic Revolutionary Party (PRD) in the Congress included the creation of a public registry of collective bargaining agreements so that workers could more easily learn whether they are represented by a union and the terms of the collective bargaining agreement. According to the submitters, Plan Abascal would increase the administrative obstacles to workers' ability to join the union of their choice, strike and engage in collective bargaining – thus exacerbating the administrative obstacles found to be in violation of the NAALC in public communications – and did nothing to address the lack of impartiality in federal and local labor boards in Mexico. In addition to arguing that Plan Abascal violated the NAALC, the submitters argued that it violated ILO Convention 87, flouted recommendations made by the ILO Committee of Experts on the Application of Conventions and Recommendations, violated Mexico's obligations under the Inter-American Convention on Human Rights and failed to address recommendations of the United Nations High Commission for Human Rights, which found that Mexico must improve respect for labor rights.

232. The US NAO/OTAI rejected the public communication in February 2006, a year after it was filed, on the basis that a review would not further the objectives of the NAALC. The Canadian NAO also rejected the public communication on the basis that the matter should be address by democratic processes in Mexico.

233. As Mexican President Vicente Fox's six-year term came to a close at the end of 2006, Fox was less and less able to achieve a consensus in the Congress. While the Institutional Revolutionary Party (PRI) often supported economically liberal policies and the Mexican union federation most closely tied to the PRI, the Mexican Confederation of Workers (CTM), entered into a pact with COPARMEX to keep wages low when NAFTA first went into effect, Fox and his conservative National Action Party (PAN) were unable to achieve enough votes in Congress to pass the Plan Abascal in the face of opposition from the progressive PRD and PRI-istas who hold the substance, if not always the application, of Mexico's Federal Labor Law in reverence. At the end of 2008 the Plan Abascal reforms to Mexico's Federal Labor Law had not been passed by the Mexican Congress.

234. Mexico's conservative party PAN achieved labor law reform at the end of the administration of Felipe Calderón in 2012. In late 2012, the Calderón Administration introduced legislation with the Mexican Congress to make several reforms to the LFT. According to *Mexican Labor News & Analysis*, the initial legislative proposal contained provisions that would have made it impossible for independent trade unions to win elections or for legal strikes to occur. On the other hand, the initial proposal included provisions that would have required transparency in union elections and finances. Neither of these proposals made it into the final law. Provisions making it easier to hire and terminate workers, permitting outsourcing and part-time employment all survived the lengthy legislative process. The final version law did nothing to reform the legal regime governing trade unions under which protection contracts are possible. In some positive developments, the LFT was amended to include provisions prohibiting workplace discrimination and harassment and now specifically prohibits pre-hire pregnancy testing. The amended LFT went into effect on December 1, 2012, the first day of the presidential administration of President Enrique Peña Nieto.

XVI. *Mexican Pilots – ASPA* (US NAO case no. 2005-02, Canada NAO case no. 2005-1)

235. In May 2005, the Mexican Airline Pilots Union (ASPA) submitted a complaint alleging that Mexico failed to effectively enforce its labor law in relation to a labor dispute between ASPA and Aviacsa Airlines. Pilots working for Aviacsa Airlines voted to affiliate with ASPA in April 2002 but the Federal Conciliation and Arbitration Board did not ratify the pilots' vote and placed obstacles to the pilots' free exercise of their freedom of association under the NAALC, ILO Convention 87, the Inter-American Convention on Human Rights and the International Covenant on Economic, Social and Cultural Rights. When ASPA filed the NAALC complaint, its unionization campaign had been ongoing for five years. Pilots involved in the campaign had been fired and intimidated by Aviacsa. ASPA also filed a complaint with the ILO Committee on Freedom of Association.

236. In July 2006, over a year after it was filed, the US NAO/OTAI rejected the complaint on the grounds that it would not further the objectives of the NAALC and because the Mexican Supreme Court issued a decision that pilots working at Aviacsa were not entitled to a craft-based pilots-only union.

XVII. *Hidalgo – Child Labor at Rubie's de Mexico* (US NAO case no. 2005-03)

237. On 15 October 2005, the Progressive Union of Workers of the Textile Industry, the Manufacturing, Cutting and Confection of Fabric and Garments in General and Related and Similar Industries in the Mexican Republic, Chicago-based US Labor Education in the Americas Project (US LEAP) and the Washington Office on Latin America (WOLA) filed a public communication with the US NAO concerning labor rights violations at Rubie's de Mexico, a factory in Tepeji del Rio, a town in the state of Hidalgo, Mexico. Rubie's de Mexico was a subsidiary of New York City-based Rubie's Costume Company which manufactures costumes, accessories, pet outfits and masks for 60 different labels, including Barbie, Star Wars, Harry Potter and Shrek. Rubie's had an exclusive license to produce Barbie costumes as a Mattel licensee. The company has a corporate presence in North America, Europe and Asia. The complaint alleged that Mexico and the state of Hidalgo failed to effectively enforce labor laws governing 10 of the 11 NAALC labor principles in relation to violations at the Rubie's de Mexico factory in Tepeji del Rio. The only NAALC principle not alleged to have been violated was principle 11 requiring the equal protection of migrant workers.

238. The *Rubie's* complaint was significant for a number of reasons. Except for an early letter from tomato industry representatives complaining of child labor practices in agriculture in Mexico, the *Rubie's* complaint was the first public communication to seriously raise the issue of child labor violations in a North American country. The complaint also made advances in the kinds of proof presented to the US NAO, as well as the level and use of governmental mechanisms at the local level. Unlike the *Puebla Tarrant/Matamoros Garment* complaint, the *Rubie's* complaint included evidence of a number of ongoing and pending cases before the conciliation and arbitration boards, as well as detailed proof about child labor law violations at the factory in the form of workers' birth certificates that had been altered by factory managers to make it appear that underage workers were in fact of age to work. The complaint was also significant because of a major public relations campaign involving the issue of child workers creating Barbie and other costumes for better-off children in the United States and elsewhere, the role played by the worldwide toy manufacturer Mattel and its Global Manufacturing Principles (GMP) and the participation of the Washington, DC law firm Jones Day which represented Rubie's Costume Company in the NAALC proceeding and submitted a 30-page response to the NAALC complaint along with over 500 exhibits.

239. The Tepeji del Rio Rubie's plant employed between 60 and 80 workers to manufacture Barbie and other costumes. According to the complaint, many of the workers in the plant were under age, forced to drop out of school and work to help their families. Workers as young as 13 performed the same work as adults. One 13-year-old boy injured his spine carrying heavy fabric rolls. Health and safety conditions the factories included cockroach infestations, dirty bathrooms, expensive and poor quality food in the factory that made the workers ill. Workers were required to buy water and toilet paper from the company, as well as their work tools including masks, gloves and belts. One worker stated that workers were required to pay $42 (450 pesos) for a work belt. Since the cost of the belt exceeded workers' weekly wages, many did not buy it.

240. In addition to child labor and workplace safety violations, the complaint alleged that workers were not probably paid for overtime, factory doors were sometimes locked to force workers to stay late to meet production quotas, women and girls were required to pay for and take pregnancy tests in order to work for the company and supervisors and managers often insulted and mistreated workers. The workers turned to relevant authorities to complain about the situation but did not receive an adequate response.

241. In February 2005, 58 Rubie's workers agreed to affiliate with the Progressive Union of Workers of the Textile Industry (FTVO-CROC) and to enter into a collective bargaining agreement (CBA) with Rubie's. The following month, the workers and the union submitted a strike notification petition with the Federal Conciliation and Arbitration Board with the objective of having Rubie's sign a CBA. The workers filed with the Federal rather than the Local Conciliation and Arbitration Board because the textile industry is one of the industries under federal rather than local enforcement jurisdiction unless the plant owner applies for a special exception.

242. Over the next two months there was a heated campaign in which Rubie's shut down the plant, almost all the plant's workers filed complaints with the Conciliation and Arbitration Board for unpaid benefits, Rubie's began to dismantle the plant, plant officials informed workers who had filed complaints to the labor board and participated in strikes would have no work, workers picketed the plant and Rubie's called Hidalgo state police to disperse the picketing workers. Throughout the campaign, the union and Rubie's continued to negotiate independently and under the auspices of the labor board. On 11 May 2005, the union and Rubie's presented a resolution to the labor board in which Rubie's agreed to sign the CBA and reinstate the workers. In exchange, the union would withdraw its petition.

243. Despite the successful negotiation of an agreement between Rubie's and the union, less than a week later the Federal Conciliation and Arbitration Board declared it did not have jurisdiction over the strike procedure and disqualified itself, giving the union a 24-hour deadline to designate a local labor board or its case would be denied. Rubie's then reneged on the agreed-upon resolution and the fired workers filed complaints seeking payment and benefits as well as reinstatement at the plant. A little over two weeks after Rubie's and the union signed the resolution, a CTM-affiliated union appeared before the federal labor board alleging it had signed a CBA with Rubie's in 2003. The FTVO-CROC filed a court appeal of the federal labor board's decision, but the court was unable to process the appeal because of the local labor board's failures to comply with procedure. Although the federal labor board declared itself incompetent to adjudicate the FTVO-CROC union petition, it continued to adjudicate individual employee complaints for severance and other payments.

244. The US OTLA accepted the Hidalgo/Rubie's complaint on 6 January 2006, almost three months after the complaint was filed. It issued a Public Report of Review on 31 August 2007, almost two years after the complaint was originally filed. For the first time in over a decade, the US OTLA did not conduct a public hearing to gather testimony and evidence regarding an accepted public communication. As part of its review of the Hidalgo/Rubie's complaint, the US OTLA consulted with Mexican government officials, workers, employers, union representatives, and an independent legal expert with knowledge of the case. The US OTLA's report noted that as had been done in the *Puebla Tarrant/ Matamoros Garment* public communication review process, the Mexican NAO declined the US OTLA's request to arrange meetings with Mexican government officials charged with enforcing labor laws. Interestingly, possibly as a result of advocacy by Rubie's outside counsel Jones Day, the US OTLA was careful to note that its review was not intended to determine whether or not Rubie's may have acted in violation of the law, and nothing in the report should be taken as an independent finding by the OTLA on Rubie's compliance or failure to comply with Mexican labor law.

245. The US OTLA found that there may have been a legal technicality in the way the Rubie's de Hidalgo plant was registered that placed it under local rather than federal jurisdiction, so that Rubie's may have fallen under a narrow exception to the general rule that textile companies are under the jurisdiction of the federal labor board rather than the local labor board. It also found, however, that the Mexican Government has stated to the International Labor Organization that when there were technical errors in worker petitions, the labor board would help workers revise the petition so that it could be filed in the proper place. The US OTLA expressed concern that valid unionization petitions were rejected based on highly technical grounds, recounting the trajectory of the Hidalgo/Rubie's union petition as it progressed through the local labor board process (after its failed trajectory in the federal labor board process), when it was rejected in July 2005 due to a flaw in the signature on the petition document. Importantly, the US OTLA found there to be several problematic aspects with the administrative procedures for registering collective bargaining agreements, including reliance on technical grounds to reject union petitions seeking collective bargaining rights and unwarranted delays resulting from ineffective communication between federal and state labor authorities. The US OTLA also found there were too few periodic inspections of the Rubie's plant between 1998 and 2005 and that although it could not independently verify that women working at Rubie's did take pregnancy tests, they were required to do so in the hiring process until 2005.

246. The US OTLA recommended consultations with the Mexican NAO on improving compliance with Mexican labor law, reducing delays and increasing coordination between federal and state labor boards; increasing the transparency of the union registration process and creating a public registry of existing CBA's; existence of inspection resources; current status of anti-discrimination and prohibition of pregnancy testing pursuant to the ministerial agreement in US NAO 9701; and obtaining access to Mexican authorities responsible for enforcing labor law. As of the end of 2008, it was not clear whether the Mexican NAO had accepted consultations.

XVIII. *USW – Coahuila Pasta de Conchos Copper Mine Disaster Case* (US NAO case no. 2006-01)

247. On 19 February 2006, an explosion in the Pasta de Conchos copper mine killed 65 mine workers in the state of Coahuila, Mexico. Temperatures inside the mine reached 600 degrees Celsius or over 1,100 degrees Fahrenheit. Only two of the miners' bodies were ever recovered. The mine was owned by the multinational conglomerate Grupo Mexico. Two-thirds of the miners who were killed worked for the subcontractor Compañia General de Hullua. Twenty-five of the miners who were killed were represented by Mexican National Union of Miners and Metal Workers (SNTMMSRM), first established in 1934. Just ten days before, miners had been told that the Pasta de Conchos mine was safe and federal safety inspectors certified that their employer had corrected 34 safety violations in the mine. Miners had been complaining to Mexican labor officials for over two years about safety violations including poor ventilation, faulty electrical switches and live wires on the ground.

248. Two days before the mine explosion, the Mexican labor department STPS issued a notice recognizing Elias Morales Hernandez and a new Executive Committee for the SNTMMSRM. In 2002 and 2004, miners themselves had elected Napoleon Gómez Urrutia and Executive Committee members to leadership terms ending in May 2008 and May 2010. Napoleon Gómez Urrutia and other elected SNTMMSRM union officers learned from the news on 28 February 2006 that they had been removed and replaced by a different set of union officials recognized by Mexico's federal labor department. Government officials alleged that Gómez Urrutia was responsible for embezzling US$50 million US from money paid to the union when Mexico's mines were privatized in 1990. Gómez Urrutia and his supporters alleged that the move was made to keep Gómez Urrutia from leading strikes as a result of the 17 February Pasta de Conchos mining disaster. Thousands of workers in the SNTMMSRM and other mining unions went on strike throughout Mexico and in the state of Coahuila to protest Gómez Urrutia's ouster from the union's leadership and to protest the conditions that led to the mining disaster. According to news reports, the Pasta de Conchos mine was not reopened.

249. On 9 November 2006, the United Steelworkers (USW) filed a public communication with the US OTLA stating that Mexico violated several provisions the Mexican Federal Labor Law (LFT) and failed to effectively enforce labor laws governing freedom of association, collective bargaining and the right to strike in violation of the NAALC when it made the administrative decision to recognize new executive leadership of SNTMMSRM in place of leadership elected by union members in accordance to union by-laws. Among the legal provisions cited by the USW include LFT Articles 369 and 370, which state that union dissolution, suspension and decertification measures must be issued by Conciliation and Arbitration boards, not through administrative measures.

250. Separately, Mexican lawyers for the SNTMMSRM led by the De Buen law firm filed local legal challenges to actions by the Mexican government in the context of SNTMMSRM union elections in a number of Mexican states. While not all of these legal challenges were successful, as a result of these efforts in September 2008 the Mexican Supreme Court issued a decision affirming Mexican workers' right to a secret ballot in trade union elections.

251. The public communication also stated that Mexico failed to effectively enforce occupational safety and health laws, resulting in the 17 February 2006 Pasta de Conchos mine explosion. According to the complaint, the last government inspection of the Pasta de Conchos mine before the disaster was in July, 2004. The company was allowed months to deal with unsafe conditions in the mine and federal officials did not physically verify the company's statements that it had effectively eliminated safety violations. Although the state of Coahuila has over 129 mines and over 1,500 miners have died in that state over the last century, there are only five federal safety inspectors allocated to the state. The public communication also stated that, unlike almost every other state in Mexico, Coahuila does not have a federal Conciliation and Arbitration Board despite the heavy presence of the mining industry and the fact that the mining industry is one of the industries governed by the federal, as opposed to the state, Conciliation and Arbitration Board.

252. In its request for remedies, the USW called upon the US OTLA to engage in cooperative consultations with its Mexican counterparts and to hold public hearings in San Antonio, Texas to discuss the trade union rights and occupational safety and health issues raised in the complaint. The USW called upon the US OTLA to require the Government of Mexico to commit to reviewing the procedure by which it changed by administrative fiat the elected leadership of the SNTMMSRM on 17 February 2006, commit to compensate the victims and the relatives of workers who died in the Pasta de Conchos mine accident and commit to transparency in OSH reporting and enforcement and to fully enforce the Mexican labor law. Citing a number of past US NAO reports on Mexico's failure to effectively enforce occupational safety and health and trade union rights laws, the USW called on the US OTLA to convene and Evaluation Committee of Experts to address Mexico's continual failure to comply with the NAALC and to convene an Arbitral Panel to issue sanctions against Mexico for its ongoing violation of its NAALC commitments.

253. Almost eight months after the public communication was filed, the US OTLA rejected the public communication in a letter dated 31 August 2007. The US NAO/OTAI had been reorganized into the US OTLA during the period between the original filing of the complaint and its rejection. The reasons given for rejecting the complaint were that several criminal and labor proceedings related to the issues raised in the complaint were ongoing, that complaints filed with the International Labor Organization (ILO) were still pending and the Mexican Ministry of Labor should be given an opportunity to address the issues raised before the US labor officials reviewed whether or not their Mexican counterparts had effectively enforced labor laws in compliance with the provisions of the NAALC. Essentially, the US OTLA rejected the claim on grounds similar to the 'exhaustion of remedies' requirement found in many international mechanisms, a requirement not present in the text of the NAALC, and the 'pending international proceedings' requirement, also not present in the text of the NAALC.

254. The *Coahuila Pasta de Conchos Copper Mine Disaster* case reflects a number of NAALC-related trends in the first decade of the 21st century. As in the 2003 *Puebla* textile factory complaint, submitters filed related complaints with the International Labor Organization. The US OTLA, as it did more frequently, delayed months before making a decision whether or not to accept a NAALC complaint, then rejected the complaint. Unlike in the past, the US OTLA did not reproduce the complaint on its website. The entire text of the complaint was published by the privately published *BNA Labor Reporter* in addition to a *BNA Labor Reporter* news report about the complaint. Finally, the US OTLA continued the nascent trend of reading into the NAALC 'exhaustion of remedies' and 'pending international proceedings' requirements not found in the NAALC's text or past NAO practice. In contrast, in the *Sprint Mexico* NAO case filed in 1995, the Mexican NAO monitored ongoing NLRB proceedings as part of its review and action plan. In the 2003 Puebla textile factories case, the US NAO conducted a full hearing and review process although the ILO conducted a simultaneous review of the case.

255. The *Coahuila Mine* case may also be an important moment in the movement of North American labor and occupational safety and health advocates toward conducting their own monitoring and report-writing activities independent of the NAALC. In the fall of 2007 at the request of Local 65 of the SNTMMSRM, the Maquiladora Health and Safety Support Network (MHSSN) organized a team of US and Mexican occupational safety and medical professionals to conduct a workplace safety assessment of the Grupo Mexico-owned open pit copper mine in Cananea, Sonora, Mexico. The team of physicians, industrial hygienists, a pulmonary technician and a registered nurse conducted workplace observations and worker interviews as well as lung function testing of 68 workers over a four day period in October 2007. In the resulting report published in MHSSN's website, the team concluded that the Cananea copper mine was in general disrepair resulting in unsafe working conditions, that workers were subject to high concentrations of quartz silica dust that exceed ten times those allowed by Mexican safety regulations and that the overall safety program, including industrial hygiene monitoring, worker training and ventilation and source pollution controls in the mine were grossly inadequate, leading to numerous worker injuries and deaths.

256. In October 2007, the Commission for Labor Cooperation Secretariat and NAOs organized a 1½ day cooperative activity in Guadalajara, Mexico entitled, 'Trinational Government Experts Workshop on the Role of Labor Ministries in the Effective Promotion of Mine Safety and Health in North America.' During this government workshop, government officials from Canada, the US and Mexico discussed innovative practices in establishing mine safety and health standards, tripartite solutions to improve mining safety and best practices in managing mine accidents and labor inspector training.

XIX. *Sindicato Mexicano de Electricistas – SME* (US NAO case no. 2011-01)

257. The first NAALC complaint filed with the US and Canadian NAOs in the Obama administration was filed in Canada in October 2011 and the US in November 2011. It was the first complaint filed in the US since 2006 and the first filed in Canada since 2008. The complaint was filed by an impressive array of close to a hundred Mexican, Canadian, US and international trade unions and advocacy groups, including the AFL-CIO, Canadian Labour Congress, Canadian Union of Public Employees and the independent Mexican trade union federation UNT.

258. On Sunday, October 11, 2009, then Mexican President Felipe Calderón issued a decree dissolving one of two government-owned power companies – Luz y

Fuerza (Light and Power) – and immediately transferred all of its operations and assets to the other government-owned power company, Comisión Federal de Electricidad (Federal Electric Commission – CFE), giving CFE a monopoly over electrici service in Mexico. The night before the decree was issued, 27,000 federal, state and local police were dispatched to immediately terminate over 44,000 Luz y Fuerza employees and dissolve the union representing them, Sindicato Mexicano de Electricistas (Mexican Electrical Workers Union – SME). The action also affected over 22,000 retirees from the company. The electric company and its trade union had been in existence for over 100 years. The stated reason for closing Luz y Fuerza was excessive cost, but the NAALC complaint cites government communications indicating that the primary reason was to dissolve the powerful SME, a powerful opponent to the privatization of electrical services in Mexico.

259. The petitioners argued that the Government of Mexico had violated its core obligations under the NAALC to effectively enforce labor laws in a transparent, independent and impartial manner. In particular, petitioners pointed out that federal labor boards had approved of the terminations of Luz y Fuerza employees despite the fact that the terminations did not comply with Mexican legal requirements that employee terminations be in writing for a narrow list of reasons. Petitioners also pointed out that there were extensive delays in administration of cases by the federal labor boards. Importantly, the petitioners argued that the Calderón Administration had interfered with the internal affairs of SME and violated NAALC Labor Principles governing the freedom of association and the right to collective bargaining. Finally, petitioners argued that President Calderón's decree led to violations of NAALC Principle 9 obligation to maintain a healthy and safe working environment, as the lack sufficient and experienced staffing on electrical installations led to workplace accidents and deaths.

260. The US OTLA accepted the complaint for review on 13 January 2012. After the OTLA initiated its investigation and met with the SME in Mexico in March 2012, the petitioners filed a supplement to their original complaint on 25 May 2012. The May 2012 supplement provided additional information about Mexican law governing the dismissal of employees and amended the original complaint to include allegations that the government of Mexico had failed to properly enforce anti-discrimination laws per Labor Principle 7 of the NAALC. Under Mexican law, workers must be given written notice of dismissal in accordance with a number of specific listed reasons. This did not happen when Luz y Fuerza was abruptly closed by the Calderón administration in 2009. The May 2012 supplement added a gender element to the original complaint, outlining protections that should have been afforded to Luz y Fuerza workers who were pregnant at the time of the abrupt closure of the company including the right to reinstatement after legally mandated paid maternity leave, as well as medical benefits. Petitioners pointed out that when Luz y Fuerza was closed down, its employees lost the medical coverage and in some cases wage indemnity (for maternity leave and work and non-work related disability) they had through the Mexican Institute of Social Security, affecting mothers, their children and employees on temporary disability. Former Luz y Fuerza workers were offered a year of work of continued medical coverage through the Mexican

Institute of Social Security but only if they agreed to sign acceptance of their termination, thereby foreclosing any opportunity they might have to be rehired by Luz y Fuerza's successor employer, the CFE.

261. In particular, the May 2012 supplement discusses in detail the issue of anti-union animus expressed by the government of Mexico and anti-union discrimination against the SME and its members, arguing that President Calderón's administration engaged in a public smear campaign against the SME and its members. Petitioners described this public smear campaign as a 'calculated strategy to demonize the SME and turn public opinion against it.' As a result of this public smear campaign, even the children of SME members and former Luz y Fuerza employees suffered bullying at school and in some cases had to leave school because their parents could no longer afford school fees. Former Luz y Fuerza workers also suffered labor market discrimination and blacklisting as in many cases they were unable to secure new employment and were denied access to jobs at CFE despite the fact that CFE employees and contractors were unfamiliar with Luz y Fuerza operations, resulting in a number of outages and problems in the electrical grid. The Mexican Secretary of Labor at the time, Javier Lozano, attributed the outages to sabotage by former Luz y Fuerza employees, but it is more likely that the outages occurred as a result of old equipment and a shortage of workers experienced with working with Luz y Fuerza installations. The petitioners cited jurisprudence from the ILO's Committee on Freedom of Association (CFA) for the proposition that a government's negative attitude against a trade union can constitute discrimination against union membership. While acknowledging that the 2004 Federal Law on the Prevention and Elimination of Discrimination (LFPED) prohibits discrimination against women, persons with disabilities and trade union members (among others), petitioners point out that the government agency designed to enforce the LFPED, the National Council on the Prevention of Discrimination (CONAPRED) lacks the authority to compel respondents to participate in conciliation of disputes. Petitioners also cited ILO CFA jurisprudence for the proposition that failure to establish effective machinery to prevent workplace discrimination against trade union members is a violation of ILO Convention 98.

262. On 2 July 2012, the US OTLA granted itself an extension to issue a report on the 2011 Luz y Fuerza complaint in light of new information in the May 2012 supplement. Meanwhile, the SME's complaints wound their way through the Mexican legal system. The Federal Arbitration and Conciliation Board (JCFA) held that the Calderón Administration had not violated the law with its closure of Luz y Fuerza. This decision was upheld by a federal district court. On 9 October 2012 the Court of Appeals overturned the federal district court's decision, issuing Decision 1337/2010 in which it held that the Decree extinguishing the government-owned Luz y Fuerza did NOT terminate the collective labor relationship by Luz y Fuerza and the SME or the employment relationship with over 44,000 employees. The Court of Appeals also held that CFE was the successor employer to the workers and must continue both individual employment relationships and the collective relationship with CFM.

263. In the wake of the October 2012 Decision 1337/2010 of the Mexican Court of Appeals, petitioners filed a second supplement to their original complaint on 8 November 2012. The purpose of the November 2012 supplement was to argue that although Decision 1337/2010 was in the union's favor, it does not dispose of the union's NAALC complaint. The November 2012 supplement focuses on the failure of the Government of Mexico to comply with its core procedural obligations under the NAALC, citing Decision 1337/2010 findings that the federal labor board failed to make decisions based on information before it that are consistent with Mexican law, demonstrating that the JCFA lacked independence and does not make legal and factual determinations in an impartial manner. Petitioners pointed out that the October 2012 Decision 1337/2010 did not address the rest of the allegations in the SME's NAALC petition related to claims related to occupational safety and health, respect for labor laws, maternity leave, the protection of the rights of women and persons with disabilities or discrimination against trade union members.

264. On January 30, 2013, the Supreme Court of Mexico overturned the appellate court's decision in 1337/2010, holding that President Calderón's 2009 Decree extinguishing Luz y Fuerza was constitutional based on the grounds of *force majeure*, reasoning that the Calderón administration's actions were based on circumstances outside its control. The Supreme Court of Mexico also held that CFE was not the successor employer of Luz y Fuerza's former employees and was not subject to the collective agreement between Luz y Fuerza and the SME.

265. As of the end of April 2014, the SME/Luz y Fuerza NAALC complaint was still pending. Neither the US OTLA nor the Canadian NAO had issued a report regarding the allegations made in the complaint. The SME and former Luz y Fuerza employees continued direct action and public protests in support of their cause. In January 2014, they held public protests outside the Supreme Court of Mexico and the Mexican Ministry of the Interior. On April 9, 2014, the SME announced on its website that the Mexican Ministry of the Interior had agreed to sign an agreement with SME to provide retirement benefits to Luz y Fuerza retirees in late April 2014.

§3. Cases Involving Alleged Workers' Rights Violations in the United States

I. *Sprint* (Mexico NAO case no. 9501)

266. The *Sindicato de Telefonistas de la República Mexicana* (STRM) filed a complaint with the NAO of Mexico in February 1995 on the sudden closing of a Spanish-language telemarketing facility of the Sprint Corp. in San Francisco, California. The complaint alleged that the shutdown was motivated by anti-union bias. The STRM collaborated with its US counterpart, the Communications Workers of America (CWA), which was the union seeking to organize the Sprint facility.

267. The NAO of Mexico accepted the submission for review and issued a Report on 31 May 1995 concluding that it was 'concerned about the effectiveness of certain measures intended to guarantee [freedom of association and the right of workers to organize]' and 'possible problems in the effective application of US law,' and recommended ministerial consultations in the matter. Ensuing consultations resulted in an agreement among the labor secretaries of Mexico and the United States and the labor minister of Canada in February 1996 calling for a three part program:

(1) a public forum to be held in San Francisco, California;
(2) a special report by the Secretariat on the effects of sudden plant closings on the principle of freedom of association and protection of the right to organize in Canada, Mexico, and the United States; and
(3) updating by the Secretary of Labor of the United States to the Secretary of Labor of Mexico on developments in proceedings under US domestic labor law of the case that prompted the submission and the ministerial consultations.

268. In February 1996 the public forum called for by the ministers was held in San Francisco with presentations by workers affected by the plant closing, by union representatives from the STRM, the CWA and unionists from Germany and Great Britain. Testimony was also offered by a law professor speaking on behalf of Sprint, and by academic analysts.

269. In December 1996 the US National Labor Relations Board (NLRB) ruled that the plant closing by Sprint was motivated by anti-union animus, and ordered the employer to rehire affected workers into openings in other divisions of the company and to provide back pay for lost wages. Sprint appealed the NLRB decision to a US federal court of appeals.

270. In April 1997 the Secretariat issued its special report titled *Plant Closings and Labor Rights*. The report explained legal frameworks and union organizing systems in the US, Canada and Mexico, and reviewed administrative tribunal and court decisions in each of the three countries dealing with plant closings and threats of plant closing to resist union organizing efforts by workers. The Secretariat found that such anti-union tactics are widespread in the United States but less prevalent in the other countries. In Canada, this is due to stronger enforcement. In Mexico, it is due to differences in the union organizing system, which rarely involves an election 'campaign' where threats of closing or decisions to close are made.

271. In November 1997 the US federal court of appeals reversed the NLRB's decision that had found Sprint liable for an unlawful plant closing motivated by anti-union bias. The court ruled in favor of the company, finding that the closing was motivated by legitimate business considerations, not by anti-unionism.[1] This decision effectively foreclosed any further action under the NAALC, since the agreement did not provide a means of overturning or reversing a ruling by domestic labor authorities.

1. See *Sprint Corporation* v. *NLRB*, 129 F.3d. 1276 (D.C. Circuit 1997).

II. *Solec, Inc.* (Mexico NAO case no. 9801)

272. In April 1998 the US-based Oil, Chemical, and Atomic Workers (OCAW) Local Union I-675 was joined by a San, Diego, California-based NGO and two independent Mexican local unions in the Tijuana region in a complaint filed with the NAO of Mexico. The submission cited anti-union activities at the Solec, Inc. facility in Carson, California, and the alleged failure of US labor law authorities to effectively enforce domestic labor law in union organizing and in health and safety matters.

273. The case involved a union organizing attempt by the OCAW at this manufacturer of solar panels sold mainly to Sanyo Corp. of Japan. According to submitters, the organizing effort was prompted by severe health and safety problems at the plant. The union won the NLRB election, but certification and bargaining were delayed by legal maneuvering on the part of the employer, advised by a professional anti-union consultant. The NAO of Mexico accepted the case for review, and issued a report in August 1999 recommending ministerial consultations. A consultation program was discussed in 2000, but was not made concrete after the complaining union reported that it gained a collective agreement at the plant and was not keen to press the case forward. Issues raised in the *Solec* case were folded into ministerial consultations coming out of other cases filed about the same time, involving migrant workers in Washington and Maine.

III. *Washington State Apple Industry* (Mexico NAO case no. 9802)

274. A coalition of Mexican trade unions and farmworker organizations filed a wide-ranging NAALC complaint in May 1998 alleging failure of US labor law to protect workers' rights in the Washington State apple industry. The submission cited the lack of legal protection for farmworker union organizing, widespread health and safety violations, discrimination against migrant workers, and employers' use of threats and intimidation in recent union representation elections in apple packing and shipping facilities.

275. The *Union Nacional de Trabajadores* (UNT), a new independent labor federation, the *Frente Auténtico del Trabajo* (FAT), another independent labor group, and the *Frente Democrático Campesino* (FDC) of Mexico filed the complaint with the Mexican NAO. In preparing the submission, they collaborated with the US Teamsters union and the United Farm Workers union, which are conducting organizing campaigns in the apple sector. The complaint called on the Mexican government to pursue multiple stages of review, consultation, evaluation, and arbitration under the NAALC.

276. At the time, the NAALC apple workers submission was the broadest case yet filed under the NAALC, citing labor law violations and inadequate enforcement in areas encompassed in 7 of the NAALC's 11 labor principles. Most earlier cases addressed union organizing issues. The Washington State apple industry complaint covered the right to organize, collective bargaining, minimum labor standards, non-discrimination in employment, job safety and health, workers' compensation, and protection of migrant workers. The filing generated a burst of publicity calling attention to conditions of migrant workers and the opportunity for advocacy presented by the NAALC.

277. The NAO of Mexico accepted the *Washington State Apple* case for review in August 1998. In December 1998 the NAO of Mexico held its first-ever hearing on a NAALC complaint. It was not a public hearing in the quasi-legal style of the US and Canadian NAOs, but rather an 'informative session' under the Mexican NAO procedural guidelines conducted in private in a roundtable setting. A delegation of workers from packing sheds and orchards in Washington State attended the hearing and presented direct testimony about pesticide poisoning, discharge for union activity, minimum wage violations, discrimination in the workers' compensation system, discrimination against migrant workers, and other violations of workers' rights.

278. The hearing garnered widespread publicity in the news media of both the United States and Mexico. The NAO of Mexico was to issue its report in February 1999, but the report was delayed by personnel changes in the department of labor and the NAO. The report was finally issued in August 1999, and on 20 August Mexico's secretary of labor formally requested ministerial consultations with the US secretary of labor. This development sparked a new round of publicity and related attention to the conditions of migrant workers in the industry.

279. In May 2000 the governments announced a program of events resulting from the consultations, including a public forum for workers, unions, employers and government officials and an 'outreach' effort by labor law enforcement personnel. The follow-up program was to be implemented early in 2001, after national elections and the advent of new administrations in the two countries. It included government-to-government meetings in Washington, DC and Mexico City, Mexico as well as public forums in the states of Washington and Maine (see below).

IV. *DeCoster Egg Farm* (Mexico NAO case no. 9803)

280. In August 1998 the CTM labor federation filed a NAALC complaint with the NAO of Mexico about abusive treatment of migrant Mexican workers at the DeCoster Egg Farm. This was the first engagement of the official pro-government labor body in a NAALC case. The egg processing facility is located in the state of Maine, in the extreme Northeast of the United States. The submission alleged violations and failure to effectively enforce laws regarding minimum wages, health and safety, housing conditions, workers' compensation for work-related injuries and illnesses, and other minimum conditions of work. The NAALC complaint followed action by the Mexican government filing a class-action lawsuit on behalf of 1,500 current and former DeCoster employees in US federal court over the same allegations.

281. In October 2000 the federal appeals court ruled that the Mexican government did not have standing to bring such a lawsuit. The suit may be pursued by individual plaintiffs, said the court, and Mexico may assist the plaintiffs financially or by paying plaintiffs' attorneys. But the doctrine of *parens patriae* allowing a state of the United States to file suits on behalf of its citizens does not extend to a foreign nation 'which asserts only quasi-sovereign interests and not its own proprietary interests.'[2]

282. The NAO of Mexico accepted the DeCoster case for review, and a report recommending ministerial consultations in the matter was issued in August 1999 at the same time as the Washington State apple case report. A follow-up program similar to that designed for the Washington State apple case was also announced for the DeCoster case. In addition to the government-to-government meetings held in Washington, DC and Mexico City and the public forum in Washington state, a public forum was held in the state of Maine.

V. *Yale Labor Department–INS Memorandum of Understanding* (Mexico NAO case no. 9804; Canada NAO case no. 98-2)

283. In September 1998 a workers' rights project of students at Yale Law School, joined by 20 local and national immigrants' rights organizations, filed complaints with both the NAO of Mexico and the NAO of Canada challenging a policy laid out in a Memorandum of Understanding (MOU) between the US Department of Labor and the Immigration and Naturalization Service (INS). Under the MOU, Labor Department inspectors who receive complaints alleging violations of minimum wage and overtime requirements of the Fair Labor Standards Act (FLSA) must determine the immigration status of workers who filed complaints. If any worker cannot produce authentic documentation, the Labor Department will inform the INS, and the worker faces deportation.

284. The effects of the MOU on effective enforcement of US labor law are obvious. Workers whose immigration status is questionable are loath to complain when their rights are violated for fear that the Labor Department will report them to the INS. This sets a vicious cycle in motion. Employers hire immigrant workers with a glance at their documentation, then cheat workers on minimum wage and overtime pay in full confidence that they will never complain to the Department of Labor. Even workers with proper documentation do not complain, because an investigation might reach their coworkers, often relatives or friends from the same country, whose documents are questionable. The students who brought the NAALC complaint hope that international scrutiny will end the policy that makes the Labor Department an informant for the INS.

285. Shortly after the NAALC complaint was filed, the Department of Labor issued a revised MOU on its dealings with the INS. Under the new MOU, DOL

2. See *Estados Unidos Mexicanos* v. *DeCoster*, 1st Cir., No. 99-2170 (11 October 2000).

agents will not inform the INS about the immigration status of any worker who files an individual complaint for unpaid minimum wages or overtime pay. However, the Labor Department may still inform INS of findings in workplaces that are inspected in routine, programmed inspections rather than in response to a complaint.

286. In December 1998 the NAO of Mexico announced that it accepted the MOU case for review. The NAO of Canada announced that it would await more information from the submitters on the effects of the revised MOU before deciding whether to accept the case for review. In April 1999 the Canadian NAO declined to accept the complaint for review on grounds that the revised MOU addressed the complaints raised by submitters. In December 2000, the Mexican NAO issued its report on the matter, recommending ministerial consultations. Since issues raised in the MOU case involved migrant workers' protection, it was expected that these ministerial consultations would be linked to those resulting from the Washington and Maine workers' cases.

VI. *Labor Policy Association and Section 8(a)(2) of the NLRA* (Canada NAO case no. 99-1)

287. On 14 April 1999 the Labor Policy Association (LPA), a management group opposed to unions, filed the first employer-initiated complaint under the NAALC. In its submission to the NAO of Canada, the LPA charged that the United States is failing to promote labor-management cooperation under the NAALC by the NLRB's application of Section 8(a)(2) of the National Labor Relations Act. Section 8(a)(2) prohibits employer domination of labor organizations.

288. The LPA was joined in the complaint by EFCO, a company whose employee participation committees were ordered disbanded by the NLRB on the grounds that these 'teams' were sponsored and dominated by management to deal with wages, hours and working conditions. Under Section 8(a)(2), only *bona fide* trade unions are allowed to represent workers on these issues.

289. Since this was the first substantive complaint[3] filed by an employer under the NAALC, it will receive careful attention here. The LPA complaint cited what it called 'the failure of the United States to uphold the principles, obligations and objectives contained in the North American Agreement on Labor Cooperation concerning labor-management cooperation and employee involvement and participation in non-union settings' and 'the failure of the United States to apply effectively and enforce its laws and resolve disputes, without undue delay, concerning employee involvement under Section 8(a)(2) of the National Labor Relations Act.'

3. An earlier complaint was filed by the Florida Tomato Exchange on 28 September 1998, raising the issue of the use of child labor in the production of fruit and vegetables in Mexico. In accordance with its procedural guidelines, the NAO held this submission in abeyance for a year for the submitters to provide further information. No additional information was provided, and the case was closed as of 4 October 1999.

290. The complaint charged that failure to properly apply the law prohibited effective employee involvement and participation in non-union workplaces, thus violating the principles, obligations and objectives embodied in the NAALC. The complaint argued that the NLRB's interpretation of Section 8(a)(2) was inconsistent with the legislative history of the NLRA and with the NLRB's mandate to interpret the Act in light of changing industrial times, and concluded that the United States is in violation of the NAALC by its ineffective and improper application and enforcement of the law.

291. At the heart of the LPA complaint was the argument that 'employee involvement is the contemporary global mode of production for the most highly productive and competitive companies' but that 'despite the widespread support for these programs, the NLRB has been, and continues to, systematically prosecute companies that promote employee involvement under an interpretation of Section 8(a)(2) that has outlived its usefulness.'

292. 'Company' unions were a serious problem in 1935 when Section 8(a)(2) was enacted, said the LPA. But 'the industrial and labor climates have significantly changed since 1935 and 'company' unions are far from prevalent … Yet, the NLRB, charged with interpreting the NLRA to respond to changes in the workplace, refuses to accept this mandate and interpret Section 8(a)(2) in light of the fundamental changes in the common mode of production since the NLRA was enacted.'

293. To bring its complaint into an area that can give rise to formation of an ECE and an arbitral panel, the LPA complaint emphasized health and safety aspects of employee involvement programs. 'The NAALC specifically addresses labor-management cooperation and employee involvement in the area of occupational safety and health,' the complaint declares. 'Although the United States NLRB applies United States federal law to prohibit effective employee involvement, other United States agencies encourage, and arguably require, employee involvement to address occupational safety and health issues.' As a result, 'effective employee participation and involvement would be in direct violation of Section 8(a)(2) of the US NLRA as interpreted by the NLRB. 'Clearly,' says the complaint, 'with the exception of the NLRB, the US Administration has long recognized the importance of effective employee involvement programs to address occupational safety and health issues. Yet, the US Administration has been unable or unwilling to bring its NLRB into accord with these policies, thereby creating the breakdown in US policy that necessitates this Submission.'

294. The LPA told the Canadian NAO that 'effective employee involvement in non-union settings is prohibited in the United States,' and asked the NAO to:

(1) accept this Submission and conduct a thorough review and investigation of the issues raised by this Submission;
(2) conduct public hearings allowing the Submitters to testify at the hearings as well as other interested and affected parties, including, without limitation,

employees employed in workplaces that allowed employee involvement but that are now prohibited from engaging in such involvement;
(3) request and engage in Cooperative Consultations with the NAO of the United States;
(4) prepare a Report requesting Ministerial Consultations be conducted between the respective Ministers and Secretaries of Labor of the Parties to the NAALC;
(5) conduct and/or supervise a Study pursuant to Part Three, Article 14 on employee involvement in workplaces;
(6) organize and convene a forum on employee involvement in the workplace to be attended by government, labor and management representatives;
(7) organize and convene an Evaluation Committee of Experts to address employee involvement in non-union workplaces including accepting for review 'written views' submitted by the parties;
(8) address the report prepared by the Evaluation Committee of Experts at a session of the Council;
(9) address the issue of employee involvement in non-union workplaces through Article 27 consultations and through a special session of the Council;
(10) organize and convene an Arbitral Panel to address employee involvement in non-union workplaces and conduct hearings and receive submissions from the parties;
(11) implement an Action plan and reconvene a panel to review the adequacy of the implementation of the Action plan;
(12) impose a monetary assessment and sanctions on the United States for its failure to allow effective employee involvement in non-union workplaces in violation of its obligations under the NAALC;
(13) issue a declaration providing that the United States has violated principles and obligations found in the NAALC;
(14) urge and encourage the United States to amend their labor law to allow employee involvement in non-union workplace settings; and
(15) require that the United States comply with the norms and principles of the NAALC to allow employee involvement in non-union workplace settings.

295. The US NAO and the AFL–CIO made written arguments to the Canadian NAO asking it not to accept the complaint for review. The AFL–CIO argued that, if anything, the LPA was complaining about *too effective* enforcement of Section 8(a)(2) of the NLRA, not a failure of enforcement.

296. The LPA complaint was rejected by the NAO of Canada on grounds that it did not raise matters related to failure to effectively enforce national labor law. In a letter to the LPA, the Canadian NAO secretary said that its submission 'did not raise issues related to the enforcement of labor legislation,' as required under the NAALC. 'After careful consideration,' said the Canadian NAO secretary,

> I have decided not to accept this *Public Communication on Employee Involvement in the United States Nonunion Workplaces* for review. In your submission, you assert that there is a failure by the United States with regard to its

obligations under the North American Agreement on Labor Cooperation ... A review of the information does not indicate a failure to comply with the obligations of the agreement, including enforcement of labor law.

297. The LPA appealed this decision. Under the Canadian NAO's guidelines, parties submitting complaints can seek a review of a rejection and ask the agency to provide its reasons for not accepting a complaint. LPA told the NAO in its appeal that the NAALC provides that the parties resolve 'to promote, in accordance with the respective laws, high skill, high productivity economic development ... by ... encouraging employers and employees ... to work together in maintaining a progressive, fair, safe and healthy working environment' and argued that 'If the United States Occupational Safety and Health Administration requires workplace safety and health teams, a requirement that furthers two objectives of the NAALC, while the US National Labor Relations Board prohibits them, then it would seem that there is a fundamental failure by the United States to comply with the obligations of the agreement.' The Canadian NAO again declined to accept the LPA's complaint for review, stating that the appeal did not contain any new information as grounds for reversing its decision.

VII. *New York Workers' Compensation* (Mexican NAO Submission 2001-1)

298. In October 2001, a group of individual immigrant workers and some immigrant rights groups including the Chinese Staff and Workers' Association (CSWA) and National Mobilization Against Sweat Shops (NMASS) filed a complaint with the Mexican NAO alleging that the United States and state of New York had failed to effectively enforce laws governing compensation to workers for on-the-job injuries. In the United States, compensation for on-the-job injuries and diseases is subject to state jurisdiction. Each state has its own workers' compensation law, usually administered and enforced by a state government agency. Except for five states that have public workers' compensation, almost all states in the US require employers to acquire private insurance to compensate workers for on-the job injuries and diseases. In addition, state workers' compensation agencies often have a public fund generated from employer taxes to provide coverage for injured workers whose employers are not in compliance with the state's workers' compensation law. Most state workers' compensation agencies aggressively enforce the requirement that employers obtain workers' compensation insurance.

299. According to the complaint, administrative law judges adjudicating New York workers' compensation cases allowed employers and insurers to abuse the administrative hearing system by overusing the privilege of postponing hearings. As a result, the process for obtaining compensation for an on-the-job injury could extend for years – in some cases alleged in the complaint, for 10 to 20 years. The problem was exacerbated in the case of immigrant workers, and the New York Workers' Compensation Board provided inadequate resources for translation and interpretation of proceedings for non-English-speaking workers.

300. Although the New York Workers' Compensation Board argued that it should not be subject to an international complaint under the NAALC, the Mexican NAO accepted the complaint in November 2001 and issued public reports of review in November 2002 and November 2004. The Mexican NAO would not comment on the substance of New York workers' compensation law and whether it had been effectively enforced, but recommended that systems for compensation for worker injuries be publicized and requested ministerial consultations between Ministers of Labor Carlos Abascal Carranza and Elaine Chao. Ministerial consultations and resolution of the NAALC complaint were still pending at the end of 2008.

301. The NAALC complaint was only one part of a movement by worker and immigrant advocates in the state of New York to reform workers' compensation law in New York and improve the administration and application of workers' compensation law. Over the years, activities included workshops, lobbying and union-organized education sessions for workers, immigrant advocates and trade union activists.

VIII. *North Carolina H-2A Workers* (Mexican NAO Submission 2003-1)

302. In February 2003, the US-based Farmworker Justice Fund (FJF) and the *Central Independiente de Obreros Agrícolas y Campesinos* (CIOAC), a Mexican farm worker union, filed a public communication with the Mexican NAO alleging that the United States failed to effectively enforce labor laws covered by 9 of the 11 NAALC labor principles in the treatment of Mexican migrant agricultural workers recruited to work in the state of North Carolina through the US H-2A visa program. The H-2A visa program is a US visa program that allows US agricultural employers to recruit migrant agricultural workers from other countries if they can demonstrate to the US DOL that there are no local workers who can fill the jobs. Approximately 10,000 workers from Mexico work in agriculture in North Carolina with H-2A visas, the majority of them on farms that produce cucumbers destined to become pickles processed and marketed by the Mt. Olive Pickle Company. A small number of H-2A workers in North Carolina work for farms that produce Christmas trees. Almost all H-2A workers in North Carolina are recruited by an employer organization called the North Carolina Growers Association (NCGA) which recruits workers directly in Mexico.

303. Workers in the H-2A visa program are excluded from the protection of more than one US labor law. As agricultural workers, workers with H-2A visas are excluded from the protection of the US National Labor Relations Act (NLRA). Moreover, regulations governing the H-2A visa program explicitly exclude workers with H-2A visas from the protection of the Migrant and Seasonal Agricultural Workers Protection Act (MSAWPA), a law that requires agricultural employers and their agents to provide migrant farm workers with details about where and for whom they will be working, as well as the payment and other terms of employment. The MSAWPA also provides a private cause of action to individual migrant farm workers to enforce its provisions.

304. In addition to outlining these legal restrictions on the rights of H-2A workers in North Carolina, the public communication outlines that employers restrict H-2A workers' access to union organizers, service providers and legal aid attorneys; deny H-2A workers medical care and access to compensation for on-the job injuries; blacklist workers from participating in the program if they file complaints about on-the-job injuries or unpaid wages; do not hire women or workers over a certain age; and manipulate the growing season and force workers to sign voluntary resignations in order to avoid paying required travel and other expenses. The complaint points out that despite these and other violations of US and state labor and employment laws, neither federal or state authorities fail to enforce the rights of H-2A workers as required under H-2A visa regulations and federal and state laws. Subsequent to filing the complaint, the FJF and CIOAC filed a supplement alleging that US and North Carolina authorities failed to ensure a safe and healthy work environment for H-2A workers. The supplement included a number of exhibits, including several 'Do Not Hire' lists prepared by the NCGA of workers in various Mexican states who are blacklisted from being hired in North Carolina under the H-2A visa program.

305. The Mexican NAO accepted the H-2A NAALC complaint in September 2003. Although In 2004 the US and Mexican labor departments negotiated two agreements to improve coordination between branches of the US DOL and Mexican consulates in North Carolina and other US states to improve enforcement of labor laws in relation to H-2A workers. The Mexican NAO issued its report on the North Carolina H-2A complaint as part of a comprehensive report released in December 2012 on US failure to effectively enforce labor laws with respect to H-2A and H-2B workers. In April 2014, the Governments of Mexico and the US signed a Ministerial Declaration addressing the issues raised in complaints filed with the Mexican NAO between 2003 and 2011. See Paragraphs 342-344.

306. In 2004, the Farm Labor Organizing Committee, a farm worker union that originated in Ohio, began collective bargaining negotiations on behalf of H-2A workers with the Mount Olive Pickle Company, the second biggest pickle processor and marketer in the United States. The historic event was the result of over eight years of advocacy by the FLOC and a multi-year boycott against Mount Olive Pickle Company. As a result of the FLOC's effective unionization drive and negotiation of a collective bargaining agreement with Mount Olive Pickle Company, the FLOC established the first US-Mexico binational trade union, conducting representational and educational activities in both the United States and in Mexico, before H-2A workers travel to work in the state of North Carolina. Almost 8,000 Mexican workers in the H-2A program are covered by this collective bargaining agreement. Despite these remarkable achievements, the FLOC still faces some obstacles. In April 2006, FLOC organizer Santiago Rafael Cruz was murdered in the FLOC office in Monterrey, Mexico. Cruz's murder had not yet been solved at the end of 2008.

IX. *Hoffman Plastics and the Inter-American Court of Human Rights Advisory Opinion on the Rights of Undocumented Workers* (Inter-American Court of Human Rights Advisory Opinion OC-18/03)

307. One of the most significant events in North American labor law in the first decade of the 21st century was dealt with not under the NAALC, but under the Inter-American human rights system.

308. On 27 March 2002, the US Supreme Court handed down a decision in trade union rights that had international significance. In *Hoffman Plastic Compounds* v. *NLRB*, the US Supreme Court ruled that undocumented migrant workers who were illegally fired in retaliation for trade union organizing activities were not entitled to the remedy of back pay for the period of unemployment resulting from the unlawful firing. Workers who are US citizens or who are legally authorized to work in the United States are entitled to the remedy of back pay for that period. The Supreme Court's rationale was that the undocumented worker engaged in misconduct by violating US immigration law and the National Labor Relations Board did not have the authority to interpret US immigration law, so it did not have the capacity to award back pay to an undocumented worker illegally fired for participating in union organizing activities. The NLRB has the discretion to reduce a worker's back pay if it finds that the worker engaged in some kind of misconduct. The US Supreme Court took away that discretion in cases involving undocumented workers.

309. In the years since the *Hoffman Plastic Compounds* case was handed down, the holding has been interpreted narrowly. Most US state and federal courts and administrative boards have ruled that all workers are entitled to minimum wage and overtime protection, the right to compensation for on-the-job injuries, freedom from discrimination on the basis of race, sex, religion, age, disability and other grounds (except for possession of work authorization). Moreover, almost every court where the question has arisen has ruled that a worker's immigration status is not pertinent to whether minimum wage and other labor and employment laws were violated. Legally, the *Hoffman Plastic Compounds* case does not take away the right of an undocumented immigrant to participate in trade union organizing activities, only the right to the remedy US citizens and workers authorized to work in the US receive. Practically, the US Supreme Court's decision in *Hoffman Plastics Compounds* changed the atmosphere in US workplaces where it is estimated over 12 million undocumented migrant workers toil – both increasing undocumented workers' fear of retaliation if they complain about labor rights violations and increasing employers' attempts to use workers' immigration status as a defense for not paying wages on time or failing to comply with the law and other labor violations.

310. In response to the *Hoffman Plastic Compounds* case, the Mexican government utilized diplomatic channels created by the NAALC structure to challenge the decision and to demand that the US DOL act more expeditiously on its commitment in the 2000 ministerial agreement to prepare foreign language guides for migrant workers and press for the publication of the CLC Secretariat's Guide to Labor and

Employment Laws in North America for Migrant Workers. On a legal level, however, the Mexican government did not avail itself of NAALC procedure to request that an Evaluation Committee of Experts (ECE) be convened either in a pending NAALC submission or directly as a result of the *Hoffman Plastic Compounds* case itself.

311. Rather, on 10 May 2002, less than two months after the *Hoffman Plastics Compound* decision was handed down by the US Supreme Court, the Mexican government made the historical decision to pursue the issue of treatment of undocumented migrant workers under the Inter-American human rights system by seeking an advisory opinion from the Inter-American Court of Human Rights on the Juridical Condition and Rights of Migrant Workers.

312. The Inter-American human rights system was created under the auspices of the Organization of American States (OAS). OAS member states adopted the Inter-American Declaration on the Rights and Duties of Man in 1948, chartered the Inter-American Commission on Human Rights in 1959 and created the Inter-American Court of Human Rights as part of the Inter-American Convention on Human Rights in 1969. The Inter-American Court of Human Rights has jurisdiction over contentious cases brought by the Inter-American Commission on Human Rights about human rights abuses by the limited number countries that have accepted its jurisdiction. It also has jurisdiction to issue legal advisory opinions interpreting Inter-American human rights law on the request of a member state.

313. In its request for an advisory opinion from the Inter-American Court of Human Rights, the Mexican government expressed profound concern about the incompatibility with the OAS human rights system of the interpretations, practices and enactment of laws by 'some states in the region' that have the effect of negating labor rights based on discriminatory criteria derived from the migratory status of undocumented workers. Mexico asked the Inter-American Court to interpret a number of Inter-American and international human rights norms on the specific issues of (a) whether an American State may establish labor legislation that provides distinct treatment to workers based on their migratory status; (b) whether human rights norms may be interpreted so that an individual's legal residence in an American state is a pre-condition for the state to respect and protect that individual's human rights and freedoms; (c) whether denial of one or more labor rights based on migratory status is compatible with American states' obligations to ensure non-discrimination and equal protection of the law; (d) whether it is valid for an American state to interpret its laws to subordinate or condition observance of fundamental human rights like the right to equality before the law and equal and effective protection of the law without discrimination as a way to achieve migratory policy goals; and (e) whether the rights to equality and to be free from discrimination are *jus cogens* – so that they apply to States who have not ratified some human rights conventions. Two particular norms Mexico referred to included the right of every person to be free from discrimination without distinction of national and social origin and the right to an effective remedy issued by a competent judicial, administrative or legislative body.

314. Five American governments, including Honduras, Nicaragua, El Salvador, Canada and Costa Rica, submitted comments and briefs to the court, as did the Inter-American Commission Human Rights and a dozen representatives of law firms, law school clinics and labor and human rights non-governmental organizations from the United States and other American countries. The comments and briefs addressed the living and working conditions of migrants in the United States as well as the juridical status of migrants under Inter-American and international human rights law. The United States submitted a note that it would not comment on Mexico's request. A public hearing was held at the seat of the Court in San José on 24 February 2003.

315. The Inter-American Court of Human Rights issued its unanimous opinion on 17 September 2003. It held that the fundamental principles of equality and non-discrimination are part of general international law and apply to all states, whether or not they are party to a specific international treaty, and are therefore *jus cogens*. It also held that states have the obligation to respect and ensure protection of the fundamental rights to equality and non-discrimination regardless of any circumstance and consideration, including a person's migratory status; that the right to due process of law, including the right to a remedy and the means to enforce rights, is recognized as a fundamental and minimum guarantee that should be offered to any migrant, regardless of migratory status; and that the migratory status of a person cannot be a justification for depriving him or her of the enjoyment and exercise of human rights, including those of a labor-related nature.

316. In one of the most important international labor rights decisions in North America before or after the advent of the NAFTA and the NAALC, the Inter-American Court of Human Rights held that the state has the obligation to respect and guarantee the labor rights of all workers, whether national or alien, and not to allow private employers to violate the rights of workers or for the contractual relationship to violate minimum international standards.

X. *H-2B Visa Workers* (Mexico NAO Submission 2005-1)

317. In April 2005 attorneys with the Northwest Justice Project in Oregon, the Andrade Law Office in Idaho and the Brennan Center in New York filed a public communication with the Mexican NAO on behalf of several immigrant workers who were brought to the United States under the H-2B visa program, which is a visa program for non-agricultural temporary guest workers. The workers, who were recruited in Panama and Mexico to work in Idaho, Arkansas, Texas and other states, suffered a number of violations of their rights under H-2B visa guidelines and US labor and employment law, such as being transported to the worksite in unsafe vehicles under inhumane conditions (for example, a small van with 14 men travelling for over 60 hours), being forced to pay for housing when the employer was supposed to provide free housing under H-2B visa guidelines, or being required to live in small tents in isolated, cold mountain areas. The employers who recruited and hired the workers violated a number of US labor and employment laws by using recruiters who were not properly registered under the US Migrant and Seasonal Agricultural Workers Protection Act (MSAWPA), failing to pay prevailing wages or provide the amount of work promised as required under H-2B guidelines, requiring workers to perform agricultural work in violation of H-2B guidelines, failing to pay the minimum wage and subtracting work-related expenses from the workers' pay so their wages fell below the minimum wage in violation of the Fair Labor Standards Act (FLSA) and failing pay wages owed. In one of the cases discussed in the public communication, a worker recruited to pack water-melons in Arkansas and Texas woke up to find himself without a leg in a Tennessee hospital after his employer required him to drive a fork lift without providing him proper training. None of these workers were able to find a lawyer to represent them in their cases.

318. The crux of the public communication was the fact that none of the workers were able to avail themselves of the protections of various state and federal laws their employers violated because federal guidelines covering the Legal Services Corporation (LSC) which provides federal funding to legal aid offices specifically prohibits those offices from providing legal services to workers with H-2B visas. Workers with H-2A temporary agricultural worker visas are entitled to legal services from federally-funded legal aid offices, as are US citizens and permanent residents. The petitioners argued that the denial of federally-funded legal aid services to H-2B visa holders violates several provisions and principles of the NAALC, including the provisions requiring NAALC signatories to ensure effective access to labor tribunals for people with recognized interests and to ensure that administrative and legal proceedings governing labor issues are fair and transparent. Because they are prohibited from obtaining free legal aid services and as demonstrated by the experiences of the workers in the public communication are unable to find private lawyers willing and able to represent them, H-2B visa holders are unable to vindicate their labor rights. Petitioners argued this is a violation of NAALC principle 11, which requires member countries to provide treatment of migrant workers that is equal to that received by native workers, as well as a violation of principles governing workers' right to minimum standards and a safe working environment. Petitioners also argued that the denial of legal representation violates several international human rights treaties, including the Inter-American Human Rights Convention (IACHR) as interpreted by the 2003 Advisory Opinion of the Inter-American Court of Human Rights on the Legal Condition and Rights of Migrant Workers, which found that the right to judicial protection is violated when fear of deportation or denial of free public legal services to immigrants prevents them from seeking to protect their rights.

319. After filing the *H-2B* public communication, activists raised funds to obtain legal representation for the workers discussed in the complaint. The response of the US OTLA to the Mexican NAO's inquiries about the complaint was that the facts were moot as the workers had in fact obtained legal representation, though not through legal aid services funded by the Legal Services Corporation.

320. The question of mootness of the individual workers' cases is not one that generally arises in the context of the NAALC. As is often pointed out by both critics and proponents of the NAALC, individual workers do not receive individual justice – whether reinstatement or monetary remedies – as a result of filing a NAALC complaint. The NAALC process allows for critique and review of the way member countries enforce and apply existing labor and employment laws. Under the NAALC framework, the actual outcome of a particular enforcement action or failure to enforce is not a ground for determining whether or not a member state has effectively enforced its labor and employment laws.

321. Approaching the NAALC complaint from the point of view of seasoned migrant worker litigators, the petitioners applied an innovative strategy upon receiving news of the US OTLA's response. The NAALC does not contain a process for appealing the decision of an NAO Secretary. In the *H-2B* case, there was in fact no decision to appeal. There is no rule against refiling or submitting additional information about an existing NAALC complaint, however.

322. In March 2006 the petitioners filed an addendum to their original petition in which they added another group of H-2B visa holders who were recruited in Mexico to work in corn packing sheds in Colorado and who suffered a number of violations to their rights under the H-2B visa program and US and Colorado labor laws. The addendum showed that in addition to being unable to obtain free legal services from federally-funded legal aid offices or private attorneys, the workers were unable to obtain redress of their complaints from state and federal agencies responsible for enforcing US labor laws, including the US Department of Labor which is responsible for ensuring that employers use recruiters who are properly registered under the MSAWPA and the Colorado state labor department which must have a Monitor Advocate who is responsible for addressing treatment of migrant workers and ensuring their rights are protected by federal and state authorities. In the addendum, petitioners pointed out that none of the personnel in the Colorado state labor department spoke Spanish so it was not possible to directly interview the workers and understand their grievances.

323. In October 2007, the Mexican NAO submitted a series of 69 detailed questions to the US NAO inquiring about the allegations made in the complaint. In December 2012, the Mexican NAO issued a report addressing the H-2B Migrant Workers' complaint as part of its comprehensive report discussing a decade's worth of complaints filed about the US Government's failure to set high labor standards and effectively enforce labor laws with respect to migrant workers. In April 2014, the Governments of Mexico and the US signed a Ministerial Declaration addressing issued raised in complaints filed with the Mexican NAO between 2003 and 2011. See paragraphs 342–344.

XI. *North Carolina Public Service Workers* (Mexican NAO case no. 2006-2)

324. In October 2006, the Mexico-based *Frente Autentico de Trabajadores* (FAT) and US-based United Electrical Workers (UE) and over 50 unions and non-governmental organizations in Canada, Mexico and the United States submitted a public communication to the Mexican NAO on behalf of 650,000 government workers in the state of North Carolina who are denied by state law the right to organize a union, exercise the right to strike and engage in collective bargaining with their state government employer. The complaint was filed with the Canadian NAO in 2008. The Canadian Labour Congress (CLC) and almost 50 other petitioners signed on to the complaint. North Carolina Statute 95-98 specifies that any collective bargaining agreement in the public sector is contrary to the public policy of the State of North Carolina and is therefore illegal, unlawful and null and void. North Carolina state law has both racial and gender elements, since a high percentage of the government employees, including sanitation workers, bus drivers, housekeepers, grounds keepers and medical technicians who are denied the right to organize are African American. A month before the public communication was filed, over 50 sanitation workers in the city of Raleigh, North Carolina went on strike for two days. The NAALC principles implicated in the North Carolina Public Workers complaint included those relating to the right to association and collective bargaining (Principles 1 and 2), minimum employment standards (Principle 6), the right to be free of workplace discrimination (Principle 7) and the right to a safe workplace and compensation for work-related injuries and diseases (Principles 9 and 10).

325. In addition to filing the NAALC complaint with the Mexican and Canadian NAOs, North Carolina government employees and their allies obtained a report in June 2006 from the non-governmental International Commission for Labor Rights (ICLR) detailing the denial of the right to associate, strike and collective bargaining, filed a complaint with the ILO Committee on Freedom of Association (CFA) in October 2005 and filed a complaint with the Inter-American Commission on Human Rights in January 2006. In addition to discussing North Carolina's non-compliance with internationally recognized rights to free association and collective bargaining, the June 2006 ICLR report found significant race and gender discrimination in hiring, promotion, pay, discipline and termination of North Carolina public sector employees, and cited academic studies and data indicating that people of color and women working in North Carolina's public sector are employed in the lowest pay grades due to lack of access to training, education and jobs. The ICLR also found there to be significant gaps in workplace safety and health measures and lack of respect for worker and union initiatives to improve worker safety in North Carolina's public sector.

326. In October 2005, the UE filed a complaint with the ILO Committee on Freedom of Association regarding the denial of the rights to associate, strike and engage in collective bargaining to public workers under North Carolina law. Although under the US Constitution, North Carolina is prohibited from denying its employees the right to freely associate, there is no specific provision in the US Constitution guaranteeing the right to bargain collectively and courts have been reluctant to read such a guarantee into the US Constitution. While the US Constitution establishes a republic of states, the US Supreme Court has upheld federal laws impinging on the ability of states to set laws state and local government public sector employees - including imposition of federal occupational safety and health, minimum wage and anti-discrimination laws on state public sector employers. The essence of the complainants' argument before the CFA was that the US Government had violated its obligations under the ILO Constitution as set forth in Conventions 87, 98 and 151 by permitting the State of North Carolina to ban collective bargaining agreements in the public sector. Convention 151 governs the rights of public employees to associate and engage in collective bargaining. In its report on Case 2460, the CFA found that voluntary negotiation of collective agreements is a fundamental aspect of the freedom of association as it demonstrates the autonomy of the bargaining partners. Addressing an argument made by the US Government that the right of North Carolina Public Sector workers to freedom of association had not been violated, the CFA emphasized that one of the fundamental purposes of organizing a trade union is to bargain collectively. Placing a ban on collective bargaining is therefore an infringement of the freedom of association. The CFA concluded that the right to bargain freely with one's employer including public employers is a fundamental aspect of the freedom of association and that any interference with this right is an infringement of ILO principles. The CFA recommended that the US Government promote the establishment of a collective bargaining framework in North Carolina.

327. The trade union movement and international support movements were still active and energized at the end of 2007 and beginning of 2008. In October 2007, the Mexican NAO submitted a series of detailed questions to the US NAO about the North Carolina Public Service Workers complaint. In April 2008, a coalition of Canadian and other unions submitted the NAALC complaint to the Canadian NAO in the wake of a meeting between the North American Labor Ministers in Ottawa, Canada. The Canadian NAO accepted the complaint in June 2008. In early January 2009, the Canadian NAO placed the complaint on hold when it appeared that the law banning collective bargaining by North Carolina public sector workers might be repealed. Review of the complaint was reopened in 2013 when it was apparent that legislation to repeal General Statute 95-98 would not be passed.

328. The Mexican NAO accepted the North Carolina Public Workers complaint and requested information from the US NAO in October 2007 about the issues raised in the complaint. It is interesting to note that as has been the case with many complaints filed with the US NAO regarding labor law matters in Mexico, the Mexican NAO comments in its final report (issued in November 2012, see below) that the US NAO did not respond adequately or in a timely fashion to its questions about US labor laws relating to the North Carolina Public Workers complaint.

329. The Mexican NAO issued its report in response to the North Carolina Public Workers' complaint in November 2012. As has been the Mexican NAO's practice, the report is a combination of assertions that the NAALC protects the sovereignty of signatory member states and bold statements indicating that the US may be in violation of the NAALC as a result of allegations made in the complaint. The report issued in response to the North Carolina Public Workers complaint stands out because of its heavy reliance on and frequent referral to the ILO CFA's conclusions and recommendations in Case 2460 as well as other jurisprudence of the CFA. In addition to citing with approval the CFA's discussion of Case 2460, the Mexican NAO begins its report by referring to NAALC fundamental obligation to set high labor standards. In its recommendations, the Mexican NAO reasserts its respect for Article 2 of the NAALC which recognizes the right of NAALC signatories to establish their own domestic laws but indicates its interesting in knowing what actions the US Government has taken to promote the right of public workers in North Carolina to engage in collective bargaining. The Mexican NAO recommended that ministerial consultations take place regarding the complaint.

330. In January 2013, the UE sent letters to US Secretary of Labor Hilda Solis and Acting Secretary of Labor Seth Harris indicating that the US NAO had ignored the Mexican NAO's request for ministerial consultations, remarking that the US NAO indicated it would not translate the Mexican NAO's report into English and asking the US Government to take action in response to the recommendations of the Mexican NAO and the ILO. In August 2013, the UE submitted an update to the Mexican NAO indicating that it had received no response from the US DOL and that in addition to ignoring the UE's letter, the US Government had done little to encourage North Carolina to repeal its ban on public sector collective bargaining. The UE's letter noted that in addition to not passing legislation repealing the public sector bargaining ban, the State of North Carolina had passed voter repression legislation, repealed the Racial Justice Act and made it illegal to base the purchase of agricultural products on an agricultural producer's status as a union or non-union employer (targeted at the Farm Labor Organizing Committee or FLOC's success in the state of North Carolina).

XII. *H-2B Carnival and Fair Workers* (Mexican NAO case no. 2011-1)

331. On 19 September 2011, three Mexican migrant workers and a coalition of US and Mexican non-governmental migrant advocacy groups and trade unions led by the Baltimore-based *Centro de los Derechos del Migrante* (Migrant Rights Center or CDM) and the Mexico City- based *Proyecto de Derechos Económicos, Sociales y Culturales* (Economic, Social and Cultural Rights Project or ProDESC) filed a complaint with the Mexican NAO arguing that the US government had failed to comply with its obligations under the NAALC to effectively enforce labor laws with respect migrants working in the carnival and fair industry under H-2B visas. The individual migrant workers were originally from the Mexican states of Zacatecas and Veracruz and worked for J&J Amusements, Inc. and Reithoffer Shows, Inc. in the US from 2007 to 2009. Under the H-2B visa program, foreign workers enter the US for temporary periods to perform non-agricultural unskilled labor. Over 47,403 workers were granted H-2B visas in 2010, 70% of whom were from Mexico.

332. The core of the complaint's legal argument is that the US violated its duty under the NAALC to ensure that its laws provide for high labor standards and to promote compliance with and effective enforcement of its labor laws. The NAALC labor principles implicated were No. 4 (minimum employment standards such as minimum wages and overtime pay) and No. 11 (providing migrant workers with the same legal protection as nationals).

333. The complainants alleged that the US government allowed carnival and fair industry employers of workers with H-2B visas to deny their employees minimum wage and overtime payments. In addition, the US government failed to conduct inspections of traveling carnivals and fairs that employed H-2B workers. H-2B workers also continue to be excluded from eligibility for free legal services available through the US Legal Services Corporation (LSC). This exclusion was the subject of a 2005 complaint filed with the Mexican NAO. Some of the labor violations the US government failed to address included not reimbursing H-2B workers for pre-employment visa-related and travel expenses, illegally withholding a portion of the workers' pay to ensure they stay for the entire period of temporary employment and requiring workers to purchase $100 uniforms. All of these employer requirements are unlawful under US labor laws and under the provisions of the H-2B visa requirements.

334. Under the US Fair Labor Standards Act, carnival and fair workers may be excluded from minimum wage requirements under certain narrow circumstances. The US government never required the traveling carnival and fair employers to prove that they actually qualified for the exclusion from the requirement to pay the minimum wage of $7.25/hour to their H-2B employees. Even so, they were required to pay their H-2B temporary employees at least the prevailing wage in the industry, which was $6.60/hour at the time. Although the H-2B workers were promised the minimum wage, in fact they were offered flat rates of $210 or $240/week. The complainants calculated that the workers were paid $3.14/hour for 12-hour days during 7-day weeks. With all of the other unreimbursed expenses and additional illegal wage deductions, the effective pay rate the H-2B workers received was between $1.61 and $1.98/hour - hovering around 25 percent of the mandatory minimum wage.

335. In addition to outlining the specific facts related to the migrant workers named in the complaint and their co-workers, the complaint goes on to discuss in detail the failure of the US government to effectively enforce minimum wage and overtime standards and systemic failure to protect migrant workers and provide them with the same legal protections as nationals. In addition to language and cultural barriers, H-2B visa workers and other migrant workers have a difficult time accessing administrative and judicial resources because they tend to work in industries that require them to work seven days a week and travel from place to place.

336. The complainants filed a supplement to their original petition on 15 August 2012. US DOL had issued revised regulations governing the H-2B visa program, but a federal court had issued an injunction prohibiting the implementation of those regulations and the complainants noted that US DOL had not taken any steps to implement the new regulations. Other progress that was made since the Obama administration came into office in January 2009 included the addition of 300 more wage and hour investigators and upgrades to equipment and technology. Despite these improvements, however, complainants found labor law enforcement to continue to be weak. They refer to a 2009 US General Accounting Office outlining failings in the US DOL Wage and Hour investigation process, and outline in detail the difficulties migrant workers encounter in trying to enforce their rights through US administrative and judicial proceedings.

337. The enforcement action the complainants recommended be taken by the US government included the dedication of more attention and funding to train wage and hour inspectors, expansion of inspections and monitoring of the fair and carnival industry, investigation and provision of remedies for a higher percentage of worker complaints, more outreach to workers and education of employers about their responsibilities and the consequences for violating those responsibilities. The complainants asked the Mexican NAO to accept the petition for review, engage an independent Mexican expert to conduct on-site inspections and prepare a detail study of working conditions in the carnival and fair industry, have public information sessions with workers and advocates in Mexico and the US, engage in Ministerial Consultations establish an ECE and if the ECE report is not adopted to request an Arbitral Panel.

338. In November 2012, the Mexican NAO issued a report of review regarding three NAALC petitions – MEX 2003-1 (regarding H-2A temporary agricultural labor visa holders), MEX 2005-1 (regarding H-2B temporary non-agricultural labor visa holders) and MEX 2011-1. The 72-page report is a study in bold critique of US labor laws and policies governing migrant workers and diplomatic treatment of an important trading partner. In the introduction to the report, the Mexican NAO points out that under US law, agricultural workers with H-2A visas do not enjoy the right to form unions, bargain collectively and engage in collective action if they wish to improve their working conditions. Similarly, the Mexican NAO cites language from the 2010 North American Commission for Labor Cooperation Secretariat report noting that all agricultural laborers are excluded from coverage under the National Labor Relations Act except in a couple of states (such as California) that have passed legislation affording legal protection to agricultural laborers who wish to form unions and bargain collectively. The Mexican NAO is careful to cite communications it received from the US NAO during the course of investigating the 2003, 2005 and 2011 H-2A and H-2B petitions in outlining shortcomings in US law. The Mexican NAO also notes that with regard to NAALC Principle 11 regarding affording migrant workers protections equal to those of nationals under US labor law, petitioners in the MEX 2003-1, 2005-1 and 2011-1 complaints indicating that H-2A and H-2B visa holders do not have the same rights as US nationals since H-2A visa holders may not file class actions and H-2B workers may not avail themselves of free legal aid services. Other limits on the exercise of labor rights by H-2A and H-2B visa holders noted by the Mexican NAO include language, seven-day work weeks and constant movement from workplace to workplace by carnival and fair workers. While expressing its respect for the NAALC and the commitment of the signatories to recognize each party's right to establish its own labor laws and to adopt, modify its own labor laws, the Mexican NAO recommended Ministerial Consultations between the US Secretary of Labor and the Mexican Minister of Labor to discuss the issues raised in all three reports.

339. Petitioners hailed calls made by the Mexican NAO for Ministerial Consultations to be a victory for migrant workers with H-2 visas. Nevertheless, on 18 February 2014, in advance of a North American presidential summit to be held in Toluca, Mexico, the petitioners filed a second supplement to their original complaint. The petitioners noted that ministerial consultations had not commenced 10 months after the Mexican NAO issued its report, so the petitioners sent letters to the Mexican and US NAOs urging them to begin consultations. While the Mexican NAO indicated that parameters of the consultations were being discussed, consultations had not yet begun.

340. In addition to urging that progress be made in ministerial consultations between the US and Mexican labor ministers, petitioners called for more transparency in the NAALC process itself. In particular, petitioners called on the US and Mexican NAOs to include H-2 workers and their advocates in consultations so that discussions will be better informed by the workers' experiences. Petitioners also called on the NAOs to afford H-2 workers and their advocates with the opportunity to comment on draft declarations and proposed resolutions as well as to provide comments in the final declaration. Finally, petitioners criticized the NAALC website for not being up-to-date and for containing very little information and documentation about past NAALC complaints, calling for all documentation related to NAALC complaints to be posted on the NAALC website within 48 hours of receipt.

341. Migrant worker advocates also filed petitions with the Inter-American Commission on Human Rights (IACHR) regarding treatment of H2 visa holders, attending a hearing in March 2013 in which one of the IACHR commissioners expressed concern about lack of protection of workers from retaliation for filing work-related complaints. On 21 February 2014, migrant worker advocates requested another hearing before the IACHR to address issues facing migrant workers not only in the US under the H2 visa programs but also in Canada under the Seasonal Agricultural Workers Program, which extends visas for temporary agricultural laborers in Mexico, Guatemala and several Caribbean nations. The coalition of migrant worker advocates involved in the request for the 2014 IACHR hearing includes members from all three NAFTA member states as well as El Salvador and Guatemala.

342. On 3 April 2014, US Secretary of Labor Thomas E. Perez and Mexican Secretary of Labor and Social Welfare entered into a Ministerial Declaration to address the issues raised in the MEX 2003-1, MEX 2005-1 and MEX 2011-1 NAALC complaints filed with the Mexican NAO. Unlike Ministerial Declarations of the past, the April 2014 Declaration purports to enter into ministerial consultations rather than constitute a final solution and response to issues raised in the

NAALC complaints. Although procedurally the Declaration commences a period of ministerial consultation, it contains a number of steps that will be taken by the governments of the US and Mexico to address issues raised in the NAALC complaints. The Declaration reconfirms the Consular Partnership Program (CPP) between Mexican Consulates in the US and US labor enforcement authorities which has been in existence for over decade . As has been the case in every other Ministerial Declaration or Agreement addressing issues related to migrant workers under the NAALC, the US DOL commits yet again to develop and prepare even more outreach materials for migrant workers. The Declaration moves beyond the commitment to create migrant worker education materials, however, by outlining concrete steps to plain joint activities involving DOL and STPS officials such as joint training programs in workplaces with H-2A and H-2B visa holders in the agricultural, food packing, forestry and carnival and fair sectors. Other joint activities will involve training for H-2A and H-2B employers and materials and workshops to raise awareness about unlawful migrant worker recruitment practices such as charging recruitment fees to workers.

343. Many of the provisions of the April 2014 Ministerial Declaration consist of potential ideas the Mexican and US labor departments plan on exploring to determine whether they might be feasible, such as collaboration with Mexican government offices in Mexico, development of processes to facilitate locating workers who have returned to Mexico whose back wages have been recovered by the Wage and Hour Division of US DOL and collaboration with the Canadian NAO on the dissemination of educational materials to migrant workers. The US and Mexican NAOs committed to developing a work plan in 60 days (by early June 2014) that will be completed by April 2015. The US and Mexican NAOs also committed to preparing a public report on the outcomes of the educational and outreach events and whether the outcomes achieved the work plan's objectives. The Baltimore-based Centro de Derechos del Migrante expressed optimism about the outcome of its NAALC complaint.

344. An innovation in the April 2014 Ministerial Declaration is paragraph 2, in which the US and Mexican NAOs expressed their intention to reach out to stakeholders – including the petitioners of the NAALC complaints – in developing outreach and educational materials. Every other past ministerial consultation process under the NAALC has been a bit of a black box into which the NAALC complaint goes until a Ministerial Declaration is signed at the end, so paragraph 2 of the April 2014 Ministerial Declaration may end up being historically significant if it hearkens an era of more commitment by NAALC signatories to formally involve petitioners and other members of the public in ministerial consultations.

XIII. *Alabama Anti-Immigration Law HB 56* (Mexican NAO case no. 2012-1)

345. On 27 April 2012, the US-based Service Employees International Union (SEIU) and the Mexico-based National Association of Democratic Lawyers (Asociación Nacional de Abogados Democráticos – ANAD) filed a petition with the

Mexican NAO alleging that an anti-immigrant law that was later passed in the US state of Alabama (House Bill 56 or HB 56) violated the NAALC Principle 11 obligation of the US to afford migrant workers labor protections equal to those afforded to US nationals. HB 56 became law in Alabama in June 2011 and was based on similar anti-immigrant legislation passed in Arizona in 2010 (Arizona Senate Bill 1070 or SB 1070). Most of the provisions of Arizona SB 1070 were ruled to be unconstitutional by the US Supreme Court in *Arizona et al.* v. *The United States*, 567 US ___ (2012). The only provision of SB 1070 to be found constitutional by the US Supreme Court was the requirement that state law enforcement officials to determine the immigration status of anyone they stop or arrest if they have a reasonable suspicion that the person might be an unauthorized immigrant. HB 56 has been referred to as the 'Show Me Your Papers' bill.

346. While HB 56 and SB 1070 contained a number of non-workplace related provisions affecting several aspects of the daily lives of unauthorized immigrants, the core allegation in the NAALC petition filed by SEIU and ANAD is that the legislation creates a climate of fear and intimidation that chills immigrant workers from forming trade unions, bargaining collectively and filing complaints with government authorities when they suffer abuse in the workplace. Thus, almost all 11 labor principles in the NAALC are implicated by HB 56.

347. In the NAALC complaint, petitioners outline how at least eight provisions of HB 56 affect the labor and employment rights of unauthorized immigrants in the US state of Alabama. These include (1) making it a crime for an unauthorized worker to apply for, solicit or perform work as an employee; (2) making it a crime to welcome an unauthorized person into one's home or church or to give a ride to an unauthorized person (the "harboring" provision); (3) allowing US citizens and authorized immigrant workers to file a lawsuit against employers who fail to hire or dismiss them while employing an unauthorized worker; (4) making it unlawful to stop a motor vehicle on a public road to hire any person to work at a different location (essentially, outlawing picking up day laborers, many of whom are unauthorized immigrants); (5) preventing the enforcement of contracts entered into by unauthorized immigrants; (6) requiring police to check the legal status of people who are driving when police have a reasonable suspicion that a person may be unauthorized; (7) making it illegal for any unauthorized worker or young person to enter college of university; and (8) requiring all business entities and employers to utilize 'E-Verify,' a federal online system for determining whether an employee or applicant is legally authorized to work in the US. In particular, petitioners point out that the harboring provision affects unauthorized workers' associational rights as both workers and trade union organizers who host meetings in their homes could be charged with a crime under Alabama law.

348. With regard to occupational safety and the right to compensation for workplace injuries, petitioners point out that HB 56 will lead to more workplace health and safety violations as immigrant workers will be driven deeper into the shadows of the economy and too afraid to report unsafe workplaces. In addition, HB 56 completely precludes unauthorized workers from receiving compensation for workplace injuries and diseases because the Alabama state workers' compensation agency must determine the immigration status of workers before allowing claims for compensation to proceed.

349. As was the case with Arizona SB 1070, most of the provisions of HB 56 were struck down as being contrary to the US Constitution by the US Court of Appeals for the Eleventh Circuit on August 20, 2012. Under the US Constitution, the federal government has plenary power to regulate immigration and international affairs, so much of HB was pre-empted by federal law. Other provisions of Alabama HB 56 were also held to be contrary to free speech, due process and equal protection clauses in the US Constitution. The State of Alabama appealed the ruling of the 11th Circuit's decision to the US Supreme Court, but the US Supreme Court refused to hear the appeal in April 2013, essentially confirming the 11th Circuit Court's decision. In late October 2013, the State of Alabama settled lawsuits filed by the US Department of Justice and immigrant advocacy groups, permanently blocking most of the work-related and "safe harbor" provisions in the law as well as the provision allowing Alabama state law enforcement officials to ascertain the immigration status of people they stop or arrest. The provisions that remain in effect are those preventing unauthorized immigrants from obtaining business licenses or enrolling in universities and requiring employers to use the E-Verify system.

350. Although many provisions of HB 56 were struck down as being contrary to the US Constitution, the SEIU argued that its NAALC complaint to the Mexican NAO was not moot because of the law's overall impact on workers. The Mexican NAO accepted the Alabama HB 56 complaint for review on 3 September 2012.

351. The SEIU also filed a complaint about Alabama HB 56 with the International Labor Organization Committee on Freedom of Association. The Inter-American Commission on Human Rights expressed concern about the negative impact the bill would have on the human rights of immigrants and migrant workers in the US.

XIV. *Porteadores del Noroeste SA de CV* v. *The Industrial Commission of Arizona* (Arizona Court of Appeals 2014)

352. While NAALC complaints regarding North American issues declined in the second decade of the 21st century, cross-border labor issues did not decline, especially in the wake of the partial and still contested implementation of NAFTA's long-haul trucking provisions allowing Mexican trucks to travel beyond 100 miles from the US–Mexico border. In July 2011, the US Federal Motor Carrier Safety Administration (FMCSA) issued regulations and initiated a pilot program to implement NAFTA's long overdue provisions opening North American borders to cross-border trucking. In 2014, Mexico's premier organization of trucking companies, *Cámara Nacional del Autotransporte de Carga* (National Chamber of Cargo Transporters or CANACAR) filed a request for arbitration under the NAFTA arguing the

FMCSA's pilot program does not go far enough in complying with NAFTA's Cross-Border Trucking provision.

353. The high level of contention over the implementation of NAFTA's trucking provisions has been an obstacle in the generation of practical intergovernmental policies and guidance for trucking companies that engage in cross-border trucking and workers' compensation administrators (which operate at a state level in the United States and a provincial level in Canada) when it comes to compensating truck drivers for workplace injuries incurred outside their home country. In 2010, Adan Valenzuela, a truck driver employed by the Mexican corporation Porteadores Del Noroeste SA de CV suffered extensive injuries when the truck he was driving rolled over in the state of Arizona. While Mr Valenzuela's employer had obtained coverage for him through Mexico's Social Security Institute (which includes wage indemnity and medical treatment for workplace injuries) as required by Mexican law, neither Porteadores nor the subcontractor that actually employed Mr Valenzuela had obtained workers' compensation insurance as required under Arizona law. Thus Mr Valenzuela received wage indemnity from the Mexican Social Security Institute as well as medical treatment in Mexico, but did not have a way to pay for the $17,000 US in medical bills incurred for medical treatment in Arizona when the accident happened and for treatment by a Mexican doctor not covered by the Mexican Social Security Institute health plan.

354. Finding Porteadores and its subcontractor to be uninsured employers, the Arizona Workers' Compensation Administration paid for Mr Valenzuela's Arizona emergency medical bills but not those of his Mexican physician out of its Uninsured Employers Fund. In response to Mr Valenzuela's claim for full payment of all the medical bills incurred as part of work-related injuries, Porteadores utilized the NAALC to argue that the NAFTA and the NAALC pre-empted Arizona law and that the state of Arizona had no jurisdiction over Porteadores to enforce Arizona workers' compensation law against Porteadores.

355. The Arizona Workers' Compensation Administration found against Porteadores, which appealed to the Arizona Court of Appeals. In a decision issued in January 2014, the Arizona Court of Appeals rejected Porteadores' NAALC-based pre-emption argument. Pointing to public policy underlying the passage of the Arizona Workers' Compensation Act, the court held that every employer that has employees working in Arizona – whether it be established out of state or out of the country – is required to obtain Arizona workers' compensation insurance. With specific regard to the NAALC-based pre-emption argument, the Court of Appeals held that Porteadores was precluded from asserting that the NAFTA and NAALC pre-empt Arizona state law. The court cited the US NAFTA Implementation Act for this proposition as well as the proposition that no state law may be held invalid on the ground that its application is contrary to the NAFTA. The court found that neither US law nor the NAFTA and NAALC pre-empt Arizona state action in Mr. Valenzuela's case. Thus, Mexican trucking employers are required to comply with Arizona state law and obtain workers' compensation insurance for their employees when operating within Arizona even if they register with Mexican workers' compensation insurance within Mexico.

§4. Cases Involving Alleged Workers' Rights Violations in Canada

I. *McDonald's* (US NAO case no. 9803)

356. Joined by the Quebec Federation of Labor and the International Labor Rights Fund, the Teamsters union and its Quebec affiliates filed a NAALC complaint with the US NAO in October 1998 over the closure of a McDonald's restaurant in St-Hubert, Quebec shortly before the union was certified to bargain for workers there. This was the first NAALC case implicating labor law in a Canadian jurisdiction.

357. Citing violations and lack of effective enforcement in matters related to labor principles 1 and 2 on freedom of association and protection of the right to organize and the right to bargain collectively, the submitters argued that McDonald's used loopholes and delaying tactics to string out union representation proceedings before the Quebec labor board for one year. The company prolonged proceedings by arguing falsely that the restaurant was part of a larger chain where workers transferred among different facilities. 'The franchise system and the fact that the franchisee controlled multiple locations opened the door to undue delays in that it allowed an artificial challenge to the definition of the bargaining unit,' the complaint argued.

358. The case also 'raises questions regarding the absence of recourses under Quebec law for anti-union motivated plant closures, as well as unwarranted delays in the certification process,' said the complaint. McDonald's routinely appealed decisions in the union's favor, then finally shut the restaurant when the union certification was about to be issued.

359. Although Quebec labor law is generally favorable to workers and unions, it is impotent in dealing with anti-union workplace closures. The Quebec courts evolved a doctrine allowing employers to close facilities to avoid unionization with impunity – the only jurisdiction in North America that does so.

360. In December 1998 the US NAO announced that it accepted the *McDonalds* case for review. When the US NAO accepted the complaint and scheduled public hearings, Quebec trade unions, employer federations, and labor department officials looked for a way out. In effect, they did not want to have Quebec's 'dirty laundry' aired in a US public hearing. They preferred to take up the matter *en famille*, based on the sentiment that Canada – and especially Quebec – is a more advanced industrial democracy than the United States and that it would be inappropriate to subject Quebec to critical review by a country where workers' rights are less respected. The unions withdrew the complaint, and the hearing was cancelled. In April 1999 the petitioners withdrew their complaint following an agreement by the Quebec government to undertake a special study of the question of anti-union plant workplace closures in the context of an overall review of the Quebec Labor Code. The labor code review was still underway as of 1 January 2001.

II. *Canadian Rural Letter Carriers* (US NAO case no. 9804)

361. A coalition of postal unions and other labor organizations, along with several NGOs, filed a complaint in December 1988 with the NAOs of both the United States and Mexico on new legislation in Canada defining rural letter carriers as independent contractors rather than employees of the postal service. The result has been to strip rural letter carriers of protection of the right to organize and the right to collective bargaining, resulting in a *de facto* exclusion of women from trade union rights because of the high number of rural letter carriers who are women.

362. Noting that Canadian courts had considered and rejected the postal workers' claim under the Canadian Charter of Rights and Freedoms, the US NAO declined to accept the letter carriers' case for review in February 1999. The submitters argued that the US NAO acted *ex parte*, receiving briefs from the Canadian government that submitters were not made aware of and did not have an opportunity to respond to. They asked for a reconsideration of this decision, but later dropped this appeal and shifted to a request for a cooperative activities program dealing with the overall issue of independent contractors and protection of the right to organize in the three NAALC countries under ILO Conventions and under NAALC obligations.

363. An international conference on this subject was scheduled for February 2001 in Toronto. The conference agenda was expanded to take up issues of other categories of workers excluded from coverage under certain labor laws, such as agricultural workers, household domestic employees, and supervisors.

Chapter 4. The NAALC and ILO Standards

364. The NAALC does not make explicit use of ILO Conventions. The 11 labor principles in Annex 1 of the NAALC are similar to but not the same as relevant ILO Conventions. They have no stated link to ILO definitions or ILO jurisprudence. The NAALC negotiators did not want to make such a link, since none of them has ratified all the ILO Conventions related to the NAALC labor principles.

365. Negotiators wanted to avoid any implication that they were adopting ILO Conventions or assuming ILO-linked obligations. They rather intended to construct a separate, self-standing declaration of principles and obligations with an accompanying system of mutual reviews, evaluations, and (for some matters) arbitration on over effective enforcement of domestic legislation. As the Ministerial Council's four-year report put it: 'The NAALC is clearly based on a fundamental recognition of the sovereignty of the parties in the labor area … the use of international standards rather than domestic laws would run counter to this fundamental concern for sovereignty.'

366. There is one reference to the ILO in the NAALC. Article 45 has the three NAALC partners establish cooperative arrangements with the ILO to enable them to draw on the ILO's experience and expertise for purposes of implementing the rules of procedure for a NAALC Evaluation Committee of Experts. Negotiators believed that such a committee is analogous to the ILO's Committee of Experts or Committee on Freedom of Association, so that advice from the ILO would be helpful. The first Executive Director of the Secretariat of the Commission for Labor Cooperation visited the ILO in Geneva, and communication on this issue was established between the staffs of the Secretariat and the ILO.

367. Notwithstanding the efforts of NAALC negotiators to avoid entanglement with ILO Conventions, submitters of several complaints under the NAALC have invoked ILO standards in fashioning their submissions and making their arguments as cases unfolded. These cases have mostly involved Mexico, although Convention 87 is also at issue in the most recent NAALC submission aimed at Canadian legislation stripping rural letter carriers of the right to unionize (the legislation defines them as independent contractors, not employees). In addition, beginning with the 2003 *Puebla Natamoros Garment* and *Tarrant* complaint, submitters often dual file NAALC complaints with the ILO Committee on Freedom of Association.

368. Mexican jurisprudence incorporates international treaties, including ratified ILO Conventions, into domestic legislation. Some of the NAALC cases involved the trade union registration system and allegations of discriminatory treatment of unions not affiliated with the central labor body loyal to the ruling Institutional Revolutionary Party (PRI). Others dealt with the requirement of a single-union monopoly in the public sector. ILO Convention No. 87 and decisions of the Committee of Freedom of Association have been critical factors in treatment of the submissions at both the initial review and reporting stage and in subsequent conferences and workshops.

369. Despite the scant reference to the ILO and ILO Conventions in the NAALC, social actors involved in NAALC matters inevitably look to the ILO for authoritative guidance on international labor jurisprudence. For example, in its request for a cooperative activity, the Canadian rural letter carriers union sought a forum on collective bargaining 'in light of international labor law under ILO Conventions and of the Parties' obligations under the NAALC' and asked the NAOs to invite experts from the ILO to participate.

370. In the wake of adoption of the ILO's 1998 *Declaration on Fundamental Principles and Rights at Work*, it was assumed that the three NAALC governments would have to incorporate greater reference to the ILO in the operation of their labor agreement. The United States, Canada and Mexico all approved the *Declaration*. They would be hard put to insist that there is no relationship between commitments under the *Declaration* and obligations on the same matters contained in the NAALC's labor principles. In both cooperative activities and in complaints yet to occur under the NAALC, one could expect even more attention to the ILO and a greater connection between NAALC and ILO discourse. Nevertheless, such an incorporation of ILO principles and the Declaration into the work of the CLC Secretariat and the NAOs had not occurred by the end of April 2014.

Chapter 5. Evaluating the NAALC

§1. Contrasting Views of the NAALC

371. In 1993 NAALC negotiators agreed on a provision requiring a review of its implementation and effectiveness after four years of operation. In 1997 the countries set out a process for such a review that included the following elements:

- preparation by the Secretariat of a general overview of the activities undertaken under the agreement since coming into force on 1 January 1994, including cooperative activities, public communications, NAO and ministerial consultations, and Secretariat reports;
- comments by each government on the operation and effectiveness of the NAALC from their Governmental and National Advisory Committees;
- an invitation for written public comments to be submitted to the Secretariat or to the NAOs;
- creation of an independent review committee made up of non-governmental labor experts chosen by each country from its National Advisory Committee or an alternate, to provide an independent advisory report to the Council on the operation and effectiveness of the NAALC;
- preparation of a draft report by the Secretariat for consideration by the Council, including a general overview; highlights from government comments and public comments, comments from the Executive Director on the operation of the Secretariat, the advisory report of the independent review committee, a summary of literature related to the NAALC, and identification of key issues for consideration by the Council;
- a final report issued by the Council and made available to the public, including the full report of the independent review committee.

372. At a Prince Edward Island ministerial meeting in October 1998, the three governments discussed the status of the four-year review of the NAALC. The labor ministers expressed general satisfaction with the results of the NAALC. They cited mainly the fruits of cooperative activities such as the increase in knowledge about each one another's labor markets and labor law systems. At the same time, they pledged to 'improve the future operations and effectiveness of the NAALC.'

373. The review was not finally approved by the Council and published on the web site of the NAALC Secretariat at www.naalc.org until June, 1999. The delay was attributed to two factors: (1) controversy and hard bargaining over the report's final language, some of which might be construed to be critical of one government or another, and (2) a split in the three-person independent review committee, which had hoped to achieve a consensus report.

374. Although they were not published until June 1999, public comments for the Commission's four-year review were received in early 1998. At that time a total of ten complaints had been submitted under the NAALC, and nine of them involved labor law matters in Mexico. This created an impression that NAFTA's labor side

Chapter 5, Evaluating the NAALC agreement was really an exercise in Mexico-bashing, not a balanced agreement subjecting each country equally to scrutiny by its partners.

375. Mexico's governmental advisory committee to its NAO summed up the sentiment of perceived 'Mexico-bashing' in its comment for the four-year report:

> NAALC members must recognize that each country has its own institutions and laws ... The public communications process should foster cooperation, not controversy between the Parties ... Some of the US NAO reviews interfere with proceedings in Mexican tribunals ... NAOs should not accept communications and the Council should not authorize research studies that call into question the labor legislation of a country ... Public hearings violate sovereignty and lead to confrontation ... they become an instrument of pressure that distorts the purposes of the NAALC.

A similar review was originally contemplated eight years after NAFTA went into effect, however in 2002 the Council of Ministers decided there would not be a tri-national report and public commentary process and each member country would determine whether and what kind of process and report would be required. The public process and reporting in each country was minimal.

§2. Trade Union Views

376. Trade unions and allied NGOs, on one hand, and business organizations, on the other hand, criticized the NAALC from diametrically opposed perspectives. An organization representing Canadian labor lawyers who represent unions stated:

> As matters now stand, workers and unions that are the victims of governmental failure to enact and enforce labour laws protecting freedom of association, in the face of free trade and economic integration, have virtually no recourse under the NAALC other than to make submissions to the NAO than to make submissions to the NAO of a signatory government which can only recommend ministerial consultations with the offending signatory government. Petitioners have no right under the NAALC to pursue their complaints concerning denial of freedom of association before an independent body such as the ECE or an Arbitral Panel. Granted, submissions to an NAO under the NAALC, and presentations at subsequently convened inquiries, have had a positive effect, by informing the public and publicizing NAALC violations. However, the fact is that, although the series of cases which have arisen during the past four years under the NAALC have demonstrated a persistent pattern of violation of freedom of association, no effective remedy is yet available to protect this basic right which is essential to the protection of the workers' dignity and the enhancement of their living standards. It is clear that, in light of the initial four years of experience, the NAALC must be substantially strengthened, so as to achieve its original promise and purpose.

377. The Canadian Labour Congress submitted a comment saying of the NAALC:

> A key concern in the NAFTA debate was weak (to say the least) respect for democratic, human and labour rights in Mexico, and low levels of labour standards and environmental regulation. Critics drew attention to the fact that NAFTA lacked a 'social dimension' and created significant new rights for capital without putting in place any corresponding set of minimum obligations to respect basic labour rights and standards, or minimum environmental and health and safety regulations. In this respect, NAFTA differed greatly from the European Community process of economic integration, which has seen some explicit attempts to establish minimum standards, as in the area of health and safety, the creation of Euro-Works councils, as well as a regional parliament and a redistributive fund to reduce the economic disparities between richer and poorer countries.
>
> It was in response to such criticisms that NAFTA was implemented along with labour and environment "side deals" which established what purports to be a minimum – or minimal – social framework. The labour side deal or NAALC, as you know, requires each country only to respect and enforce its own labour laws, and does not require a country to respect a common set of basic labour rights as defined in conventions of the International Labour Organization. It thus falls far short of the idea of 'binding social clauses' inserting recognized core labour rights and enforceable standards in trade agreements as called for by the international labour movement. While the labour side-deal did establish procedures for governments to examine complaints on labour rights and standards and thus to publicize abuses, it falls far short of the mechanisms necessary to truly remedy market failures and halt the downward pressures on wages and standards.

378. Echoing the view of the Canadian Labour Congress, Quebec's Confederation of National Trade Unions (CSN) said 'we must unfortunately conclude that the approach of the NAALC ... has been a failure.' The Quebec Workers' Federation said 'The NAALC is a toothless accord that collapses under bureaucratic weight.'

379. In the United States, the US NGO that was most active in filing NAALC complaints, the International Labor Rights Fund, first praised the work of the US NAO, saying 'the ILRF is very enthusiastic about the quality of work done by the US NAO within the narrow mandate provided by the NAALC.' but when on to declare that 'the NAALC is fatally flawed due to the lack of effective enforcement mechanisms':

> Our concerns are focused on the general lack of concrete, measurable progress made in improving enforcement of labor laws following a NAALC proceeding. The right to associate is the most fundamental right for workers. If workers have the ability to organize free and independent unions, they have a voice in the setting of the terms and conditions of their employment. Most of the

NAALC cases filed against Mexico have raised issues of freedom of association, and have emphasized the corrupt system of state-sponsored unions in Mexico under the dominance of the PRI. The sole remedy under the NAALC for violation of the fundamental right to associate, no matter how pervasive or frequent, is Ministerial Consultations under Article 22. Such consultations have been held with Mexico specifically on the right to associate in at least four of the cases filed to date, yet systematic change has not occurred. New violations are occurring constantly.

The lack of significant progress on the question of the right to associate highlights the fundamental flaw with the NAALC: it relies upon the commitment of each member of NAFTA to enforce its own domestic labor law within its territory, thereby assuring that the labor law enforcement process would remain unchanged. "Consultations" are not sufficient to deter the significant economic incentive companies have to exploit workers. Indeed, not a single company involved in any NAALC case has appeared to testify at a NAO proceeding. The companies have no concern about an adverse outcome. And the Mexican government is loathe to crack down on General Motors or Sunbeam, two companies specifically cited by witnesses at the hearing on case No. 9701 for engaging openly in illegal pregnancy testing to screen employees and applicants, for fear the companies will seek a more employer friendly location.

The structure created by NAALC does not necessarily require that labor law enforcement would not be improved. The problem remains one of unexercised discretion, which is why most critics of the NAALC process insist that the clear solution is mandatory, enforceable standards. The Ministerial Consultations held to date in response to previously filed petitions challenging non-enforcement of Mexican labor law have not resulted in concrete, measurable improvement simply because the US has not provided adequate incentives to encourage change (or sufficient penalties for failing to improve enforcement). Nothing in the NAALC would prevent, for example, the US from linking financial assistance to Mexico with improved enforcement of labor laws.

380. Human Rights Watch, another active NAALC petitioner, stated that 'to the extent that the NAALC leads to public awareness in Mexico about longstanding labor rights problems, we find the accord positive,' but at the same time cautioned that 'the indirect benefits of the submission process are not necessarily as strong as they could be ... NAALC suffers from a lack of political will on the part of the Mexican government to improve its labor rights situation.'

381. The AFL–CIO declared that its 'overall assessment of the NAALC is that for the first four years of its existence, it has failed to bring about substantial improvement in worker rights and standards in the three NAFTA countries. The NAALC, thus far, has been ineffective in promoting the concerns of workers beset by stagnant wages and job insecurity, which have been exacerbated by economic integration in North America.' The US labor federation cited several areas of criticism:

> The NAALC contains no agreement on adherence to internationally recognized worker rights. The NAALC simply commits each nation to 'effectively enforce' its domestic labor laws. Labor laws which are inadequate to protect the rights of workers do not qualify for any corrective action at all. The silence of the NAALC on upward harmonization of labor laws constitutes a serious flaw.
>
> The second objective in the NAALC is to promote a list of labor principles. Unfortunately, the NAALC creates a three-tier system in which only three areas of labor standards are subject to dispute settlement. This is unacceptable.
>
> Even in the areas subject to dispute settlement, the consultation and dispute resolution procedures are so lengthy and tortuous as to discourage complaints and petitions. The provisions in NAFTA governing intellectual property stand in stark contrast to this long and tortuous process. Not only is immediate action possible in the case of intellectual property rights violation, but pirated goods are stopped at the border.

382. Similarly, the Communications Workers of America (CWA) declared 'the NAALC has failed to live up to its goals.' The United Auto Workers (UAW) asserted that 'the NAALC has failed North American Workers.' Independent (i.e. not affiliated with the ruling PRI) Mexican union organizations said the NAALC 'has not represented a real social counterweight to free trade' and 'has shown serious limitations as an instrument' for improving workers' rights.

§3. Employer Views

383. Conversely, some employer critics see the NAALC providing a powerful new weapon for trade unionists and anti-corporate campaigners. They point to the complaint procedure and the attendant publicity and public scrutiny of employer conduct. Commenting on the Washington State apple industry NAALC complaint, an industry spokesman, said 'unions on both side of the border are abusing the NAFTA process in an effort to expand their power ... NAFTA's labor side agreement is an open invitation for specific labor disputes to be raised into an international question' and 'could open the door to a host of costly and frivolous complaints against US employers.' He said 'the labor section of NAFTA should be revised or industry support for future trade agreements will be severely eroded.'

384. Business organizations called for the NAALC to emphasize cooperative activities. The US Council for International Business (CIB), the principal US employers' organization involved in international labor affairs, argued that the NAALC 'has unduly emphasized [submissions] over positive cooperative activities ... it sets the wrong tone and focus.' The US CIB went on to say:

> Each country's National Administrative Office and the NAALC Executive Secretariat deserve much credit for a wide range of information exchange and cooperative programs on labor and employment issues. Unfortunately, the value of these cooperative activities is undermined by the highly visible

emphasis on handling complaints and individual cases. Regrettably many of the complaint submissions focus on specific incidents of alleged improper conduct of individual employers rather than whether a signatory country is effectively enforcing its labor and employment laws. The submissions are filed, and accepted by the NAO, even before domestic administrative and judicial procedures have been exhausted. Thus the NAO often looks at the wrong behavior – individual company behavior in specific instances – rather than the issues addressed by the NAALC – effective enforcement of national laws. And by its conduct the NAO encourages a public misconception about the purpose of the NAALC and feeds unrealistic political expectations.

The acceptance of a public submission under the US NAO procedures should be an exceptional act. Given the spirit of the NAALC, public submissions should only be accepted after domestic procedures have been exhausted and, when accepted, result primarily in joint studies and in technical cooperation and assistance. To accept prematurely submissions for review undercuts they very purpose of the NAALC which is to build cooperation and to ensure that there is compliance and effective enforcement of each Party's labor laws. Under the practice of the US NAO, it appears that there is virtually no written submission that the US NAO will not accept.

The obligations of the NAALC apply to the three signatory countries, not to companies or their employees. Yet, although companies are not parties to the NAALC, they are targets of the proceedings. The cases are known by company names–GE, Honeywell, Sony, and Sprint–when the issue in all the cases has been the effective enforcement of law in Mexico or the United States. In the OECD and the ILO, it has been the consistent practice to not name companies in disputes because they are not parties. This practice should be followed under the NAALC.

The USCIB believes that public hearings as means of gathering information is too confrontational and not in keeping with the purposes of the NAALC. Instead, more informal means in the spirit of cooperation should be employed. Indeed, neither the ILO nor the OECD permit hearings under the procedures of their supervisory machinery, but seek, instead, to resolve matters through investigation, exchange of information and dialogue.

385. In the same vein, Mexico's Enterprise Coordinating Council (CCE), Coordination of Foreign Trade Enterprise Organisms (COECE), and Confederation of Chambers of Commerce (CONCAMIN) criticized the 'publicity' surrounding NAALC cases in connection with 'premature' acceptance of cases. They called public hearings by the US NAO 'contrary to Mexican sovereignty' and argued that no submission or related report should contain the name of a specific company. A prominent consultant who has earlier served in the Mexican trade ministry attributed the NAALC solely to pressure from anti-NAFTA protectionist groups in the United States and characterized actions of the US NAO in accepting cases and holding hearings on events in Mexico as a 'distortion' of the NAALC.

§4. Independent Review Committee's Views

386. Similar divergences appeared in an independent advisors' report by prominent labor law experts from each country. The US and Canadian experts agreed that:

> The submission process has provided a heretofore unknown cross-border scrutiny of the actual implementation of labor law in each of these countries. … The process is an instrument available to the Parties to identify systematic violations in the application of the labor laws of the other Parties. … The process, however, leads to little concrete action. Although the investigation and hearing has produced substantial evidence that the law has been violated, that procedures lack impartiality, and that the law is not being enforced, no remedy or correction follows.
>
> In part, this is because of the provisions of NAALC and the premises of the submission process. … The submission process is designed, as it must be under NAALC, as a fact-finding process, not an educative process with power to order a remedy. Any action must be taken through Ministerial Consultation. The submission process can, however, lead to recommendations. The Public Report does make recommendations for Ministerial Consultation, and the Ministers can agree on recommended action. Those recommendations, however, have not included any undertaking to take formal or informal corrective action, either to provide some measure of relief to victims of unlawful action or to correct systemic defects. The recommendations in the Public Reports and as a result of Ministerial Consultation have been limited to making joint studies, holding seminars, organizing conferences, calling public meetings, and the Ministers exchanging information and keeping each other informed. It is to be feared the further recurrence of conclusions of this nature in cases involving the same labor law principles will gradually lead to disillusion amongst concerned circles, at least in the United States and Canada.
>
> This self-limitation of the NAOs and Ministers is most troublesome where there is evidence of a failure to provide for fair and transparent procedures. NAALC imposes positive procedural obligations. Unfair procedures violate the Agreement, even though they comply with domestic law. Yet neither the United States NAO nor the Ministers seem willing to declare that certain procedures violate the Agreement, much less recommend changes.
>
> This reluctance to make full use of the Agreement is further indicated by the failure to make use of an Evaluation Committee of Experts to methodically inquire into the enforcement of health and safety laws and other technical labor standards.

387. However, their dissenting Mexican colleague took an opposite tack. He declared, 'I however, firmly believe that cooperation represents the very essence of the Agreement and that controversy and its subsequent resolution should be the exception. … Submissions may not be considered as a mechanism for altering the manner in which national laws are enforced or modified. The enforcement or modification of laws is strictly subject to the sovereignty of each of the NAALC signatory countries.' He went said that the work of the US NAO, in particular, 'is clearly characterized by a marked slant and a total lack of equilibrium … the specific cases were analyzed from an ethnocentric standpoint … the available information does not offer any evidence as to the existence of systematic omissions in the enforcement of labor legislation by the Mexican government.'

388. The Mexican expert went on to say:

> I am also of the opinion that none of these submissions should have been accepted. … If public communications are ultimately aimed at identifying the systematic violation of labor legislation enforcement by any of the Parties, it is clear that this measure may not be utilized if legal proceedings are still in process and if the disputing parties have yet to exhaust the legal resources at their disposal.
>
> When viewed from an institutional standpoint, it would seem that the manner in which these submission procedures have been handled has generated a rather perverse triple effect. Since they are solely focused on Mexico, it would seem that this country has become the accused of the tripartite relationship and that the enforcement of its labor legislation is all that really merits scrutiny. Second, the indiscriminate acceptance of submissions has given greater weight to conflict *vis-à-vis* cooperation, thereby encouraging false expectations regarding the corrective capabilities of the Agreement in specific cases. Finally, and as has also been the case of the Secretariat, the United States and Mexican NAOs have been obliged to, relegate those activities not directly linked to the development of submission procedures.

389. The dissident Mexican member of the independent advisory group concluded by defending Mexico's official, corporatist unions and condemning collaboration between US trade unions and independent Mexican unions in using the NAALC process:

> The original goals of the NAALC run the risk of becoming adulterated by the perspective which nongovernmental United States trade unions have attempted to impose upon it. This strategy has three main objectives: (a) to focus attention on Mexico, which is considered an unfair competitor *vis-à-vis* the attraction of regional investment; (b) to encourage a negative vision of judicial labor proceedings and the enforcement of labor law in Mexico; and (c) to seek strategic alliances, especially with the so-called independent trade unions.
>
> Despite the fact that they are willing to adjust their general strategies as a means of adapting to profound national and international changes, the large traditional unions which still represent the vast bulk of Mexican trade unionism do not wish to cast off measures and forms of action that have proved beneficial to the organized labor movement. The fact that Mexican trade unionism emerged, grew, and achieved advanced labor legislation, social security, a workers' housing program and a close alliance with the post-revolutionary state is often overlooked. In contrast to its United States and Canadian counterparts, since the 1930s Mexican trade unionism has participated in the definition of the policies that have sculpted its development and are indeed

important to its interests. … Since the NAALC has not fully comprehended the historical role played by Mexican trade unions in the policy-making process, it therefore remains aloof and distant from the traditions of the Mexican labor movement. This is essentially a situation comprising two different political and labor cultures. The reluctance of the majority trade union organizations to accept an Agreement considered as little more than a potentially disruptive factor that could well upset the equilibrium achieved with great effort over the course of many years may consequently be understood.

However, it should be noted that there are certain exceptions to this pattern of conduct within the majority Mexican trade unions. The new or independent organizations … have discovered an additional form of action by using the NAALC submission procedures and, above all, the United States NAO to further their cause. … In other words, by submitting complaints before the United States NAO, the independent trade unions have sought to broaden their sphere of action *vis-à-vis* their conflict with traditional trade union organizations.

The political designs of the independent trade unions have found a certain echo and indeed reply in the protectionist dispositions of United States trade unionism. This factor has led to agreements such as the Alliance for Strategic Organization, concluded between United Electrical Workers union (UE) and the *Frente Auténtico del Trabajo* (Authentic Labor Front – FAT) for the consolidation of joint action in the in-bond industries situated along the northern Mexican border. Other United States trade unions have initiated similar projects with independent Mexican organizations, especially those functioning in the areas of clothing and textile manufacture, telecommunications, foodstuffs and transportation. While the convergence of this type of interest and form of action may be clearly perceived in the submission procedures so far initiated, the fact that conflict is stressed over and above cooperation would also seem to indicate a desire to imbue the NAALC with a character that it simply does not possess.

It is therefore not coincidental that the majority of the complaints submitted before the United States NAO have focused on the freedom of trade union association (Article 49). While this is undoubtedly a highly important principle, it is not however included in the three principles considered as part of the mechanism created for the resolution of controversy (Article 27). Since trade union freedom is precisely the point of contact between the tactical interests of United States trade unionism and independent Mexican organizations, it is therefore logical that this issue serve to test the limits of the Agreement.

§5. Academic Views

390. Between the contrasting critical perspectives of labor and business, many academic analysts see substantive, positive results in the NAALCs addressing of workers' rights in the region. The NAFTA Committee of the Industrial Relations Research Association, for example, said 'the NAALC has had several positive effects that make it worth exploring further as a mechanism to shed light on labor rights violations in the three countries.' The Committee cited improved ability of policy makers to understand labor relations practices and laws, valuable research reports from the Secretariat, the broad subject matter of the 11 labor principles, opportunities for unions to collaborate across borders with each other and with advocacy groups outside of the labor movement, and the positive effects of 'sunshine' generated by the publicity surrounding NAALC cases.

391. Other analysts have noted that 'Despite the skepticism of critics, the NAALC and the institutions it has spawned have had some modest successes in labour's favor. Although the agreement contains procedures that are far from ideal, they do have the capacity to advance the struggle for labour rights.'[4] Another commented 'It is clear that the NAALC's primary contribution to the transnational labor rights regime to date has been to create a forum for regional public awareness of labor rights issues ... Despite its limitations, the NAALC stands as a groundbreaking step toward regional collaboration in the development of labor rights.'[5]

4. See Roy J. Adams and Parbudyal Singh, 'Early Experience with NAFTA's Labor Side Agreement', 18 *Comparative Labor Law Journal* 161 (Winter 1997).
5. See Sarah H. Cleveland, 'Global Labor Rights and the Alien Torts Claims Act', 76 *Texas Law Review* 1533 (May 1998).

Chapter 6. Continuing Controversy over NAFTA and the NAALC

392. The debate in the United States over NAFTA, job losses and wage reductions was mostly a low-intensity war until the 2008 US presidential campaign, which began in the fall of 2007. In the Democratic primary, candidate Barack Obama challenged Hillary Clinton on the issue of NAFTA, which her husband Bill Clinton shepherded through Congress in his first term in office. Both Obama and Mrs. Clinton promised working class voters to reopen the NAFTA and improve protections for workers and the environment. The debate about NAFTA has broken into large-scale conflict when international trade issues rise to the top of the Washington agenda, which they did in 2005 with the Senate's ratification of the Dominican Republic Central American Free Trade Agreement (CAFTA-DR) and in debates over controversial bilateral FTA's like the US–Colombia FTA, which was subject to congressional debate in late 2007 and early 2008. The intensity of the controversy reached another high in 2013 and early 2014 as the 20th anniversary of NAFTA and NAALC coincided with the end negotiations of the Trans-Pacific Partnership (TPP), a free trade agreement spanning at least four continents and including all three NAFTA partners as well as Australia, Brunei, Chile, Japan, Malaysia, New Zealand, Peru, Singapore and Vietnam. Widespread public perception of NAFTA's damage to US jobs and wages and continued anti-NAFTA campaigning by the trade union movement were key factors in the defeat of fast track negotiating authority for President Clinton in 1997 and 1998. Before then, no American president had ever been denied fast-track authority by Congress. As of the end of April 2014, the US Congress had not passed renewed fast track legislation and the TPP had opponents in both the Republican and Democratic parties as a result of the lack of transparency in the negotiation process. Even the US Congress did not have access to working drafts of the TPP.

393. As with any heated public policy debate, perceptions and facts are at sharp odds in the NAFTA jobs and wages debate. The AFL–CIO and allied organizations argued that some 500,000–600,000 US jobs have been destroyed by NAFTA. In contrast, the Clinton administration and business supporters claimed that NAFTA-related trade supported 2.3 million US jobs, and that many of the 14 million new American jobs since 1993 owed themselves to expanded trade thanks to agreements like NAFTA.

394. The framework and terms of the debate did not change with the 20th anniversary of the NAFTA. In its 2014 NAFTA at 20 report, the AFL-CIO argued that while NAFTA and similar FTAs facilitate more trade, they contain no measures to ensure that the gains are widely shared and FTA investor protection provisions hinder the development and support of social and environmental protection policies. In addition to finding that US trade policy does not create quality jobs or enhance social mobility, the AFL-CIO pointed out that trade union membership declined in all three NAFTA nations between 1994 and 2014 and that multinational corporations benefit disproportionately as a result of free trade policies. In its 2014 report NAFTA's 20-Year Legacy and the Fate of the Trans-Pacific Partnership, Public Citizen argued that not a single job had been produced in the US as a result of

NAFTA. In contrast, the 20th anniversary US Chamber of Commerce NAFTA report described the NAFTA as "triumphant," arguing that trade with Canada and Mexico supports nearly 14 million jobs in the US. A February 2013 report issued by the US Congressional Research Service was more ecumenical on the subject of NAFTA's impact, noting the continued deep divide in views of the NAFTA and pointing out that not all economic improvements and downturns, job losses and job creation that have occurred in North American member states over the past two decades can be attributed to the NAFTA.

395. Each side in the debate has accused the other of reliance on ideology, passion and perceptions rather than facts. Controversy is exacerbated by the malleability of numbers in arguments about jobs gained or lost under NAFTA. The argument is further complicated by the difficulty of disaggregating effects of NAFTA on employment and wages from the effects of Mexico's peso devaluation at the end of 1994. One widely noted US study concluded that 'it has become clear that many of NAFTA's most important effects are not easily quantified or observed, and the full effects of the Agreement will take many more years to make themselves known.'

396. Judging from congressional reactions to fast track, NAFTA critics believed they had won the debate at the end of 2000. Fast track authority was renewed in 2002 but expired in July 2007 without being renewed again. NAFTA opponents pointed to closed US factories, many employing hundreds of workers whose jobs were shifted to Mexico. In contrast, jobs created in warehousing, distribution, professional services and other fields were spread too thinly through the economy to affect the public debate. The balance of US trade with Canada and Mexico had shifted from one with a slight deficit with Canada and a surplus with Mexico at the time that NAFTA was negotiated to a large and growing deficit with both countries by the end of 2000. With China's accession to the World Trade Organization in 2001, the manufacturing sector in Mexico began to suffer job losses to China as well.

397. Prominent articles in important regional newspapers were typical of historical NAFTA discourse in the United States. A light bulb manufacturer near Boston, Massachusetts employing 600 workers closed and moved production to Mexico. Most of the employees were women and members of minority groups. Their average salary was approximately $12.00 per hour and total compensation exceeded $20 per hour, taking benefits into account. They lost everything with the plant closing and move to Mexico.

398. Speaking to the *Boston Globe*, the state government's director of international trade said 'The job loss here is very regrettable, but NAFTA has opened markets for us that weren't there before.' She pointed out that Massachusetts-based exports to Mexico, mostly in growth industries such as computers and telecommunications equipment, increased 30 per cent from 1997 to 1998.

399. The union leader at the plant stated 'There is no more American Dream. What we have now is the Mexican Dream.' A regional union official said 'The bitterness workers feel now is not that they're losing jobs because of a lack of sales, but because the government greased the skids for the transfer of our jobs to other countries.' A worker added 'It's our politicians and our government. They are the ones to blame on this.' The newspaper article's text was accompanied by photographs of victimized women workers and their children pondering their future after the loss of a good job with good health insurance and other benefits. In a battle for the public's hearts and minds, the image of suffering workers far outweighs a bureaucrat's recitation of statistics.

400. The drama of job losses attributed to NAFTA takes on added layers of impact and irony because many of the most widely publicized plant closings take place on the US side of the border with Mexico and affect mostly low-paid Mexican and Mexican-American women workers. In El Paso, Texas, Levi Strauss & Co. closed large facilities employing thousands of workers who made modest wages of $6–8 per hour. Many smaller firms along the border in California, Arizona and Texas also shut down and joined the exodus to Mexico, lured by wages one-tenth the US level and new, advantageous access to the US market under NAFTA.

401. In all, some 10,000 workers in El Paso lost their jobs because of plant closings and moves to Mexico. The adjustment assistance program designed just for these types of situations proved ineffective, since it contemplated retraining for 'high tech' and service sector employment. In El Paso, most of the affected workers had only labored as garment sewers their entire lives and spoke little or no English.

402. These examples of the effects of NAFTA can be multiplied many times through all parts of the United States since the trade agreement went into effect. In their continuing emphasis on drama, the mass media is drawn to evocative portrayals of shuttered plants and ex-employees who gave a lifetime's work to a company that moved their jobs to Mexico. The cumulative effect on public consciousness and on politicians' wariness on trade issues is strong, even in a time of overall economic growth, high employment levels, and a rising stock market.

403. Amid all the claims and counterclaims, the North American Integration and Development (NAID) Center at the University of California at Los Angeles has conducted what are generally seen as credible, if not conclusive, studies on the employment effects of NAFTA. The NAID Center studies attempt to assess NAFTA alone, rather than NAFTA as a proxy for all the pushing and pulling of the US labor market. NAID Center studies have found that the net effect on jobs lost or jobs gained because of NAFTA was negligible. One study found that rising US exports to Mexico created 44,000 new jobs, while imports from Mexico caused a loss of 35,000 US jobs – a net gain of 9,000 US jobs. More recent studies have found a slight shift in the other direction, with a small net loss of US jobs.

404. Despite such research efforts, it is really not possible to distinguish between the employment effects of NAFTA and the effects of the peso devaluation in late

1994. The Clinton administration and business leaders argued that NAFTA prevented Mexico from resorting to protectionist measures, as it had after a devaluation in the early 1980s. They also pointed to the fact that US total exports to Mexico kept rising even after the peso devaluation, in contrast to a sharp drop in the 1980s. But these claims are too abstract to affect public perception compared with evocative accounts of closed factories and portrayals of real, live workers on the street because their employers closed the plant and moved operations to Mexico.

405. In evaluating the agreement's impact on jobs, anti-NAFTA activists in the United States use two measures. First, they turn on its head a claim used by the Clinton administration during the campaign for NAFTA's passage that every $1 billion worth of exports creates 20,000 new, high-paid jobs for American workers. The basis for this claim is questionable, but it became a mantra of the pro-NAFTA public relations effort in 1992 and 1993.

406. When NAFTA was adopted the United States exported some $40 billion worth of goods to Mexico and had a $5 billion trade surplus with Mexico. Since then, US exports to Mexico have doubled under NAFTA. However, imports from Mexico have tripled, from $35 billion to more than $100 billion, and the earlier trade surplus has shifted to a deficit of more than $20 billion. Meanwhile, Canada's trade surplus with the United States exceeds $30 billion. Anti-NAFTA critics now charge, using the earlier pro-NAFTA formula, that every $1 billion worth of imports from Mexico has *destroyed* 20,000 good jobs. With a $50 billion deficit with Canada and Mexico, NAFTA critics can claim that 1 million jobs have been lost because of the trade agreement.

407. Second, critics point to official US Department of Labor figures showing that more than 250,000 US workers have been found eligible for special, NAFTA-related trade adjustment assistance (TAA) benefits because their jobs are affected by imports from Mexico or Canada. NAFTA-TAA benefits include extended unemployment insurance payments and extra job retraining assistance. From this base of 250,000 jobs claimed lost, critics argue that as many or more workers are not informed of the special NAFTA-TAA benefits program or are unfairly denied eligibility for benefits. This raises the total estimate of jobs lost due to NAFTA to the number greater than half a million, using NAFTA-TAA figures.

408. As with anecdotal evidence of plant closings, the argument that 'even the Labor Department admits that more than 250,000 jobs have been destroyed by NAFTA' affects public opinion and political support for new trade initiatives. However, this argument is incomplete because the number 250,000 reflects *all* workers – including managers and supervisors – employed by firms where at least *some* lay-offs, but not necessarily large lay-offs or full plant shutdowns, have occurred in connection with NAFTA trade. Some of these workers indeed were employed at plants that closed or had layoffs, but many others never lost their jobs. They simply work at firms where at least some layoffs occurred, but they are still working. What has been determined is that if they lose their jobs in the future, they would be eligible for NAFTA-TAA benefits.

409. It is not possible to determine further using NAFTA-TAA figures how many workers actually lost jobs because of NAFTA-related trade. Many of those who were laid off quickly found other work and never bothered to apply for TAA benefits. Others were not aware of the special NAFTA-TAA program and applied for regular unemployment insurance benefits.

410. In any event, the US economy is so huge and labor market churn is so extensive that to speak of 250,000, half a million, or even a million jobs 'destroyed' in the first five years of NAFTA requires further examination. Every *week* in the United States, 300,000 workers apply for unemployment insurance because they lost their jobs or had working hours reduced. A greater number finds new work – those coming off unemployment, and those entering the labor force. Every *month*, more than 13 million workers – about 10 per cent of the workforce – lose a job, change a job, or enter the labor force. The economy shows a net gain of 20 million jobs in the past decade.

411. But overall positive employment gains mask problems that trade union advocates and analysts still attribute to trade in general and to NAFTA in particular. In November 1997, for example, at the time of the fast track vote in Congress, Eastman Kodak announced plans to eliminate 10,000 jobs at its Rochester, New York headquarters site. Levi Strauss & Co. said it would shut down 11 manufacturing plants in the United States affecting thousands of workers, including many more in El Paso, Texas. Fruit of the Loom said it would end all US-based production and shift work to Mexico and Central America, putting thousands more out of work.

412. The composition of the labor market and the preservation of manufacturing employment are key concerns for US trade unions and their allies. Manufacturing jobs tend to provide higher wages and benefits than service sector jobs, and are more highly unionized. Low unemployment rates and high job creation rates in the United States in recent years mask widespread job losses in manufacturing, with corresponding effects on trade union density. The percentage of US workers represented by unions has fallen to 14 per cent from a high of 35–40 per cent in the 1950s. Only 10 per cent of private sector workers are represented by trade unions.

413. The biggest jobs increase in 1998 was in temporary employment agencies supplying business services. A half-million manufacturing jobs were eliminated in 1999 and 2000. Many big manufacturing companies continued to declare large-scale 'downsizing.' One of the most ominous examples came from the largest, most successful US exporter, the Boeing aircraft company, which announced plans to lay off 40,000 workers in 1999. Boeing's announcement, like many others, has almost nothing to do with NAFTA. But these media bombshells usually attribute such moves to the global economy and stresses and strains of international trade, of which NAFTA is the single most evocative symbol in the public mind.

414. Twenty years of experience with NAFTA did not abate the heated academic and political debates about the economic impact of NAFTA and other free trade agreements in North American policy-making. Nevertheless, after the first 12 and 14 years of NAFTA there appeared to be some consensus on certain facts and issues despite widespread disagreement about the causes of economic improvement or decline and job losses in North American countries – especially about Mexico–US immigration and the state of the Mexican economy. Thus, while economists with the World Bank ascribe causation for increased migration to the US from Mexico to the porous US–Mexico border and economists with the Economic Policy Institute (EPI), Migration Policy Institute (MPI) and agricultural labor market economists ascribe causation to the impact of free trade-related policies in Mexico, both agree that migration from Mexico to the United States increased since the advent of NAFTA.

415. Similarly, though expressed in different terms, the World Bank and the EPI both found in 2005 and 2006 that wages between the US and Mexico had not converged. This presented a problem for the World Bank, which conducted its analysis from a prediction that free trade should cause a convergence of returns on both capital and wages. Despite a lack of convergence of wages, some prices did converge – resulting in the phenomena important to labor and human rights advocates focused on stagnating wages in Mexico and increasing price of food and other goods.

416. Economists and advocates on both sides of the debate also agreed on the level of administrative and legal sophistication in Mexico, though in different arenas. Thus, while World Bank economists called for increased flexibilization of Mexican labor laws, they found Mexico's legal and regulatory framework in the financial sector to be inadequate – especially in the area of securities regulation and bankruptcy laws – and that it hampered investment, economic efficiency and technological progress. The World Bank's analysis of this issue echoes the frustration expressed by worker rights advocates with local labor boards and implementation of labor laws reflected in numerous NAALC complaints filed over the years.

417. As free trade agreements and globalization proliferated after 2000, Mexico began losing manufacturing jobs to other countries, especially China. Though coming from different points of view, both free trade advocates and human and labor rights advocates agreed that Mexico's infrastructure and educational system and human infrastructure investment did not adequately prepare Mexico for this change in the world economy. Education and health indicators in Mexico did not improve over the first 14 years of NAFTA, affecting not only the quality of life of ordinary Mexicans but also Mexico's competitiveness in the global economy, in which relying on a low wage manufacturing strategy and close proximity to US markets and transportation systems are no longer sustainable strategies.

418. Although there continues to be disagreement about whether NAFTA caused some of the economic problems in North America, there is agreement that NAFTA has not resulted in reducing the economic disparities that exist between the US and

Canada on the one hand and Mexico on the other. The failure of NAFTA to substantially improve the lives of ordinary Mexicans and reduce immigration from Mexico to the US has led to calls even by the business community for social investment similar to investment by the EU in Spain and Portugal to improve the economic fortunes of Mexico and its citizens.

Chapter 7. The NAALC and International Labor Solidarity

§1. Cross-border Collaboration

419. Metaphorically, the NAALC can be seen creating a series of sliding platforms crossing the space of one, two or three countries where trade unionists and their allies can stand to defend workers' rights in the North American context. These platforms can cross borders in equal proportion, or be anchored mostly in one country. They rest first on the Agreement's unique, accessible cross-border complaint mechanism. Workers who suffer abuses, and their defenders, have to file a complaint with the government of *another* country, not the country where violations occurred. Under the agreement, 'any person' can file such complaints. There are no citizenship requirements or requirements that a complainant be an injured party or have a material stake in a case.

420. The result is that social actors that use the NAALC seek partners in the country or country where they intend to file complaints. Indeed, most of the more than twenty cases filed so far have involved transnational coalitions of unions and allied human rights and community groups who find in the Agreement's institutional mechanisms new opportunities to develop relationships and joint action.

421. Before the NAALC was created, cross-border trade union relationships mostly consisted of thin contacts at two levels. One was between high-level union leaders who attended conferences and conventions and agreed on resolutions of support without much follow-up. The other consisted of sporadic local union-to-local union contacts and occasional worker-to-worker delegations that usually were aimed at helping the poor Mexicans. These links paled in comparison with the business-to-business contacts delegations that occur every day in North American commerce.

422. The new NAALC platforms allow transnational social actors to demand investigations, public hearings and government consultations on workers' rights violations. Advocates now have the opportunity to strategize and plan together in a sustained fashion, gathering evidence for drafting a complaint, crafting its elements, setting priorities, defining demands, launching media campaigns, meeting with government officials to set the agenda for a hearing and to press them for thorough reviews and follow-up, preparing to testify in public hearings, engaging technical experts to buttress a case with scientific elements (a health and safety case, for example), influencing the composition of independent experts' panels and the terms of reference of their investigation, and other concrete tasks that go far beyond adopting resolutions or arranging serial worker-to-worker meetings.

423. As noted by the Mexican member of the independent review committee, even before NAFTA, the United Electrical Workers union (UE) and the Mexican *Frente Auténtico del Trabajo* (FAT) fashioned a 1992 strategic organizing alliance. Much like the FAT, the UE is a small, independent union outside the main national labor federation but with strong local unions in workplaces around the country and a national contract with General Electric. The UE is respected among American trade unionists for sticking to its founding principles. Top union officers' salaries match those of working members. Officers are elected for one-year terms in an annual convention. Rank and file democracy and mobilization are the UE's main strategies for organizing, bargaining, and political action, rather than reliance on professional organizers, lawyers and lobbyists. In December 2008 a UE affiliate in Chicago, Illinois gained nationwide attention when its members conducted a sit-in when their factory, Republic Windows and Doors, closed its doors with three days, notice because it could not obtain financing from Bank of America. Public pressure on Bank of America, which received US $15 billion in a government bank bail-out program in late 2008, resulted in a victory for the Republic Workers who received two months of severance pay and health care coverage they had been previously denied.

424. The Teamsters union also worked with the FAT without the formality of a written agreement. The two US unions helped FAT organizing attempts in *maquiladora* factories of General Electric and Honeywell. The assistance flows both ways, though. In 1995 FAT organizers helped the UE win an organizing victory at a large manufacturing plant in Milwaukee, Wisconsin with a high complement of immigrant Mexican workers.

§2. Inside an NAALC Case

425. An intimate look at just one case, the *Washington State Apple* complaint, demonstrates how the NAALC can nourish cross-border coalition-building among trade unions and allied organizations. The Washington state apple case is a rich example 'platform-building' by strategic use of the NAALC and how it can foster new ties of solidarity and sustained work among labor rights advocates in the United States and Mexico. More than 50,000 Mexican workers labor in the orchards and processing plants of the largest apple-growing region in the United States. Employers resisted their efforts throughout the 1990s to form trade unions, to bargain collectively, to have job health and safety protection, to end discrimination, and to make other workplace gains.

426. In 1997 the Teamsters union and the United Farm Workers agreed to develop a NAALC case on these issues. They reached out for support to Mexican unions, farmworker advocacy groups, and human rights organizations. A complaint was drafted, translated and redrafted to the satisfaction of the newly formed network. In May 1998 the question was then posed: who should sign the complaint, which would be filed with the Mexican labor department? Put another way, who would be publicly identified as the parties that triggered international scrutiny of labor abuses in Washington State that might result in sanctions against apple exports to Mexico? Mexico is the largest single export market for Washington apples, and since the complaint addressed health and safety violations among many others, it was susceptible to sanctions.

427. The two US unions were each trying to organize apple workers, one in the orchards and one in the processing plants. They wanted to avoid employers' countercharges that they were out to destroy apple workers' jobs. On the Mexican side, the independent union allies in the *Unión Nacional de Trabajadores* (UNT), the *Frente Auténtico del Trabajo* (FAT), the *Frente Democrático de Campesinos* (FDC) and other groups working with their US counterparts were sensitive to government and official union accusations that they were 'puppets' of protectionist US unions. At the same time, from an inside-Mexico competitive standpoint, they wanted to be seen as frontline defenders of migrant workers in the United States, ahead of the official unions and ahead of the PRI government.

428. After careful consultations through personal visits, telephone conference calls, e-mail exchanges and other communications among key leaders and staffers of all these organizations, the complaint was officially signed by just the Mexican organizations, not by any US groups. An American NGO, the International Labor Rights Fund, became the public face of a media campaign in the United States, issuing press releases and sending an investigator to the apple growing region to meet with workers about the cases and to interview potential witnesses for a hearing to be held in Mexico, with behind-the-scenes help from the unions. An experienced organizer from the FAT came to the apple regions of Washington to help the unions in their organizing efforts. The AFL–CIO's Solidarity Center pledged financial support to send Washington apple workers to Mexico for the hearings. Less than one month after the Washington State apple complaint was filed in Mexico, the CTM – the official, pro-government union federation in Mexico – filed its own first-ever NAALC complaint over treatment of migrant Mexican workers at an opposite corner of the United States, in the Easternmost state of Maine.

429. In December 1998 a hearing in the case was held in Mexico City. Advocates faced another strategic decision: should worker witnesses be Mexican migrants alone, which would obviate the need for translation and allow more workers to testify, or should non-Mexican, English-speaking workers also participate (many Anglo workers are employed in the processing plants, not in the orchards, which are entirely Mexican migrants) at the cost of a more complicated hearing process.

430. US advocates first suggested an all-Mexican, Spanish-only project. But Mexicans thought the effort would be strengthened by presenting united interests of both Mexican and American workers. Long-time Anglo workers joined the delegation and the unions provided interpretation for them during press conferences, during meetings with Mexican workers and trade unionists, and at the hearing at the Mexican labor department. Their shoulder-to-shoulder stance with Mexican coworkers lent a powerful image of solidarity to the public face of the campaign.

431. The hearing in Mexico City itself was a dramatic example of the reach of the NAALC 'platform' and the leaping of spatial, language and cultural boundaries in the North American context. Half a dozen officials from an agency of the Mexican government heard, in their own language, accounts of labor rights abuses by a delegation of Mexican workers employed in the United States thousands of miles to the North in an industry for which Mexico is a major consumer market. The hearing was prompted by a complaint initiated by US trade unionists in Washington State, Washington DC and California (site of the United Farm Workers union headquarters; the Teamsters union headquarters are in Washington, DC), then filed by allies in Mexican labor and human rights organizations in Mexico City after lengthy cross-border planning.

432. At the hearing, the Mexican workers were joined by Spanish-speaking US trade union representatives and human rights attorneys, by Mexican independent union and farmworker advocates, and by English-speaking co-workers who deliver their own duly interpreted testimony in English.

433. The Mexican labor department later issued a report demanding consultations between the labour secretaries of the two countries. They agreed on a program, due to be implemented in early 2001, of public outreach and public hearings chaired by US and Mexican officials from the two federal governments and from the state government. The forums would take place in the apple-growing region of Washington, where large numbers of workers are prepared to testify about conditions in both Spanish and English.

434. In succession, the NAALC provided concrete means of pressing the apple growing industry to improve conditions or risk losing the Mexican market, pressing the government of Mexico to conduct a thorough review of the complaint, hold public hearings for workers from the United States, and issue a strong report seeking ministerial consultations; pressing the *officialista* Mexican labour unions to take their own action on behalf of Mexican migrants in the United States by filing the NAALC complaint on Maine, pressing the US government to agree to public events in Washington State and to devote its own energies to seeking improved conditions, and pressing the state government to take steps in matters of state competence to improve conditions, especially with regard to safety and health. While cycling from national to transnational arenas, every step was accompanied by a media campaign that kept the dispute in the public eye and shaped a new, rights-based discourse linked to North American economic integration.

§3. Coalition Building

435. In similar fashion, the Communications Workers of America (CWA) has developed close ties with the *Sindicato de Telefonistas de la República Mexicana* (STRM), the national telephone workers union of Mexico. The two unions have held a series of joint educational seminars and coordinated strategy in dealing with moves by AT&T, Sprint and other US telecommunications companies into the Mexican market.

436. A broad coalition of metalworker unions joined the complaint in the *Echlin/ ITAPSA* case – auto workers, steel workers, machinists, electrical workers and others in all three countries. They generated extensive participation by union leaders and workers in public hearings in both the United States and Canada. A similar coalition of trade unions and NGOs has maintained international support for Han Young workers, including informational picketing of Hyundai auto sales locations in the United States and Canada to inform the public about the labor dispute and the NAALC case.

437. All these steps required careful coordination to shape common positions. As those involved got to know each other better, contacts proliferated. Trade unionists and union economists, lawyers and other staffers from the three NAALC countries now regularly send delegates to each others' conventions, conferences and other activities. They are trading bargaining information, translating papers and studies and finding new ways to link their movements.

438. The labor side agreement is not the only force driving these actions. But the NAALC creates a framework for concrete work – developing strategies, drafting submissions, planning testimony, writing press releases, setting up demonstrations, meeting with government officials, participating in the Agreement's cooperative activities program and events that flow from ministerial consultations. All the time, social actors are learning about each other's countries and labor movements.

439. In trinational meetings in Mexico in December 1998, in Washington in May 1999, and in Toronto in February 2001, union leaders and labor lawyers from the three NAFTA countries who have been involved in NAALC cases formulated and refined a common strategy for working together in new NAALC cases challenging the three governments to live up to the 11 labor principles they adopted.[6] Elements of their strategy include:

- more participation in NAALC cooperative activities;
- case selection that targets systematic problems, not just single-workplace incidents;
- more use of simultaneous complaint filings with two or three NAOs on the same topic;
- more consultation among advocates from all three countries prior to filing a complaint;
- demands on their governments to strengthen the NAALC through reforms that include:
  - eliminating the three-tier division of the 11 labor principles for purposes of ECE and arbitral panel treatment;
  - more budget and staffing for the Secretariat and the NAOs;
  - creation of a code of conduct that will obligate corporations, not just governments, under NAALC disciplines and with NAALC sanctions;

6. Results of this *Encuentro Trinacional* include creation of a website at www.unam.mx/iie/ cambios/ html.

– requirement for all corporations active in NAFTA commerce to file labor relations information with the Secretariat (location, number of workers, union status, copies of contracts, wages and benefits etc.) which shall make such information publicly available on the internet.

440. The scope of cross-border union activism on trade and labor rights should not be overstated. Among US unions it involves only the most internationally active unions, still a minority of the overall labor movement. In Mexico it involves mainly small, independent opposition labor groups. Cross-border activism does engage a greater proportion of Canadian unions, but their effect is limited by the combination of scant trade between Canada and Mexico alongside Canadian trade unionists' desire to remain a counterweight to the larger US labor movement in international labor affairs.

441. While international labor activity has progressed, it does not yet embody a broad movement of rank and file workers and allied citizens' movements. Activism is more in the nature of transnational networks of labor rights partisans. At this stage, still early in the process of labor movements' responses to globalization, international contacts, foreign language skills, legal expertise, capacity for strategic intervention, and other characteristics of labor internationalists drive cross-border labor work more than an aroused consciousness among masses of workers. But this type of specialized activism is a necessary precursor to broader workers' movements in international affairs, and one can see foretelling of wider activism in today's targeted actions.

§4. Cross-border Bargaining

442. The same caution should apply to discussions of cross-border collective bargaining in North America, and to prospects for convergence of labor law and labor relations systems. In the United States and Canada, genuine cross-border bargaining takes place only in professional sports. Major league baseball, basketball and hockey all include teams in both countries. Players' associations in each sport negotiate with team owners' groups for a single contract applicable in both countries.

443. When it was a single organization in the two countries, the United Auto Workers bargained with the 'Big Three' North American auto companies, General Motors, Ford and Chrysler, for workers in the United States and Canada. But this cross-border bargaining venture broke up in the 1980s with a bitter split in the UAW with the Canadian branch – now the Canadian Auto Workers (CAW) – accusing US union leaders of getting into bed with company bosses to force concessions and labor-management cooperation programs on UAW members. The breach has only recently begun to repair itself. Leaders of each union are invited to each other's conventions, and a renewed effort at coordination and strike support marked 1997 strikes in General Motors plants in the United States. However, any resumption of joint bargaining is still far in the future.

444. Some major unions are still true 'internationals' with American and Canadian members in the same organization, notably the Teamsters, the Steelworkers, the United Food and Commercial Workers (UFCW), the Service Employees International Union (SEIU), and several construction unions. But there is still no genuine cross-border bargaining by these unions with employers operating in both countries. What does take place are varying versions of cross-border information sharing along with organizing and strike support. These actions are not necessarily a result of NAFTA, but increased cross-border trade under NAFTA makes them more compelling. In 2005, the Teamsters, UFCW, SEIU and other major unions broke away from the AFL–CIO and established an alternative US trade union movement called *Change to Win*.

445. There was no cross-border bargaining involving US and Mexican unions until 2004 when the Farm Labor Organization Committee (FLOC) negotiated a collective bargaining agreement with the North Carolina-based Mount Olive Pickle Company that covers workers in both the US and Mexico. As part of its cross-border activities, the FLDC educated H-2A visa workers recruited in Mexico before they travel to North Carolina to work for Mount Olive. With this exception, however, there is a growing network of contacts and collaborative projects already described, but nothing has reached a stage of direct dealing across a bargaining table with multinational employers operating in the United States and Mexico. Mexican trade unionists have been present at some recent collective bargaining negotiations such as those between the United Electrical Workers and General Electric in 1997, but only with observer status, not for any bargaining purposes.

446. Incipient contacts that envision cross-border bargaining can be found in the railroad and construction sectors. In November 1997 rail union leaders from the United States and Mexico began coordinating efforts to confront rail transportation companies that move freight across the border. In particular, investment in newly privatized Mexican rail lines by US companies spurred this new union collaboration. The unions declared an intention to eventually confront railroad employers in a single bargaining setting.

447. The president of the Brotherhood of Locomotive Engineers stated that rail maintenance workers in Mexico earn $12 per day, while US workers make nearly $70,000 per year. He expressed concern that maintenance work would be shifted from the United States to Mexico unless Mexican wages are rapidly raised. In a break with most union leaders' position, however, he said he is not opposed to NAFTA because more trade means more freight traveling by rail, and ultimately more stable employment for railroad workers.

448. In November 1998 leaders of the US Laborers International Union of North America (LIUNA) and the Mexican Construction and Excavation Workers Union (SITRACE) signed an accord for cooperation in efforts to unionize Mexican construction workers who migrate to the United States for jobs. SITRACE agreed to provide its members with information and encouragement to join LIUNA when they go to the United States, and LIUNA agreed to step up efforts to protect migrant

Mexican workers in US work sites and to provide skills training for Mexican workers. The agreement went on to envision a new 'international union of workers of the Americas' to raise cooperation to a continental scale.

449. The AFL–CIO has created a Mexico committee composed of key affiliates like the autoworkers and garment workers to focus on NAFTA-related issues with a substantial budget for Mexico-related work. This committee is beginning with research into details of the operations of US-based multinational corporations in Mexico, and of those few Mexican companies (in the cement and food processing sectors, for example) that are expanding operations inside the United States.

450. In August 1998 the AFL–CIO placed a new representative in Mexico City to nurture relations with the Mexican labor movement. In November 1998 this effort bore fruit with the signing of a formal agreement between the AFL–CIO and the CTM, Mexico's main pro-government union federation. The two central bodies agreed to collaborate in opposing negative aspects of NAFTA and in rooting out 'contracts of protection.' This is a common feature of the Mexican labor scene where employers pre-arrange a contract with an individual or a paper organization trafficking in such contracts to 'protect' the employer from organization by a bona fide trade union.

451. Despite the intuitive appeal of cross-border bargaining, many obstacles impede its prospects in North America. Labor movements in Mexico and Canada are concerned about potential domination by US unions which would usually have the largest membership in a firm and thus be in a position to dictate bargaining strategy and settlement terms. Employers would have to accede to cross-border bargaining, and they have little incentive to do so. Governments would have to promote cross-border bargaining, and they show no interest in it.

§5. Prospects for Convergence

452. The labor relations systems of the three NAALC countries have not moved closer together if the measure of movement is specific, identifiable changes in laws amounting to harmonization. Their labor law and labor relations systems are deeply rooted in each country's history of social movements and political and legislative struggles. The NAALC is still new and not fully tested. Any systematic convergence is going to be a long and complicated process that allows for education, adjustment and acceptance as it unfolds.

453. Nonetheless, some movement toward the US system of market-oriented labor relations and collective bargaining can be discerned. A conservative government in Alberta, for example, has introduced legislation reflecting US labor law's 'right-to-work' feature prohibiting collective agreements that require dues payments from all represented workers. A conservative government in Ontario repealed the province's method of establishing a union's majority status by signing authorization cards, and moved instead to a US-style election process. Quebec has virtually eliminated its continental European model of extending terms and conditions of employment negotiated by peak bargainers from union federations and employer associations in certain sectors to all enterprises in the sector, whether or not they are unionized.

454. Mexico's similar *contrato-ley* system of extending contract terms to designated sectors has also been largely eclipsed. In Mexico, it is universally acknowledged by employers, unions, and analysts that enterprise-based collective bargaining is resulting in a new model where 'flexibilization' overrides the constraints of the Federal Labor Law (FLL). Flexibilization features that run counter to the FLL include changes in job descriptions and job classifications to combine and eliminate jobs, redefining and reducing rights to holidays, vacations, and sick leave, employing temporary and part-time workers, defining employees as 'confidential' to deprive them of collective bargaining rights, changing work schedules to avoid overtime payment, and so on. The labor law authorities accept such *de facto* deviation from the law so as not to jeopardize continued investment in Mexico.

455. Any convergence of labor law and labor standards in North America will involve a long, slow process. Mexico's substantially lower level of economic development, resulting in wages approximately one-tenth of US and Canadian levels, is an enormous obstacle from the start. But even leaving economic disparities aside, each country's labor law system is different. The jurisdictional powers of federal and state or provincial governments, the roles of administrative authorities and courts, the degree of tripartism, the extent of industry-wide bargaining versus enterprise-based bargaining – all these and many more features of labor law and practice in the three NAALC countries vary widely, and sometimes in full contradiction with one another.

456. Even those elements of each country's labor law system that arguably violate the principles and obligations of the NAALC are deeply rooted. In Mexico, discrimination against unions not part of the PRI power structure is still common. In the United States, the striker replacement doctrine and employers' continuing, apparently undeterred ability to campaign aggressively against workers' attempts to organize are still in effect. Canada has not relaxed its penchant to legislate an end to strikes or to strip categories of workers of the right to bargain collectively. Substantial change in these and other labor law practices are not on the horizon even with enhanced international scrutiny under the NAALC.

§6. Key Criticisms and Responses

457. The NAALC does not set common new standards to which countries must adjust their laws and regulations. Instead, it recognizes 'the right of each Party to establish its own domestic labor standards.' This lack of common standards the first main criticism leveled by NAALC opponents in the trade union and allied NGO community. They argue that leaving labor rights and labor standards at the national level rewards a party with lower standards and forecloses any 'upward harmonization' of labor standards.

458. The NAALC does not create a supranational labor board to take evidence and decide guilt or innocence in labor disputes or to order remedies against violators. This is left to domestic authorities. Nor does it create a supranational labor court to take appeals from decisions of national courts and overrule decisions that arguably fail to enforce the NAALC. Decisions by national judiciaries cannot be disturbed by the NAALC. These features, too, are a source of repeated criticism that the NAALC has 'no teeth' because it cannot get workers reinstated to their jobs or have unions registered or recognized when national authorities and courts fail to take such measures.

459. While correct in principle, these criticisms overlook the realities of a three party political negotiation where one country, the United States, dominates the economic relationship and the other two are jealous about guarding their sovereignty (as is the United States, for that matter). Even if levels of development were similar, it is unrealistic to expect a new labor rights-trade agreement to immediately create a supranational power that will take effective decisions out of the hands of domestic authorities. Labor law and practice in the United States, Canada and Mexico reflect complex differences, beginning with basic matters of labor law jurisdiction. US labor law is mostly a federal matter, with a limited role for the states. Mexican labor law is governed by a federal statute, but with enforcement powers largely shared by the states. In contrast, Canadian labor law is almost totally provincial, with a limited role for the federal government.

460. These differences did not happen casually. They result from national histories replete with regional conflicts, civil wars, economic depressions and class struggles. Three governments sitting down to negotiate the NAALC in 1993 were not going to undo these differences and defer to a new, untested supranational labor law authority.

461. Common standards and upward harmonization are laudable goals. Even an integrated labor law enforcement system for the NAALC's labor principles might emerge if North America moves toward a form of political union. But such developments can only result from a long evolutionary process. They cannot be imposed in a first-ever labor agreement linked to trade relations among vastly unequal trading partners.

462. Another target of NAALC critics is the procedural mechanism it creates. Procedures for arriving at a point of economic sanctions – the only discernible 'teeth' – are so long and complicated. They contain so many opportunities for settlement short of the application of sanctions that it is difficult for sanctions ever to be applied under the NAALC.

463. However, fashioning a labor rights-trade linkage agreement making sanctions a remote rather than an immediate prospect is really the only realistic means of reaching an agreement. No country will agree to make it easy to apply economic sanctions, regardless of levels of development. The fact that a sanctions provision is included at all in the NAALC is a signal achievement creating an important precedent for a social clause in international trade and investment regimes.

464. Critics say that the NAALC's cooperative activities program is just quasi-academic conferences, workshops, and seminars with no concrete effect. But this reproach fails to take into account the importance and the need, in an entirely new agreement and a novel working relationship among the governments, for an extended period of collaboration and learning about each other's complex labor law regimes. Labor ministry officials, legislators, trade unionists, employers, researchers, NGOs, journalists and other actors can all benefit from information and analysis obtained at the various cooperative activities under the NAALC. Over time, their increased knowledge of labor law matters from a North American perspective rather than a national perspective could bring progress toward improved labor standards and strengthened national enforcement systems. This could lay the ground for movement toward common, higher standards.

465. Cooperative activities are vital for the NAALC's success. If the agreement consisted solely of a complaint mechanism, or if social actors ignore cooperative activities and concentrate only on complaints, the agreement cannot be sustained, particularly where one party exercises 90 per cent of the economic weight in the trading relationship that gave rise to the NAALC. The important gain in the creation of the NAALC's complaint mechanism, where the three countries opened themselves up to critical reviews, evaluations, and dispute resolution, can only be preserved and advanced if the countries also have wide opportunity to work together cooperatively. An international agreement that only provides forums for accusations and criticisms cannot survive. Indeed, it could not have been born.

§7. Impact of the NAALC

466. As indicated above and summarized here, the overall impact of NAFTA's regional labor arrangements can be measured in the following areas:

(1) There has been a substantial increase in knowledge and understanding of each other's labor law systems among the three countries' trade union, management, government, academic, practitioner, journalist and NGO communities.
(2) There has been a substantial development, starting practically from zero, in cross-border engagement among these communities. Cross-border labor and NGO alliances are proliferating. The three governments' labor departments have undertaken an extensive cooperative activities program and several consultations in complaint matters. Academic centers have sponsored many trinational conferences. Labor law practitioners in all three countries have begun

developing and offering specialties representing unions and employers in proceedings under the NAALC. Journalists have taken a keen interest in all of these developments, so publicity about regional labor arrangements is multiplying.

(3) The NAALC complaint system has begun to have an impact both in specific cases and in a broader, 'climate-changing' way whose consequences are yet to be fully appreciated. For example, the pregnancy testing case has already led to a halt to this practice by some firms in the *maquiladoras*, and the just-launched education and outreach program agreed by the ministers may have further effects. Several independent unions in Mexico obtained registration in connection with NAALC submissions where they would otherwise have been frustrated.

467. Sometimes the NAALC has had an effect without a case being filed. In Canada, for example, the conservative provincial government of Alberta proposed a plan to privatize occupational safety and health enforcement in 1996. Labor advocates argued that the government was abdicating its enforcement of labor laws on workplace safety and health, and announced plans to file a NAALC complaint. The government dropped the proposal.

468. In a broader context, independent trade unions in Mexico credit the NAALC submission mechanism with giving them a political opening to engage the government and other labor forces in a new arena. This has been one factor among many contributing to a realignment of labor centrals in Mexico and a related movement away from the traditional corporatist system to a more open, transparent atmosphere in labor affairs there. As one Mexican analyst puts it,

> The NAALC has encouraged new experiences of transnational trade union cooperation ... to identify common interests even among divergent hopes to attract and retain employment ... There is no doubt that the combination of external pressures like those brought to bear through the NAALC – with all its limitations – with the emergence of internal forces posing alternatives to the traditional corporatism has proven sufficient to put an end to the status quo in this terrain and increase the opportunities for an autonomous and truly representative trade unionism.[7]

§8. Is the NAALC a 'Model'?

469. The NAALC contains many procedural and substantive flaws giving rise to valid criticisms. These include its lack of harmonized standards, the absence of concrete remedies for workers whose rights are violated, and the lesser treatment afforded fundamental rights of association – organizing, collective bargaining, and the right to strike. However, even justifiable criticism should be measured not against a theoretically ideal but practically unattainable agreement linking trade and

7. See Graciela Bensusán, *Integración regional y cambio institucional: la reforma laboral en el norte del continente*, in *Estándares laborales despues del TLC* (FLACSO-Fundación Friedrich Ebert 1998).

labor rights. Criticism must take into account the reality of international relations and trade and labor controversies in the global economy today.

470. That reality begins with a strong concern for sovereignty that is generally shared by all countries, rich and poor. Sovereignty is an especially sensitive matter among NAALC partners, given the relative weight of the United States in continental affairs, on one hand, and the 'American exceptionalism' attitude prevalent in the United States that subordinates international treaties and other obligations to US national interests. The sovereignty issue is joined by a fear on the part of developing countries that a labor rights-trade linkage will be used for protectionist purposes by larger, richer countries to deprive them of a comparative advantage in lower labor costs.

471. These are not just concerns of government officials. They are deeply held in all sectors of society, including trade unions and NGOs. Many Mexican and Canadian labor policy analysts look at the state of US labor law and the low level of unionization in the United States, and shudder at the prospect of harmonized labor laws. They are not about to give up laws created by their own legislators and administered, however imperfectly, by agencies accountable to their own executive branch and reviewed by their own courts, to an untested supranational agency that might be dominated by the economic interests of the United States. Nor are American workers, let alone employers or members of Congress, disposed to hand over basic labor lawmaking and adjudication to supranational authorities.

472. The approach developed in the NAALC, emphasizing cooperation and effective enforcement of domestic labor law, is a more practical and attainable starting point for an accord linking labor rights and trade. Any system of law is only as good as its enforcement system. US experience with a resurgent 'sweatshop' industry in major American cities should give pause to demands that developing countries 'raise' their standards to the levels of industrialized countries before labor law enforcement is strengthened in every country.

473. While preserving sovereignty, the NAALC countries opened themselves up to international scrutiny of their labor law enforcement regimes, first through reviews by another country's NAO, then by independent evaluation or dispute resolution bodies made up of independent, non-governmental experts from all three countries. This represents an extraordinary degree of candor in international relations that should not be scorned because it falls short of an ideal agreement.

474. The NAALC's broad subject matter is another positive feature. The labor principles include 'core' standards, but they go farther to embrace other matters vitally important to workers – safety and health, minimum wages, hours of work, compensation for workplace injuries and illnesses, migrant worker protection.

475. The NAALC is 'user-friendly,' with both cooperative activities and complaint mechanisms open to participation and invocation not only by unions and employers, but also by NGOs and concerned citizens. None of these need to have a material interest in a matter, and they can approach any of the three NAOs for attention to the issues they want to raise. The curious, even counterintuitive NAALC mechanism requiring complaints about events in one country to be submitted to authorities in another country drives a process of communication and collaboration across national borders by trade unions, NGOs and other social actors.

476. The NAALC is not a 'model' in the sense that its institutional arrangements should be replicated in other international settings. More direct incorporation of ILO standards and expertise is vital for sustained labor rights advocacy, and the NAALC will have to move in this direction. Negotiators for a social dimension in the Free Trade Agreement of the Americas (FTAA) will have to take into account important features of Mercosur's labor arrangements. Indeed, Mexico, Canada, or the United States might have new ideas for the FTAA based on the NAALC experience. But the NAALC's spirit of respect for sovereignty alongside openness to international scrutiny and mutual accountability, the reach of its labor principles beyond a 'core' formulation, its openness to civil society involvement, and its encouragement of international labor solidarity and collaboration provide important lessons for governments and social actors grappling with the challenge of linking trade and international labor rights in the 21st century.

477. While it might be argued that the NAALC closed its twentieth-year anniversary on a low note institutionally, after 20 years the controversial NAFTA labor side agreement's positive impact on the incorporation of labor in trade agreements cannot be denied. Each of the three NAFTA partners continued to negotiate bilateral and multilateral free trade agreements. By the end of 2013, Mexico had implemented 12 trade agreements with 44 nations, the US had implemented 13 agreements with 19 nations and Canada had implemented 9 agreements with 13 nations. After 1994, almost no trade agreement negotiated by the US or Canada was without a labor provision. In the United States, at least one complaint filed under the labor chapter of an FTA (the Dominican Republic-Central American Free Trade Agreement - or CAFTA-DR) almost reached the arbitration stage, and a number of other petitions resulted in promising reports and follow-up actions that greatly expanded on and improved the area of FTA labor jurisprudence initiated by NAALC reports in the 1990s and 2000s. Since the reports issued in response to complaints filed under post-NAALC labor provisions of US and Canadian FTAs form part of the jurisprudence and practice that may be considered and applied in subsequent NAALC reports, the 2014 update to this monograph introduces a new chapter discussing these labor provisions, complaints and reports.

478. In addition to the incorporation of labor provisions in Canadian and US FTAs, the NAALC ushered in an era in which the idea that labor must be included as an integral component in international trade and financial policy discussions is no longer contested many international policy and legal circles. The world of international trade and labor policy has been almost completely transformed in the 20 years since the NAALC went into effect. While the World Trade Organization (WTO) for the most part did not incorporate labor standards into its legal framework, relations between the ILO and Bretton Woods Institutions such as the World

Bank, International Monetary Fund (IMF) and International Financial Corporation (IFC) thawed somewhat. Since 2008, G20 Labor Ministers have been meeting with G20 Finance Ministers together and separately to tackle employment and financial issues in the wake of the 2008 Financial Crash and subsequent Global Financial Crisis. The ILO has been a prominent presence in these meetings. Since 2009, the IFC and the ILO have partnered on an international program called Better Work with the aim of improving labor compliance and competitiveness in global supply chains. Better Work operates in Cambodia, Haiti, Indonesia, Jordan, Lesotho, Nicaragua and Vietnam. In early 2014, Better Work was on the cusp of becoming operational in Bangladesh, after a series of horrific factory disasters in that country in 2012 and 2013. The issue of youth unemployment, which was recognized as a major international crisis after the 2008 economic crash and subsequent Arab Spring, became a factor in deepening the relationship between the ILO and other international organizations as the international community strives to create jobs for unemployed youth the world over. In June 2012, the ILO, OECD, IMF and the World Bank issued a joint report entitled Boosting jobs and living standards in G20 countries, demonstrating just how different global financial policy making is in 2014 as compared to the pre-NAALC era.

Chapter 8. The OECD Guidelines: An Alternative to NAALC and the Labor Provisions of Free Trade Agreements

§1. Background on the OECD Guidelines

479. Canada, Mexico and the United States are all members of the Organization for Economic Cooperation and Development (OECD) and adherents to the OECD Guidelines for Multi-National Enterprises (OECD Guidelines). Canada and the US were members when the OECD came into existence in 1962 and Mexico became a member in 1994, the same year NAFTA went into effect.

480. The OECD is an economic organization that replaced the Organization for European Economic Cooperation (OEEC), an inter-governmental organization established in 1948 to administer the US Marshall Plan to redevelop Europe after the devastation of World War II. Its original membership included most European nations as well as Turkey, the United Kingdom, Canada and the United States. Over the years membership expanded to include countries with developed economies like Australia, New Zealand and Japan as well as aspiring developing economies like Mexico, South Korea and the Czech Republic. As of the end of 2007 there were 30 country members of the OECD.

481. Although the OECD's primary function is economic and it is described as a 'Rich Man's Club' because of the high number of developed countries in its ranks that are the base for operations for most of the world's multi-national enterprises, the OECD has played a longstanding role in labor and other affairs and provides an interesting contrast to the NAFTA.

482. The OECD's founding treaty promotes policies designed to achieve the 'highest sustainable growth and employment and a rising standard of living in Member countries,' and to contribute to sound economic expansion in Member as well as non-Member countries in economic development. Structurally, the OECD conducts regular consultations with two standing non-governmental committees, the Trade Union Advisory Committee (TUAC) and the Business and Industry Advisory Committee (BIAC). The OECD's 1850-person Secretariat, based in Paris, conducts research and publishes reports on a number of subjects key to inter-country trade including labor, environment, corruption, corporate governance and education. In 1996, the OECD published a path breaking report *Trade, Employment and Labour Standards: A Study of Core Worker's Rights and Labour Standards* that found that the economic impact of implementing core labor standards is minimal. This report resulted from a joint project between the OECD Secretariat's Employment, Labour and Social Affairs (ELSA) Directorate, its Trade Directorate and its Directorate for Financial and Fiscal Affairs (DAFFE).

483. The OECD Guidelines for Multi-National Enterprises (OECD Guidelines) are a set of voluntary principles for multi-national enterprises (MNEs) that were first implemented in 1976 as a result of world shock at instances of unethical corporate behavior such as the involvement of the US corporation ITT in the violent overthrow of the democratically-elected President of Chile Salvador Allende in 1973. The Guidelines include a procedure by which complaints can be made to member countries about the behavior of MNEs. During the 1980s, trade unions filed a number of complaints under this procedure about MNE activities in contravention of the Guidelines but stopped filing complaints in the 1990s when they found that neither governments nor corporations appeared to take heed of OECD pronouncements regarding the complaints.

484. The OECD Guidelines require MNEs to uphold certain ethical norms of behavior in the areas of corporate governance and transparency, avoidance of corruption, promotion of socially and environmentally friendly development, protection of the environment and respect for certain agreed-upon labor norms, especially freedom of association and right to collective bargaining, prohibition of child and forced labor and freedom from discrimination. Between 1998 and 2000, the OECD conducted a review of the Guidelines, revamping them in a process that involved OECD country members as well as representatives from the labor, business and NGO communities. There were two key changes to the newly revamped Guidelines published in 2000: the addition of human rights obligations and the extension of the Guidelines' scope beyond the territory of OECD member countries. These two changes brought about a resurgence of the use of the Guidelines, especially by non-governmental organizations in the human rights arena.

§2. Complaint Procedure under the OECD Guidelines

485. Like the NAALC, the OECD Guidelines establish a mechanism for addressing complaints about labor rights violations. Superficially, the two mechanisms are remarkably similar. Just as the NAALC requires each member state to establish a National Administrative Office (NAO) in its labor ministry, the OECD Guidelines require each member state to establish a National Contact Point (NCP). The NCP can either be a single designated office or individual in a particular government ministry or a committee of individuals from various governmental ministries. NCPs are similar to NAOs in that both serve as contact points for the public to file complaints/public communications about violations of the commitments in their respective agreements. The scope of the NCP's jurisdiction is broader than that of the NAO's, however, because NCPs may accept communications about any of the subjects in the OECD Guidelines, including labor rights, human rights, environmental issues and corporate governance. NAOs and NCPs are similar in that both are required to publicize their mandate and respective constitutive agreements and to serve as contact points for the exchange of information between member states.

486. The NAALC and the OECD Guidelines differ, however, in their basic underlying theory and focus, the level of transparency in their complaint mechanisms and in the manner in which they handle complaints/public communications. While the NAALC requires an analysis that focuses on member state action or inaction in effectively enforcing labor and employment laws, the OECD Guidelines require an analysis that focuses on the behavior of the corporation itself and whether the corporation is complying with the norms of ethnical behavior set forth in the Guidelines. The corporation-focused framework of the OECD Guidelines affects the scope of jurisdiction of NCPs, providing more options for unions, nongovernmental organizations and other members of the public to file complaints/ public communications.

487. A member state's NCP may have jurisdiction over a complaint/public communication if the subject corporation or its parent is located, headquartered or seeks financing in the member state's territory. For example, in 2002 the International Textile, Garment and Leather Workers' Federation (ITGLWF) filed an OECD Guidelines complaint about labor rights abuses at two Guatemalan factories ChoiShin and Cimatextiles with the Korean NCP (where the factories' parent corporation is headquartered) and the US NCP (where the global brand clothing retailer that sourced from the factories, Liz Claiborne, is headquartered), as well as the Dutch NCP, since Dutch/Netherlands government funds were used for a Central America *Maquila* program that included workers from the two subject Guatemalan factories. While the NAALC requires that complaint/public communication be filed with the NAO(s) of a member state(s) other than the one where the labor rights violation took place, the OECD Guidelines are less clear on this subject and it is possible that a complaint/public communication will be addressed by the NCP of the country where the violation took place. Thus, if a case similar to the ChoiShin/ Cimatextiles (Guatemala) case described above occurred in Mexico, it could be filed with NCPs in Mexico, Korea, the United States and in any OECD member state where the corporation or its parent is headquartered or obtains financing.

488. NAOs and NCPs are similar in that neither the NAALC nor the OECD Guidelines set forth a purely adjudicative dispute resolution process for handling communications and complaints from the public. NAOs engage in two different aspects of administrative problem-solving, however. Over the years, the NAO process has proved itself to be more of an investigatory process in which the NAO gathers information from a variety of sources to compile a public report of its findings. The NCP process is more of a mediation or conciliatory process in which the NCP attempts to resolve the issue between the complainant and the subject corporation(s), only making the process and facts public if the various parties are unable to come to a resolution of the dispute. If the NCP (or NCPs if the complaint was filed with more than one NCP) is unable to broker a resolution, the complaint is transmitted to the OECD Investment Committee (formerly the Committee on Multinational Enterprises – CIME) which may issue a written interpretation of the application of the OECD Guidelines to the facts in the complaint. The interpretation is not considered to be a formal decision in the case as understood in the adjudicatory context. In the 1980s there were over 20 such interpretations issued by the OECD Investment Committee's predecessor, the CIME, in the context of international labor issues.

489. The two approaches in the initial phase of the NAO and NCP process have an effect on the level of transparency of the complaint/communication process under the NAALC and the OECD Guidelines. The transparency of the NAO investigatory process is a function of the bureaucratic culture of the government and the labor ministry of each NAALC member state. Thus it is possible to find copies of NAALC public reports of review of complaints as well as Ministerial Agreements purportedly resolving those complaints on the US and Canadian NAO websites – and in many cases, even a copy of the NAALC complaint itself – though not always on the Mexican NAO website. It is also possible for members of the public to visit the information office of the US NAO to view and obtain copies of documents in the public file for NAALC complaints. Traditionally, the US NAO has conducted public hearings regarding NAALC complaints, though in recent years the investigatory process became less transparent than in the past. The transparency of the NAO investigatory process is a function not only of the bureaucratic culture of the federal labor ministry but of the particular administration in power at the time a complaint is filed and investigated. The NAO process does not suffer a complete transparency deficit until the point when one member state requests ministerial consultations from another member state after a public report of review has been issued. At that point, it is virtually impossible for members of the public to learn what is going on in the ministerial consultation phase of the NAALC process, which has no time limit and may last for years.

490. The NCP process is a less transparent process from the moment a complaint is filed, reflecting in part the more closed bureaucratic culture of the OECD and in part the confidential nature of mediation and conciliatory dispute resolution processes. Thus it is difficult for members of the public to obtain copies of complaints filed under the OECD Guidelines. Unless a complaint proceeds to the OECD Investment Committee, there may be no official public pronouncement or publication of information about complaints filed under the OECD Guidelines. The OECD Trade Union Advisory Committee (TUAC) publishes periodic reports about the progress and outcomes of labor complaints filed under the OECD Guidelines (though not the complaints themselves). In the human rights arena, a non-governmental organization OECD Watch has addressed the transparency deficit in the OECD Guidelines process by compiling a complete database of the human rights complaints filed under the OECD Guidelines since 2000. Members of OECD Watch have access to this database via the internet.

§3. Recent North American Complaints Filed under the OECD Guidelines

491. In addition to the *Markey Tex/Coco Tex* complaint that was dual filed under the NAALC and OECD Guidelines in 2004, there have been at least nine other complaints filed under the OECD Guidelines regarding labor abuses in Mexico since the resurgence of use of the OECD Guidelines beginning in 2000. There have also been at least one complaint filed regarding labor abuses in Canada and one filed regarding labor abuses in the United States. While both the US and Mexican NCPs have been criticized by human rights, labor and CSR advocates for their lack of responsiveness and low level of activity in response to complaints filed under the OECD

Guidelines, Canadian and Mexican trade unions have utilized the OECD Guidelines as part of a strategy to address a host of complex situations involving mining operations owned by Canadian and other international companies in Mexico - in particular, the Excellon and PKC Group cases filed in 2012. The Excellon case demonstrates that complex situations involving international investment and operations implicate not only labor issues, but land use, environmental, community development and securities reporting matters. Mexican trade unions and the International Campaign against Employer Protection Contracts started utilizing the OECD Guidelines to file complaints with the Mexican NCP about violations of trade union laws by Mexico-based corporations in cases like the 2008 Grupo Modelo case and the 2011 América Móvil case.

I. Mexico: the *Continental (Euzkadi)* case (2002–2005)

492. In May 2002, two German NGOs filed a complaint with the German NCP about the closure of a Continental (Euzkadi) plant in Mexico that was executed without previously informing the workers. The German NCP met with a trade union in Mexico but then transferred the case to the Mexican NCP since the incident occurred in Mexico. The issue was resolved in January 2005 (32 months later), when an agreement was reached under which the plant was reopened as a cooperative in a joint venture between the Mexican union and Llanti Systems, a Mexican investor group. This outcome contrasts with the outcomes of almost every single NAALC complaint filed about labor abuses in Mexico since 2000, where the factory in question shut down and did not reopen. On the other hand, in its report of the Continental (Euzkadi) Mexico case, the TUAC noted that the Mexican NCP was criticized for not playing a constructive role in the case. This experience is echoed by the US NAO's complaints that the Mexican NAO did not facilitate its investigation of NAALC complaints in Mexico.

II. Mexico: the *Michelin/Uniroyal* case (2004–?)

493. In February 2004 a group of Mexican workers filed a complaint with the Mexican NCP about the closure of two Michelin plants which was executed without prior notification or compensation to the workers in 2000. There was an agreement made between Mexican union SNTU and the company providing compensation to the workers, but some workers criticized this agreement because it did not provide the amount of compensation set forth in the collective bargaining agreement. In 2002, one of the plants reopened and the workers applied for reinstatement but were rejected. French unions filed a complaint with the French NCP regarding the case. As of the end of 2013, the matter was considered to be suspended.

III. Mexico: the *Grupo Modelo* case (2008–2010)

494. In June 2008, the *Frente Autentico de Trabajo* (FAT) and other Mexican trade unions filed a complaint with the Mexican NCP arguing that the beer producer Grupo Modelo had failed to comply with the OECD Guidelines by denying trade union representation to employees at a bottling plant in the Mexican state of San Luis Potosí. The complaint was supported by the International Campaign Against Protection Contracts. In January 2008, the bottling plant fired over 800 workers including the FAT union leadership, then entered into a protection contract with a different union. The Mexican NCP initiated consultations with relevant federal and state government officials to assess the case but according to the Trade Union Advisory Committee (TUAC) to the OECD, did not make efforts to mediate the case. In January 2010, the Mexican NCP rejected the case due to lack of evidence.

IV. Mexico: the *América Móvil* case (2011–2012)

495. In September 2011, the Unión Nacional de Trabajadores (UNT) with the global trade union federation UNI Global and unions in Guatemala, El Salvador and Guatemala filed a complaint with the Mexican NCP arguing that the Mexico-based telecommunications company América Móvil had violated the OECD Guidelines by unfairly dismissing trade union leaders and members in its operations in Guatemala, El Salvador and Nicaragua. The case was rejected by the Mexican NCP in June 2012. There was no public Final Report, although according to the TUAC, the petitioners have a copy of the report issued by the Mexican NCP in support of its decision to reject the case.

V. Mexico: the *Excellon La Platosa* mine case (2012–2013)

496. In May 2012, the *Sindicato Nacional de Trabajadores Mineros, Metalúrgicos, Siderúrgicos y Similares de la República Mexicana* (National Union of Mining, Metallurgical, Iron and Steel Workers of the Mexican Republic – SNTMMSRM) and the *Proyecto de Derechos Económicos Sociales y Culturales* (Economic, Social and Cultural Rights Project – ProDESC) and their Canadian allies the Canadian Labour Congress, United Steelworkers and MiningWatch Canada filed a complaint under the OECD Guidelines with the Canadian and Mexican NCPs alleging not only that Excellon was not complying with its labor and employment obligations under the Guidelines but that the British Columbia-based company had failed to comply with international obligations related human rights, land and natural resources rights, corporate accountability and disclosure and protection of the environment in the operation of the La Platosa mine in the State of Durango, Mexico.

497. The La Platosa Mine case underlines how complex the impacts of foreign investment and operation of an international company can be – and how those impacts implicate a number of overlapping areas of international obligation. In May

2004, Excellon's Mexican subsidiary entered into a land rental agreement with the La Sierrita ejido in the State of Durango, Mexico in order to operate the La Platosa silver mine in exchange for 300,000 Mexican pesos per year for a term of 30 years. An ejido is a traditional communally owned piece of land. During 2007 and 2008, the parties entered into intense negotiations to improve the terms of the land rental agreement for the ejido community. Under the new agreement signed in 2008, Excellon agreed to pay 5.5 million Mexican pesos a year to rent 1,100 hectares of communal land for its mining operations. Excellon also obligated itself to initiate a Social Development Fund with 3 million Mexican pesos and contribute another 500,000 pesos a year to the fund throughout the term of the lease. Other clauses obligated the company to grant concessions to the ejido to transport minerals from the mine to the smelter and personnel to the mine and to provide food services in the mine's cafeteria. Excellon was also to provide scholarships for students living in the ejido, extend first hiring preferences to qualified members of the ejido community and provide training to allow them to advance in the company. In the environmental protection arena, Excellon was to construct a water treatment plant that would treat water from the mine so it was suitable for agricultural use by La Sierrita. Finally, the 2008 agreement required Excellon to seek prior consent before expanding its mining activities on communal lands.

498. The complaint filed by trade unions and NGOs under the OECD Guidelines contains two core allegations. The first allegation is that Excellon failed to comply with a number of provisions of the 2008 contract, including those requiring the company to provide a food services concession to the ejido, construct a water treatment plant, provide scholarships for students and implement hiring preferences for community members. Critically, the company engaged in unauthorized exploration on ejido lands. The untreated water emanating from the mining operation contained excessive amounts of arsenic and saline so that it was undrinkable and damaged agricultural lands of not only the *ejido* but neighboring private property and surrounding areas.

499. The second allegation is that Excellon failed to comply with its labor and employment obligations under the OECD Guidelines. As has been discussed in numerous NAALC complaints and reports, Excellon entered into a protection contract with an 'official' trade union to provide representation to its workers at La Platosa mine, thereby preventing its workers from exercising their fundamental rights to freedom of association and collective bargaining. The petitioners point out that that the practice of entering into protection contracts in Mexico has been criticized by the United Nations High Commission for Human Rights and the Special Rapporteur on the Independence of Judges and Lawyers, since Mexican labor boards lack impartiality and autonomy as a result of the participation of 'official' unions on Mexican labor boards. As a result of this lack of impartiality and autonomy, unionization votes tend to be marked by fraud and intimidation of workers who seek to exercise their freedom of association.

500. In 2010, workers at La Platosa mine began to organize an independent union under the auspices of the SNTMMSRM, establishing SNTMMSRM Section 309.

In response to this organizing campaign, Excellon signed a second protection contract with a union called the 'Presidente Adolfo López Mateos' union. Leaders of Section 309 were intimidated and assigned to menial work to keep them separated from the rest of the workers. As the result of complaints filed with the Durango state labor board, the state of Durango recognized that Excellon's subsidiary was allowed under the law to end its two existing protection contracts and collectively bargain with SNTMMSRM Section 309. Despite this, Excellon never met with Section 309 and never entered into collective bargaining with the union. Moreover, the company continued to support the unions with which it entered into protection contracts in 2011 and 2012.

501. As a result of Excellon's ongoing disputes with La Sierrita ejido and its workers, the ejido conducted a blockade of the company. Markedly, the petitioners point out that the blockade is having a negative effect on Excellon's earnings, which in turn has a negative effect on its shareholder price and the earnings of investors. Thus, the complaint is designed not only to pressure Canadian and Mexican government officials to exercise leverage over Excellon, but to leverage company investors to pressure the company to comply with international and Mexican labor laws and to comply with the provisions in the company's contract with La Sierrita ejido.

502. Petitioners asked that the NCPs conduct an investigation into Excellon's activities around La Platosa mine, utilize their 'good offices' to help the parties resolve the issues, consult with the parties and with one another, and make recommendations to Excellon to ensure respect of human rights in La Sierrita *ejido* and SNTMMSRM. As is often the practice under the OECD Guidelines, the complaint devolved to the NCP of the country where the facts occurred – in this case, the Mexican NCP. On 28 November 2012, the Mexican NCP rejected the SNTMMSRM's complaint.

503. Unlike the NAALC and other US and Canadian FTA labor chapters, the OECD Guidelines do not require NCPs to issue reports discussing the facts raised in complaints, making it difficult to ascertain whether or not 'good offices' were utilized by Mexican and Canadian officials to resolve the disputes discussed in the Excellon La Platosa complaint. Nevertheless, it appears as though the complaint and related campaigns in Canada and Mexico have had an impact. For example, in June 2012, then CEO of Excellon Jeremy Wyeth resigned in the wake of the complaint and protests made by ejido community members at a Board meeting. In particular, company shareholders were troubled by a mismatch between Excellon's public statements about events in the state of Durango and the facts raised by ejido community members and their allies - a mismatch implicating disclosure requirements under Canadian securities laws. Within Mexico, the ejido filed a complaint with the National Agrarian Commission to have its contract with Excellon rescinded. Other complaints were filed by the ejido and neighboring property owners for environmental degradation and other damage to their property caused by Excellon's mining operation. Litigation was ongoing in 2013 and 2014. In 2013, a delegation of Canadian trade union members and NGO representatives conducted a review of on-the-ground situations at the La Platosa mine in La Sierrita and at other mines operated by Canadian companies in Mexico as part of an overall campaign to improve the corporate accountability of Canadian mining activities in Mexico.

VI. Mexico: the *PKC Group* case (2012–2013)

504. In August 2012, the Mexican trade union SNTMMSRM and the international trade union federation IndustrialALL filed a complaint with the Mexican and Finnish NCPs arguing that the Finnish auto parts company PKC Group had failed to comply with labor and employment obligations under the OECD Guidelines with respect to its auto parts manufacturing plants in Ciudad Acuña near the US-Mexico border. The petitioners asked that the Mexican and Finish NCPs conduct a thorough assessment of the facts, consult with PKC Group and SNTMMSRM and facilitate dialogue between the parties to find a solution to the dispute.

505. PKC Group had entered into a protection contract with the CTM without notice to or involvement of its workers. In 2011, the factory workers formed Section 307 of the SNTMMSRM and applied to the local labor board to have the union recognized so it could enter into collective bargaining on their behalf. In January 2012, PKC Group managers informed the workers that they were represented by the CTM and that PKC Group was paying their union dues on their behalf. As is frequently the case in Mexico, the organizers of SNTMMSRM Section 307 were fired for their union related activities, and were still struggling for reinstatement in 2013.

506. The Mexican NCP rejected the PKC Group complaint on 17 May 2013. As with the Excellon La Platosa Mine case, it is unclear whether any steps were taken to attempt to resolve the dispute using alternative dispute resolution or other means.

507. The OECD complaint in the PKC Group had a particular wrinkle which may provide another option for combating the protection contract system in Mexico. In addition to setting forth guidelines for responsible corporate behavior in the areas of labor and employment relations, human rights, environmental and other areas of corporate accountability, the OECD Guidelines call on multi-national enterprises to engage in good financial corporate governance and to avoid bribery. As members of the OECD, both Finland and Mexico are signatories to the 1999 OECD Convention on Combating Bribery of Foreign Public Officials. In their complaint, IndustriALL and SNTMMSRM outline a number of statements made by PKC Group's CEO on Finnish television about PKC Group's participation in the protection contract system in Mexico. They also point out that the leader of the CTM in the State of Coahuila is both President of the state labor commission and a member of the federal chamber of deputies. Thus, payments to the CTM and its officers by PKC Group might be considered to be prohibited bribes to a government official for the corrupt purpose of hindering freedom of association among PKC Group's employees. Such payments would present a significant corporate compliance issue subject to anti-bribery prosecution. For example, if PKC Group were a US company or had its stock on a US stock exchange, it might be subject to prosecution or civil legal action under the US Foreign Corrupt Practices Act (FCPA).

VII. Canada: the *UPM Kymmene* case (2004–2005)

508. In November 2004, the Communications, Energy and Paperworkers' Union of Canada filed a complaint with the Canadian NCP complaining that the Finnish company UPM Kymmene violated its obligations under the OECD Guidelines when it closed a pulp mill in Canada because it did not share required information with the union about the closure or negotiate with the union and work with the government to mitigate the effects of the closure. The company also suspended the union president and vice president. The Canadian NCP decided it would be inappropriate to get involved because the case was being addressed by provincial labor authorities.

VIII. Canada: the *Accor* case (2010–2012)

509. In November 2010, the International Union of Food Workers (IUF) filed a complaint with the French and Canadian NCPs arguing that the French hotel corporation Accor had violated the OECD Guidelines by actively opposing the recognition of trade unions at three Accor-owned Novotel hotels in Canada and failing to recognize or engage in collective bargaining with the independent trade union organized by workers at an Accor-owned hotel in the African nation of Benin. The IUF asked that the NCPs engage with Accor to make the hotel chain recognize duly organized trade unions at the Canadian hotels and enter into negotiations to conclude a collective bargaining agreement with the trade union at its hotel in Benin. The French NCP accepted the complaint and found that Accor had not complied with its labor-related obligations under the OECD Guidelines. The case was closed in December 2012. Resulting outcomes were mixed. A collective bargaining agreement was concluded with the hotel in Benin, but anti-union campaigns continued at the Canadian-based Novotel hotels.

IX. United States: the *Trico Marine Services* case (2001–2002)

510. In February 2001, the International Transport Workers' Federation (ITF) and five US unions filed a complaint with the US NCP about an anti-union campaign of Norway-based Trico. Although the complaint was not filed with the Norwegian NCP, the Norwegian oil and petrochemical workers' union NOPEF started a boycott of Trico and persuaded the oil company Norsk Hydro to halt negotiations with Trico on the chartering of vessels. In November 2002 NOPEF and Trico signed a consent decree allowing Trico's US workers to unionize. The TUAC noted that the US NCP did not take an active role in the case. The US NCP concluded its involvement was not warranted because of ongoing National Labor Relations Board (NLRB) proceedings.

511. In addition to OECD Guidelines complaints filed about labor abuses in North American territories, both the Canadian and US NCPs have received complaints about labor abuses in other countries. In 2001 and 2005, the Canadian NCP received complaints about the failure of Canadian-based corporation Bata to conform to OECD Guidelines in France (2001) and Sri Lanka (2005). In 2002, the Canadian NCP received a complaint from the Canadian Labour Congress (CLC) about participation of Canadian-based Ivanhoe Mines in forced labor and environmental degradation in Burma. The Canadian NAO closed the case in 2006 without convincing Ivanhoe Mines to engage in dialogue, achieving a resolution or issuing recommendations on the situation as required by the Guidelines. The TUAC found that the Canadian NCP did not contribute to the resolution of these cases.

512. In 2001, the AFL–CIO filed a complained with the US NCP about US companies trading with the Government of Burma but did not receive a response from the US NCP. In November 2001, the International Transport Workers' Federation (ITF) filed a complaint with the US NCP about the failure of US-registered Liberian International Ship and Corporate Registry (LISCR) to comply with the OECD Guidelines by helping the Liberian government purchase and transport arms in violation of a UN arms embargo. The US NCP conducted discussions with LISCR but despite the existence of the UN arms embargo and the existence of verifiable reports, the US NCP closed the case in 2002. As with the Canadian NCP, the TUAC noted that the US NCP did not contribute to resolution of these and other complaints brought under the OECD Guidelines.

Chapter 9. Labor Provisions of Post-NAFTA Free Trade Agreements in North America

§1. Background on Post-NAALC Labor Provisions in North American FTAs

I. Canadian Labor Cooperation Agreements

513. Six of the eight post-NAFTA free trade agreements currently in force between Canada and eleven trading partners have separate Labor and Environmental Cooperation Agreements. These six trading partners are Chile (1997), Costa Rica (2002), Peru (2009), Colombia (2011), Jordan (2012) and Panama (2013). On 5 November 2013, Canada signed an FTA with Honduras. This FTA also has separate Labor and Environmental Agreements and has been submitted to the Canadian Parliament for ratification. Although the Canada-Honduras FTA is not yet in effect, its Labor Cooperation Agreement will be discussed with Canada's other LCAs for comparative purposes. Canada also has an FTA with Israel (1997) which does not mention labor matters, and an FTA with the European Free Trade Association (Iceland, Liechtenstein, Norway and Switzerland) which went into force in 2009. The Canada-EFTA FTA does not have Labor or Environmental Cooperation Agreements, but the FTA contains a clause in which the parties affirm their 'commitment to economic and social development and the respect for the fundamental rights of workers and the principles set out in the International Labour Organization's Declaration on Fundamental Principles and Rights at Work' and 'the need for mutually supportive trade and environmental policies in order to achieve the objective of sustainable development.'

514. All seven of the Labor Cooperation Agreements (LCAs) negotiated by Canada (including the as-yet-not-in-force Canada-Honduras LCA) contain the same set of core obligations present in the NAALC. Under Canada's LCAs, signatories obligate themselves to promote compliance with and effectively enforce their labor laws through appropriate government action; ensure that persons have appropriate access to administrative, quasi-judicial, and judicial tribunals to enforce their rights under labor law; ensure that labor proceedings are fair, equitable and transparent and that labor tribunals are independent and impartial; ensure that all labor-related laws and regulations are published; and make information about labor laws and enforcement measures public. Canadian LCAs with five post-NAFTA trading partners – Peru, Colombia, Jordan, Panama and Honduras – have non-derogation clauses prohibiting signatories from lowering labor standards to increase trade. The earliest two post-NAFTA LCAs between Canada and trading partners (Chile and Costa Rica) do not have non-derogation clauses.

II. US Free Trade Agreement Labor Chapters

515. All of the twelve post-NAFTA free trade agreements currently in force between the US and 17 trading partners have labor chapters in the text of the FTA.

These FTAs include bilateral trade agreements with Jordan (2000), Chile (2004), Singapore (2004), Australia (2005), Morocco (2006), Bahrain (2006), Oman (2009), Peru (2009), Panama (2011), Colombia (2012) and South Korea (2012). The US is also a member of the multilateral Dominican Republic-Central American Free Trade Agreement (CAFTA-DR) with El Salvador (2006), Guatemala (2006), Honduras (2006), Nicaragua (2006), the Dominican Republic (2007) and Costa Rica (2009). In addition, the US has a pre-NAFTA FTA with Israel (1985) which does not have a labor chapter. All post-NAFTA US FTAs also have environmental chapters within the text of the FTA.

516. As with the Canadian Labor Cooperation Agreements (LCAs), the labor chapters of all of the post-NAFTA US FTAs maintain a set of core obligations related to the effective enforcement and application of labor laws, maintenance of procedural guarantees in and access to administrative and judicial labor tribunals and public awareness of laws and complaint mechanisms. While all post-NAFTA US FTA labor chapters have some form of non-derogation clause, these clauses can be divided into three groups. Under the US-Jordan FTA labor chapter (the first US FTA negotiated after the NAFTA), the signatories recognize that it is "inappropriate to encourage trade by relaxing domestic labor laws," so they commit to "strive to ensure" that they do not waive or otherwise derogate from existing laws to encourage trade. The non-derogation language in the second group of FTA labor chapters (including Chile, Singapore, Australia, Morocco, Bahrain, Oman, Peru and CAFTA-DR) is equally contingent and non-binding, as the signatories agree to "strive to ensure" to not waive or derogate from labor standards to encourage trade or investment. Rather than referring to existing laws setting national labor standards, in this set of FTA labor chapters the non-derogation clauses refer to "internationally recognized labor rights." This set of labor chapters also expands possible conditions under which derogation might be considered from encouragement of trade to encouragement of trade, establishment, acquisition, expansion, or retention of an investment in the territory of a signatory member state. Non-derogation language in the third set of FTA labor chapters (Panama, Colombia and South Korea) is expressed as an obligation. Rather than committing to "strive to ensure" non-derogation in these FTA labor chapters, the signatories agree that neither party "shall waive or otherwise derogate from, or offer to waive or otherwise derogate from" statutes or regulations implementing the fundamental labor rights discussed in the labor chapter in a manner affecting trade or investment between the signatories."

III. Mexican Free Trade Agreements

517. Mexico has 12 FTAs with 44 nations, including Costa Rica (1995), Nicaragua (1998), Chile (1999), the European Union (2000), Israel (2000), 'The Northern Triangle' (Guatemala, El Salvador and Honduras – 2000), the European Free Trade Association (2001), Uruguay (2004), Japan (2004), Colombia (2011) and Peru (2011). None of Mexico's non-NAFTA FTAs contains labor provisions similar to those in US and Canadian FTAs. The Japan-Mexico FTA contains provisions for temporary entry of business persons, but specifically excludes provisions that would afford citizens of signatory states access to their respective labor markets.

§2. ILO Standards and Labor Provisions in Post-NAALC North American FTAs

518. While the core treaty obligations in post-NAALC FTA labor provisions related to enforcement and application of labor law, due process in labor adjudication proceedings and publicly available information differ little from those in the NAALC, the definition of "labor law" within the labor provisions has changed. Since the negotiation of the 2000 US-Jordan FTA, the definition of labor law has changed from existing labor laws to international labor standards. In all US FTAs since then, the scope of international labor standards has been defined by the 1998 ILO Declaration on Fundamental Principles and Rights at Work and its Follow-Up. These core labor standards are defined as freedom of association, the effective recognition of the right to collective bargaining, the elimination of all forms of compulsory labor, the prohibition of child labor and the elimination of employment discrimination. Signatories commit themselves to adopt and maintain statutes, regulations and practices implementing these core labor standards. Definitional clauses in US FTA labor chapters supplement the definition of internationally recognized labor rights to include acceptable conditions of work with respect to minimum wages, hours of work and occupational safety and health. In most post-NAFTA US FTAs, signatory states obligate themselves to 'reaffirm their obligations as members of the ILO.'

519. Since the 2000 US-Jordan FTA, the three-tiered hierarchy of labor rights set forth in the NAALC (with collective labor obligations subject to the lowest level of dispute resolution) has been abandoned. The scope and number of areas of labor law covered by post-NAALC US FTAs has shrunk since the NAALC, as areas of labor law such as compensation for work-related injuries and diseases and protection of migrant workers are no longer covered by post-NAALC labor chapters in US FTAs. Moreover, all US FTAs that entered into force after the US–Jordan FTA limited the definition of US labor law to laws emitted by the federal government or the US Congress. The US–Jordan FTA is silent on this issue. As seen in NAALC jurisprudence, a high number of petitions filed with NAALC partners about inadequate labor law enforcement in the United States have a state (defined here as sub-federal) law element, including the 1998 *Washington Apple* and *DeCoster Egg Packing* cases involving the states of Washington and Maine. Other NAALC complaints about inadequate labor law enforcement in the US focus entirely on state law action, such as the 2001 *New York Workers' Compensation* case, the 2005 *North Carolina Public Workers* case and, more recently the 2012 complaint about anti-immigrant law passed in Alabama in 2011. Thus, the NAALC is the only labor chapter of a US FTA which enables the public to file a petition with a US trading partner about inadequate enforcement of labor law at the state/sub-federal level. Since some labor laws – such as those governing compensation for work-related injuries and diseases, time and manner of payment of wages and associational and collective bargaining for state government employees – are solely a matter of sub-federal jurisdiction in the US, the public would have no mechanism to petition a US trading partner to address effective enforcement at the state level if the NAALC were to be superseded, for example, by the labor chapter of the Trans-Pacific Partnership if that labor chapter adopts the same definition of US labor law as other post-NAFTA US FTAs.

520. Canada also changed the definition of 'labor law' in its post-2000 FTAs. The 1997 Canada–Chile Labor Cooperation Agreement (labor side agreement to the Canada–Chile FTA) is structured exactly the same as the NAALC, including the three-tiered approach to dispute resolution under the petition process set forth in the NAALC and the inclusion of the term 'technical labor standards' excluding collective labor rights from the term. The parity between the Canada–Chile FTA and the NAALC may be due to the fact that in the late 1990s, entry of Chile into the NAFTA was a definite possibility.

521. Beginning with the 2001 Canada–Costa Rica FTA and LCA, however, Canadian LCAs incorporated the 1998 ILO Declaration on Fundamental Principles and Rights at Work into its definition of 'labor law' in its FTAs. Unlike the US, however, Canada did not abandon the labor principles that are present in the NAALC but not in post-NAALC US FTAs. For example, the Canada–Costa Rica LCA has two annexes outlining labor principles to be upheld by the signatories. Annex 1 covers the labor principles outlined in the 1998 ILO Declaration (right of association, right to collective bargaining, elimination of forced and child labor and elimination of workplace discrimination). Annex 2 covers minimum employment standards, prevention of occupational injuries and illnesses and compensation in cases of occupational injuries or illnesses. The Canada-Costa Rica LCA does not include a specific provision protecting the labor rights of migrant workers. The 2009 LCAs between Canada and Peru and Colombia define 'labor law' as including rights outlined in the 1998 ILO Declaration as well as minimum conditions of work, occupational safety and health and protection of migrant workers. The 2009 Canada–Peru and Canada–Colombia LCAs do not specifically include compensation for workplaces injuries and diseases as a labor principle. The 2009 Canada-Jordan LCA definition of labor law includes both the 1998 ILO Declaration and all four labor principles originally included in the NAALC, including minimum employment conditions, occupational safety and health, compensation for workplace injuries and diseases and protection of migrant workers. The 2013 as-yet-not-ratified Canada–Honduras LCA includes the same labor principles as the Canada–Jordan FTA.

§3. Cooperation and Aid under Labor Provisions of Post-NAALC North American FTAs

522. As in the NAALC, all post-NAFTA labor chapters and LCAs in US and Canadian free trade agreements establish labor cooperation mechanisms including Ministerial and department-level exchanges. Such cooperative activities can include seminars, training sessions, working groups, conferences, joint research projects (including sector studies) and technical assistance.

§4. Complaint Procedures under the Labor Provisions of Post-NAALC North American FTAs

523. Except for the labor chapter in the US-Jordan FTA, which is subject to the same enforcement mechanism as other chapters in the FTA, all US and Canadian post-NAALC labor chapters and LCAs establish complaint procedures which are very similar to those of the NAALC at the preliminary stages. Thus, signatory states are to establish a National Contact Point (NCP, terminology adopted from the OECD MNE Guidelines complaint process) in their respective labor ministries to accept complaints filed by members of public alleging that another trading partner has violated its obligations under the FTA labor chapter or LCA. In the cases of Canada and the US, the offices that served as NAOs under the NAALC now serve as the NCPs under the post-NAALC FTAs. As with the NAALC, once the NAO/NCP accepts the complaint for review and issues its report, the Minister of Labor can request Ministerial Consultations as a way to resolve matters raised in the complaint.

524. With regard to complaints filed under US FTA labor chapters, if the Minister of Labor of the signatory state that issued the report finds that the trading partner about which the complaint has been made has not done enough to resolve matters raised in the complaint, it can refer the matter to the US Trade Representative (USTR) to issue a Request for Arbitration. If the Arbitration Panel determines that the signatory has failed to meet its commitments under the FTA labor chapter, trade sanctions may ensue.

525. Under Canadian LCAs, if the parties are unable to resolve matters raised in complaints by means of ministerial consultations, one party may request the establishment of a Review Panel consisting of three panelists who are independent recognized experts in labor law willing to subject themselves to a Code of Conduct without affiliation with any of the parties involved in the review process. The Review Panel can issue an Initial Report subject to comment by the respective parties, then a Final Report, which shall be available to the public. If the Panel determines in its final report that a signatory has engaged in a persistent pattern of failure to effectively enforce its labor laws, that party is required to make its best effort to follow the recommendations in the Final Report. On the second anniversary of the Final Report, the signatory that requested the Review Panel may request that the Review Panel be reconvened. If the recommendations have not been adopted and it appears as though the persistent failure has continued, reasonable an appropriate measures can be taken. These reasonable and appropriate measures do not include fines or trade sanctions.

§5. Complaints Filed under Post-NAALC North American FTA Labor Provisions

526. Since 2008, five complaints have been filed under post-NAALC US FTA labor chapters. These include complaints filed under the US-Peru FTA, the US-Bahrain FTA and three complaints filed under the CAFTA-DR related to Guatemala, Honduras and the Dominican Republic. The US OTLA has issued four reports in response to these complaints. Only the report on the CAFTA-DR complaint related to Honduras remained pending at the end of April 2014. No complaints have been filed alleging that the US has violated the labor provisions of non-NAALC FTAs. Nor have any complaints been filed under Canadian LCAs regarding labor violations by Canada or its trading partners.

I. CAFTA-DR: Guatemala (US OTLA 2008–01)

527. The first complaint filed under a non-NAFTA labor chapter was the Guatemala complaint filed under the CAFTA-DR in April 2008 by the AFL-CIO and several Guatemalan trade unions. The complaint actually consisted of five complaints as it outlines failure by the Government of Guatemala to effectively enforce labor laws in 5 trade-related sectors of the Guatemalan economy. Allegations in the complaint relate to systemic labor law violations in the port, banana production, fruit and vegetable processing, garment manufacturing and public sectors. Examples of specific violations and failure of the Government of Guatemala to effectively enforce its labor laws included failure to protect trade unionists from violence and threats of violence; not bringing the killers of trade unionists to justice, not compelling garment manufacturers to pay over $1 million in unpaid social security contributions; not enforcing court edicts ordering reinstatement for unlawfully terminated workers; failing to compel employers to bargain in good faith with trade unions; allowing companies that violate employment and customs laws to reincorporate under new names and continue operating without legal consequences; and failing to dispatch labor inspectors or challenge employers that refuse entry to labor inspectors.

528. The OTLA accepted the Guatemala CAFTA-DR petition in June 2008 and issued its report in December 2008. Based on its investigation, which included interviews of workers, trade unions, employers and government officials as well as analysis of documentary evidence, the OTLA confirmed the bulk of the complainants' allegations about Guatemala's failure to effectively enforce its labor laws, and found there to be a number of systemic flaws in Guatemala's labor rights enforcement regime - including breakdowns in communications between judicial and administrative authorities regarding enforcement of court orders in labor cases.

529. Despite its findings of serious, systemic failures by the government of Guatemala to effectively enforce its labor laws, initially the OTLA did not call for ministerial consultations between the US and Guatemalan governments. Since the government of Guatemala cooperated with the OTLA's investigation of the

CAFTA-DR complaint, the OTLA allowed the Government of Guatemala an opportunity to address failings in its labor law enforcement regime. In June 2010, the OTLA requested ministerial consultations when it appeared that insignificant progress had been made. These consultations occurred in September and December 2010. As progress was still elusive in early 2011, the USDOL called for a meeting of the labor and economic ministers of the CAFTA-DR member states in June 2011. Dissatisfied that this meeting did not have the desired effect on improvement of Guatemala's labor enforcement regime, in August 2011 the US Trade Representative (USTR) made the historic call for the first arbitral panel to address a member state's failure to comply with its obligations under the labor chapter of a free trade agreement. In April 2013, the USTR and US DOL settled the dispute with the Government of Guatemala before the arbitral panel set to work. Per the settlement agreement between the two nations, the Government of Guatemala agreed to a comprehensive labor enforcement plan in which it committed to strengthen its labor ministry by sanctioning employers and ordering remediation for labor law violations; provide additional resources for labor inspections and ensure labor inspector access to worksites; ensure payment to workers in the event of factory closures; adopt mechanisms to improve enforcement of court orders; and ensure that export companies comply with labor laws. Of particular interest is the commitment of the government of Guatemala to revoke tax benefits of export companies that fail to comply with labor and employment laws.

530. Although workers continue to struggle for recognition of their labor rights in Guatemala, the legal significance of the 2008 Guatemala CAFTA-DR complaint cannot be ignored. Not only was the 2008 Guatemala complaint the first to be filed under the CAFTA-DR, it was the first to reach the arbitral stage of the dispute resolution mechanism set forth under the labor chapter of a multilateral FTA. The 2008 Guatemala CAFTA-DR complaint and its resolution are also significant because of a number of subtle changes in the way in which the OTLA and other US government authorities - especially the USTR - respond to complaints about violations of obligations under a FTA labor chapter. In particular, the OTLA's report acknowledged that labor law enforcement does not involve only labor authorities, but can also involve trade and commercial authorities - for example, involving trade and commercial authorities in enforcement of labor laws by denying export licenses to companies that do not follow labor laws.

II. Peru: the *SINAUT* case (US OTLA 2010–2013)

531. In December 2010, the Peruvian National Union of Tax Administration Workers (SINAUT) filed a complaint with the US OTLA alleging that the Peruvian Tax and Customs Administration (SUNAT) failed to recognize SINAUT's right to collectively bargain on both economic and non-economic issues. The US OTLA accepted the complaint for review in July 2011 and issued its report in August 2012.

532. In its report, the US OTLA confirmed the trade union's allegations that the Peruvian tax and customs authority would not comply with the trade union's requests under the law for arbitration when the two parties were unable to finalize the terms of a collective bargaining agreement. The OTLA found Peruvian law on the subject of whether arbitration in such a case was mandatory or voluntary to be ambiguous. In September 2011, this ambiguity was resolved by the Government of Peru through a series of executive decrees that clarify that arbitration per the request of a party in such a case is mandatory under Peruvian law. The OTLA noted that this series of decrees established a more robust mechanism for application of trade union and collective bargaining laws in Peru's public sector. As a result of these legal changes and cooperation by Peruvian authorities in the OTLA's review and investigation of the complaint, the OTLA declined to request ministerial consultations and the matter was closed.

533. The 2010 Peru *SINAUT* complaint is legally significant because the US OTLA accepted the complaint and issued a report discussing the fundamental rights to freedom of association and collective bargaining in a case involving a public employer without a connection to international trade and private commerce - although it could be argued that the fact that the union employees involved administer customs laws might provide an international trade and commerce nexus. Employer groups criticized the US OTLA's decision to accept the complaint under these circumstances. Nevertheless, the case establishes that labor enforcement mechanisms under US FTAs can be utilized to improve labor rights in both the public and private sectors, regardless of an international trade nexus.

III. Bahrain: the *Pearl Roundabout* case (US OTLA 2011–01)

534. The 2011 Pearl Roundabout complaint filed under the US–Bahrain FTA is the first labor complaint filed under a US FTA that does not involve a Latin American trading partner. It is also the first labor complaint filed under one of the four FTAs the US has with Arab nations, and the only FTA labor chapter complaint related to worker rights violations in the wake of the Arab Spring. The complaint was filed by the AFL-CIO with the US OTLA in April 2011 and accepted in June 2011. The OTLA issued its report in December 2012 and requested ministerial consultations with the Government of Bahrain in March 2013.

535. In the wake of the military crackdown against protestors in the Pearl Roundabout in the capitol of Bahrain in February and March 2011, over 2,400 employees of public, private and parastatal entities and universities were suspended from work and/or terminated for having participated in demonstrations and strikes (in some cases, even when they had not participated in demonstrates and strikes) - or in the case of public health sector workers, providing medical care to protestors. Both the General Federation of Bahraini Trade Unions (GFBTU) and the Bahraini Teachers' Society (BTS) had called for general strikes in support of the demonstrators and to protest the military crackdowns. Trade union leaders in particular were targeted for termination, and the President of the BTS was sentenced to 10 years of prison.

536. The complaint alleged that the Government of Bahrain had failed to comply both with its FTA labor obligations regarding organizing and collective bargaining rights and with its obligation to prohibit workplace discrimination. The OTLA noted that almost all of the workers terminated and suspended in the wake of the Pearl Roundabout demonstrations were Shi'a, not Sunni. Bahrain has signed ILO Convention 111 but does not have a law prohibiting workplace discrimination. In its report, the OTLA confirmed the allegations made by complainants through interviews and review of documentary evidence.

537. The 2011 Pearl Roundabout complaint is significant not only because of its geographic scope, but because the manner in which the complaint was handled by the US OTLA broke significantly from past practice. As a result of negotiations by the OTLA and other international actors (such as the ILO) with the government of Bahrain, many of the workers who lost their jobs in the wake of the *Pearl Roundabout* protests – though in many cases not in the same or equal position and many workers still have negative marks on their employment records. Prior to the 2013 report in the 2011 *Pearl Roundabout* complaint, the policy and legal stance of the OTLA had been that labor chapters of FTAs were not designed to "get workers' jobs back." The Pearl Roundabout case shows that even if getting workers their jobs back is not a primary goal of complaint review under an FTA labor chapter, it can be a secondary or tertiary goal that is attained through negotiation and application of diplomatic pressure during the review, reporting and ministerial consultation processes. The Pearl Roundabout case also demonstrates that review of a case under an FTA labor chapter by the US OTLA can be conducted in partnership with other international authorities examining matters raised by the same set of facts raised in complaints to various international fora. The actual means by which workers were rehired in this case was through ILO-sponsored tripartite dialogue between the GFBTU, the Bahrain Chamber of Commerce and Bahraini government authorities. While it might be argued that facilitation of tripartite dialogue leading to the rehiring of affected workers may have worked in the 2011 Pearl Roundabout case because the employers involved were public sector workers, the example set in this case can equally be applied in cases involving the private sector utilizing similar means of diplomatic pressure and negotiation.

IV. CAFTA-DR: Dominican Republic – the *Haitian Sugarcane Workers* case (US OTLA 2011–03)

538. In December 2011, Father Christopher Hartley, a Catholic missionary serving the community of Haitian migrant workers in the Dominican Republic, filed a complaint with the US OTLA charging the Dominican Republic with failing to effectively enforce labor and employment laws with respect to Haitian migrant workers in the Sugarcane industry, especially with regard to international employment standards governing forced and child labor. Except for the 2005 Rubie's complaint which resulted in ambivalent findings regarding child labor allegations and the 1998 Florida Tomato Exchange child labor complaint which was declined due to lack of specific allegations, the 2011 Haitian Sugarcane Workers case is the first filed under the labor chapter of an FTA focusing extensively on child and forced labor. The US OTLA accepted the complaint in February 2012 and issued its report in September 2013.

539. The complaint in the Haitian Sugarcane Workers case differs from most of those filed under the NAALC, CAFTA-DR and other US FTAs in that rather than being a lengthy detailed brief outlining labor law violations and government labor law enforcement failings, the complaint is sparsely pleaded and refers to a number of existing international and US DOL and State Department reports discussing child labor and worker abuses in the sugarcane sector in the Dominican Republic. The complaint specifically requested that workers be protected from government and employer retaliation as a result of participation in the CAFTA-DR complaint. It is estimated that about 40,000 Haitians work in the Dominican Sugarcane industry. The majority of these workers are undocumented. The essence of the complaint is that Haitian migrant workers in the Dominican Sugar Industry are paid so poorly, work so hard and are so isolated and indebted to their employers and company stores that they are, in essence, subject to forced labor. Moreover, entire families including men, women and children must work in order to eke out minimal survival. The OTLA's acceptance of this complaint and the manner in which it conducted its review represent a departure from past practice, where a significant burden has been placed on complainants to allege labor law violations and tie them to government actions and inactions. This departure from past practice is important, because it is a signal that complainants lacking in funding and resources to prepare an extensive brief may still have the opportunity to have their complaints reviewed.

540. In its report, the OTLA outlined the methodological and procedural shortcomings of the Dominican labor inspection process on sugarcane plantations. Of particular concern was the fact that while the workers spoke Haitian Creole, the Dominican labor department did not employ inspectors with the ability to speak Haitian Creole or utilize interpreters. Other shortcomings in the process included conducting worker interviews in the presence of employer representatives and not discussing topics related to trade union rights and collective bargaining. In addition to noting inadequate wage and overtime compensation, the OTLA found that employers failed to keep adequate wage and hour records due to a piece- or weight-based system and that weights for sugarcane cut tended to be inaccurately recorded. It was also unclear whether documented and undocumented Haitian workers on Dominican sugarcane plantations were eligible for social security under the Dominican social security system, although social security taxes were deducted from sugarcane workers' wages.

541. The US OTLA report in the 2011 Haitian Sugarcane Workers case sets a standard for what constitutes forced labor, something which was not done in response to forced labor claims in NAALC complaints. Some of the indicators of forced labor in the Dominican Sugarcane industry include: deceptive hiring practices, extremely low wages, forced overtime, being required to purchase staples at inflated prices from company stores, being threatened with deportation, loss of housing and employment for meeting with co-workers or refusing to work illegal overtime. The OTLA noted in its report that at least two workers were terminated as a result of speaking with the OTLA delegation. According to the report, these workers were rehired as a result of OTLA intervention – another break in the OTLA's prior practice and policy that workers cannot regain jobs as the result of a complaint filed under the labor chapter of an FTA. The OTLA report confirmed reports by numerous witnesses of children as young as 12 working in sugarcane cutting, planting and other tasks and noted that many Haitian children born in the Dominican Republic lack any type of documentation or birth certificate from either Haiti or the Dominican Republic – making it difficult for employers and government authorities to enforce child labor protections.

542. Rather than request ministerial consultations with the Dominican Republic regarding the complaint, the OTLA made a number of recommendations for improvement of labor law enforcement in the sugarcane industry and established a timeline for progress in adoption of these recommendations by the Government of the Dominican Republic. These recommendations included conducting workplace outreach and inspections in Haitian Creole, training inspectors to identify forced and child labor and other workplace violations, formally and publicly committing to maintaining the confidentiality of workers who complain about labor law violations and strengthening enforcement of existing Dominican laws addressing forced and child labor. The OTLA planned to assess progress in March 2014 and September 2014 (six months and a year after its report). Presumably, the OTLA will request ministerial consultations if sufficient progress and improvement have not been achieved by September 2014.

543. In addition to methodological and legal precedents established in the OTLA's review and report on the 2011 Haitian Sugarcane Worker case, the case is important because it involved extensive cooperation between the OTLA and the Child Labor division of the US DOL. The OTLA relied heavily on the expertise and existing child labor reporting of the Child Labor Division and the OTLA and the Child Labor Division developed a special $10 million program to address child labor problems in the Dominican Sugarcane Industry relating directly to the allegations in the complaint and the findings in the report. Such close cooperation between these two US DOL departments and the resulting tailor-made child labor assistance program augur well for future utilization of FTA labor chapters to address child labor among US trading partners.

V. CAFTA-DR: Honduras (US OTLA 2012–01)

544. In March 2012, the AFL-CIO and over a dozen Honduran trade unions and the Honduran Women's Rights Center (*Centro de Derechos de Mujeres* – CDM) filed a complaint with the US OTLA arguing that the Government of Honduras had failed to comport to its obligations under the CAFTA-DR labor chapter. Like the 2008 Guatemala CAFTA-DR petition, the 2012 Honduras CAFTA-DR petition contains an extensive catalog of workplace violations and failures by the Government of Honduras to effectively enforce labor laws in at least four sectors of the Honduran economy, including in the garment and auto parts manufacturing industries, agriculture, port operations and the public sector. Much of the failure to effectively enforce labor laws discussed in the complaint occurred in the wake of the 2009 military coup in Honduras and the inauguration of President Porfirio Lobo, who took office in January 2010. No fewer than 11 murders of trade unionists took place in Honduras between 2009 and the 2012 filing of the CAFTA-DR complaint. In addition to arguing that the Government of Honduras failed to effectively enforce existing labor laws, the complainants argued that the Government of Honduras violated its CAFTA-DR labor chapter violations by amending its labor laws to reduce adherence to internationally recognized labor rights.

545. Many of the allegations in the complaint relate to attempts by workers to organize trade unions in garment and auto parts manufacturing plants. Complainants assert that the Government of Honduras failed on more than one occasion to grant official recognition to newly organized trade unions, failed to sanction employers for establishing company unions and firing trade union organizers and in at least one case facilitated the official registration of a management-dominated worker organization. Other failures involved inadequate workplace inspections, whereby the Government of Honduras did not utilize all of the power available to it to facilitate the entry of labor inspectors when employers refused to allow inspectors to enter their premises.

546. In particular, the complaint makes the unique argument that Honduran Labor Law violates the CAFTA-DR obligation to protect employees from workplace discrimination, as it sets a minimum wage for the garment sector which is significantly below that in other sectors, essentially systematizing gender discrimination through national wage law and policy. The complaint cites a 2009 CDM report outlining various forms of systemic workplace discrimination against women which has been inadequately addressed by Honduran labor law and administrative and judicial enforcement measures, including verbal and physical abuse against working women on the job, denial of meal and restroom breaks, sexual assault, sexual harassment, pre-hire pregnancy tests of female job applicants and dismissal of pregnant women.

547. The OTLA accepted the petition for review in May 2012. In November 2012, the OTLA granted itself an extension of the time allowed to issue a report in response to the complaint. Like the 2008 Guatemala complaint filed under the CAFTA-DR, the 2012 Honduras CAFTA-DR complaint is designed to trigger the establishment of an arbitral panel.

Selected Publications

Adams, Roy & Singh, Parbudyal. 1997. 'Early Experiences with NAFTA's Labour Side Accord.' *Comparative Labour Law Journal*, 18:161.

AFL-CIO. 2014. NAFTA at 20. Washington, DC.

Alexander, Robin. 1998. 'Experience and Reflection on the Use of the NAALC' (in *Memorias: Encuentro Trinacional de Laboralistas Democraticos* D.F.: Universidad Nacional Autonoma de Mexico).

Bazar, Jason S. 1995. 'Is the North American Agreement on Labor Cooperation Working for Workers' Rights?' *California Western International Law Journal*, 25:425.

Befort, Stephen F. and Virginia E. Cornett. 1996. 'Beyond the Rhetoric of the NAFTA Treaty Debate: A Comparative Analysis of Labor and Employment Law in Mexico and the United States.'*Comparative Labor Law Journal*, 17:269.

Bierman, Leonard and Rafael Gely. 1995. 'The North American Agreement on Labor Cooperation: A New Frontier in North American Labor Relations.' *Connecticut Journal of International Law*, 10:533.

Blackett, Adelle. 1999. 'Whither Social Clause? Human Rights, Trade Theory and Treaty Interpretation.' *Columbia Human Rights Law Review*, 31:1.

Bremer, Laurie J. 1999. 'Pregnancy Discrimination in Mexico's Maquiladora System: Mexico's Violation of its Obligations under NAFTA and the NAALC.' *NAFTA: Law and Business Review of the Americas*, 5:567.

Brooks, Tequila J. 2010. Four Key Trade Union Movements in Puebla, Mexico 2001-2008: A Comparative Analysis of the Efficacy of Non-Governmental and Inter-Governmental Complaint Mechanisms in Addressing Worker Rights Issues in Mexico's Garment Manufacturing Industry. SSRN http://ssrn.com/abstract=1652930.

—— 2005. 'Cross-Border Workers' Compensation and Social Security Policy in North America: An Analysis of the NAFTA Trucking Dispute through the eyes of a Workers' Compensation Practitioner,' International Association of Industrial Accident Boards Journal, pp. 121-147.

—— 2005. 'An Introduction to Mexican Workers' Compensation Laws for the U.S. Workers' Compensation Practitioner,' The Workers' Compensation Compendium 2005-06 (John F. Burton, Jr. et al., Eds.), Volume I, Workers' Disability Income Systems, Inc., Princeton, New Jersey, pp. 415-422 (reprinted from IAIABC Journal Fall 2003).

Carr, Barry. 1996. 'Crossing Borders: Labor Internationalism in the Era of NAFTA' (in Gerardo Otero, ed., *Neo-liberalism Revisited*), Westview Press.

Cohn, Marjorie. 2012. 'Racial Profiling Legalized in Arizona.' Columbia Journal of Race and Law, 1:2, pp. 168-186.

Selected Publications

Compa, Lance. 2014. 'From Chile to Vietnam: International Labour Law and Workers' Rights in International Trade,' Chapter in Critical Legal Perspectives on Global Governance: Liber Amicorum David M. Trubek, Gráinne de Búrca, Claire Kilpatrick and Joanne Scott, eds. Hart Publishing.

—— 2002. 'A Glass Half Full: The NAFTA Labor Agreement and Cross-Border Labor Action'

in George J. Andreopoulos, ed., Concepts and Strategies in International Human Rights. Peter Lance Publishing.

—— 2001. 'NAFTA's Labor Side Agreement and International Labor Solidarity'

in Peter Waterman & Jane Wills, eds., Place, Space and the New Labour Internationalisms. Blackwell Publishers.

—— 2000. 'Works in Progress: Constructing a Social Dimension of Trade in the Americas' (in The Social Dimension of Economic Integration, US Department of Labor, Bureau of International Labor Affairs).

—— 1999. '*El ACLAN: un recuento de tres años.*' (in Graciela Bensusán, ed., Estándares laborales despues del TLCAN Mexico City, Ebert/FLACSO).

—— 1999. 'NAFTA's Labour Side Agreement Five Years On: Progress and Prospects for the NAALC' *Canadian Labour & Employment Law Journal*, 7:1.

—— 1999. 'International Labor Rights and NAFTA's Labor Side Agreement.' XXX *LASA Forum* No. 2 (Latin American Studies Association).

—— 1998. 'The Multilateral Agreement on Investment and International Labor Rights: A Failed Connection' *Cornell Journal of International Law*, 31:683.

—— 1998. '*Comercio de América del Norte: Dimensión Social o Decepción Social?*' (in Maria Silvia Portello de Castro & Achim Wachendorfer, eds., *Sindicalismo y globalización: la dolorosa inserción en un mundo incierto*, Caracas, Venezuela, Editorial Nueva Sociedad).

—— 1998. '*Perspective américaine sur l'Alena et le mouvement syndical*' (in Rodrigue Blouin & Anthony Giles, eds., *L'intégration économique en Amerique du Nord et les relations industrielles* (Université Laval).

—— 1998. 'The North American Agreement on Labor Cooperation and International Labor Solidarity' (in *Memorias: Encuentro Trinacional de Laboralistas Democraticos*, 185. D.F.: Universidad Nacional Autonoma de Mexico).

—— 1998. 'A Fast Track for Labor' *The American Prospect* (September–October, 1998).

—— 1997. 'NAFTA's Labor Side Accord: A Three-Year Accounting' 3 *NAFTA: Law and Business Review of the Americas*, 3:6 (Kluwer Law International/ Southern Methodist University School of Law).

—— 1997. 'Another Look at NAFTA' *Dissent* magazine (Winter 1997).

—— 1995. 'The First NAFTA Labor Cases: A New International Labor Rights Regime Takes Shape' *United States-Mexico Law Journal*, 3:159 (University of New Mexico Law School).

—— 1995. 'Going Multilateral: The Evolution of US Hemispheric Labor Rights Policy Under GSP and NAFTA' 10 *Connecticut Journal of International Law*, 10: 337.

—— 1995. ' … And the Twain Shall Meet? A North-South Controversy Over Labor Rights and Trade' *Labor Research Review*, 23:51.

—— 1994. 'Los Sindicatos Norteamericanos y el Tratado de Libre Comercio' *Revista de Trabajo* (julio-agosto 1994) (Ministry of Labor of Argentina).

—— 1994. 'American Trade Unions and NAFTA' (in Hideo Totsuka et al., eds., *International Trade Unionism at the Current Stage of Economic Globalization and Regionalization* (Proceedings of the International Conference held at Saitama University, Japan, 6–9 April 1994).

—— 1993. 'Labor Rights and Labor Standards in International Trade' 25 *Journal of Law and Policy in International Business*, 25:165.

—— 1993. 'International Labor Rights and the Sovereignty Question: NAFTA and Guatemala, Two Case Studies' *American University Journal of International Law and Policy*, 9:117.

Audley, John J., Papademetriou, Demetrios G., Polaski, Sandra and Vaughan, Scott. 2004. *NAFTA's Promise and Reality Lessons from Mexico for the Hemisphere*. Carnegie Endowment for International Peace, available at www.ceip.org/pubs.

Bacon, David. 2004. *Children of NAFTA Labor Wars on the US/Mexico Border*. University of California Press, Berkeley, California.

Brower, Adam. 2008. 'Rethinking NAFTA's NAALC Provision: The Effectiveness of its Dispute Resolution System on the Protection of Mexican Migrant Workers in the United States.' *Indiana International & Comparative Law Review*, 18:153.

Centro de los Derechos del Migrante, Inc. & The American University Washington College of Law. 2013. Taken for a Ride: Migrant Workers in the US Fair and Carnival Industry.

Cook, Maria Lorena. 1997. 'Regional Integration and Transnational Politics: Popular Sector Strategies in the NAFTA Era.' (in Douglas Chalmers, Carlos Vilas, Katherine Roberts-Hite, Scott Martin, Kerianne Peister, and Monique Segarra, eds., *The New Politics of Inequality in Latin America: Rethinking Participation and Representation*. Oxford Press).

—— 1995. 'Mexican State-Labor Relations and the Political Implications of Free Trade.' *Latin American Perspectives*, 22:77.

—— 1994. (and Harry C. Katz, editors) *Regional Integration and Industrial Relations in North America*, Cornell University.

Cook, Maria Lorena, Lance Compa, Enrique de la Garza, Morley Gunderson, Russel Smith, Mark Thompson, and Anil Verma, 1997. 'Making Free Trade More Fair: Developments in Protecting Labor Rights.' Final Report of the IRRA-NAFTA Committee for 1996–1997.

Council of Ministers, 1999. 'Review of the North American Agreement on Labor Cooperation.' Www.naalc.org/english/publications/review.htm.

Damgaard, Bodil. 1998. 'ACLAN: Experiencias y Tendencias Despues de Cinco Anos.' (in *Memorias: Encuentro Trinacional de Laboralistas Democraticos* D.F.: Universidad Nacional Autonoma de Mexico).

Delp, Linda et al. 2004. *NAFTA's Labor Side Agreement: Fading Into Oblivion?* University of California Los Angeles Center for Labor Research and Education, available at http://www.labor.ucla.edu/publications/nafta.pdf.

Diamond, Stephen. 1996. 'Labor Rights in the Global Economy: A Case Study of the North American Free Trade Agreement.' (in Lance Compa & Stephen Diamond, eds., *Human Rights, Labor Rights, and International Trade*. University of Pennsylvania Press).

Selected Publications

Dreiling, Michael. 1997. *Forging Solidarity in the Struggle over the North American Free Trade Agreement: Strategy and Action for Labor, Nature, and Capital.* Dissertation, University of Michigan Press.

Economic Policy Institute, Institute for Policy Studies, International Labor Rights Fund, Public Citizen's Global Trade Watch, Sierra Club, & US Business and Industrial Council Education Foundation. 1997. *The Failed Experiment: NAFTA at Three Years.* 26 June a Joint Study.

Englehart, Fredrick. 1997. 'Withered Giants: Mexican and US Organized Labor and the North American Agreement on Labor Cooperation.' *Case Western Reserve Journal of International Law*, 29:321.

Esquivel, Magdeline R. and Dr. Leoncio Lara. 1999. 'The Maquiladora Experience: Employment Law Issues in Mexico.' *NAFTA: Law and Business Review of the Americas*, 5:589.

Finbow, Robert G. 2006. The Limits of Regionalism NAFTA's Labour Accord. Ashgate Press.

Folsom, Ralph H. and Michael Wallace Gordon, David Lopez. 2000. *NAFTA: A Problem-Oriented Coursebook*, West Publishing.

Gacek, Stanley. 1999. 'The Political Context for the NAALC–The Viewpoint of the AFL–CIO and the US Labor Movement.' (in *Memorias: Encuentro Trinacional de Laboralistas Democraticos* D.F.: Universidad Nacional Autonoma de Mexico).

Gallagher, Kevin P. and Zarsky, Lyuba. 2007. The Enclave Economy: Foreign Investment and Sustainable Development in Mexico's Silicon Valley (Urban and Industrial Environments). The MIT Press.

Gomez, Napoleon. 2013. Collapse of Dignity: The Story of a Mining Tragedy and the Fight Against Greed and Corruption in Mexico. BenBella Books.

Graubart, Jonathan. 2008. Legalizing Transnational Activism The Struggle to Gain Social Change from NAFTA's Citizen Petitions. Pennsylvania State University Press.

Griffith, Kati L., 2001. Discovering 'Immployment' Law: The Constitutionality of Subfederal Immigration Regulation at Work (May 26, 2011). Yale Law & Policy Review, Vol. 29, pp. 389-451.

Grimm, Nicole L. 1998. 'The North American Agreement on Labor Cooperation and its Effects on Women Working in Mexican Maquiladoras.' *The American University Law Review*, 48:179.

Guerra, Maria Teresa and Anna L. Torriente. 1997. 'The NAALC and the Labor Laws of Mexico and the United States.' *Arizona Journal of International and Comparative Law*, 14:503.

Hertel, Shareen. 2006. Unexpected Power Conflict and Change among Transnational Activists. Cornell University Press.

Herzstein, Robert E. 1995. 'The Labor Cooperation Agreement among Mexico, Canada and the United States: Its Negotiation and Prospects.' *United States-Mexico Law Journal*, 3:121.

Human Resources and Development Canada. 2011. Summative Evaluation of the International Trade and Labour Program Final Report. Ottawa, Ontario.

Isa, John P. 1998. 'Testing the NAALC'S Dispute Resolution System: A Case Study.' *The American University Journal of Gender & Law*, 6:615.

Katz, Sheila and Mark Rowlinson, Claude Melançon and Stephanie Bernstein. 1998. 'NAALC in Canada' (in *Memorias: Encuentro Trinacional de Laboralistas Democráticos*. Universidad Nacional Autónoma de México, Mexico City).

Keck, Margaret and Kathryn Sikkink. 1998. *Activists Beyond Borders: Advocacy Networks in International Politics*. Cornell University Press.

Koerner, Reka S. 1999. 'Pregnancy Discrimination in Mexico: Has Mexico Complied With the North American Agreement on Labor Cooperation?' *Texas Forum on Civil Liberties & Civil Rights*, 4:235.

Kohout, Michal. 2008. 'The New Labor Culture and Labor Law Reform in Mexico.' *Latin American Perspectives*, 35:135.

Lall, Paul D. 2000. 'Immigrant Farmworkers and the North American Agreement on Labor Cooperation.' *Columbia Human Rights Law Review*, 31:597.

Leary, Virginia. 1997. 'Nonbinding Accords in the Field of Labor.' (in Edith Brown Weiss, ed., *International Compliance with Nonbinding Accords*. American Society of International Law).

Lederman, Daniel, Maloney, William F. and Serven, Luis. 2003. *Lessons from NAFTA for Latin America & the Caribbean*. The World Bank, Washington, DC, available at http://lnweb18.worldbank.org/LAC/LAC.nsf/ECADocByUnid/32E02C48D1A7695685256CBB0060CA65?Opendocument.

Levinson, Jerome. 1999. 'Certifying International Worker Rights: A Practical Alternative.' *Comparative Labor Law & Policy Journal*, 20:401.

Lowe, Sarah. 1997. ' The First American Case Under the North American Agreement for Labor Cooperation.' *University of Miami Law Review*, 51:481.

Maquiladora Health & Safety Support Network. 2007. 'Workplace Health and Safety Survey And Medical Screening of Miners At Grupo Mexico's Copper Mine Cananea, Sonora, Mexico.' Maquiladora Health & Safety Support Network, Berkeley, California, available at www.igc.org/mhssn.

McGuinness, Michael Joseph. 2000. 'The Politics of Labor Regulation in North America: A Reconsideration of Labor Law Enforcement in Mexico.' *University of Pennsylvania Journal of International Economic Law*, 21:1.

—— 1998. 'The Landscape of Labor Law Enforcement in North America: An Examination of Mexico's Labor Regulatory Policy and Practice.' *Law and Policy in International Business*, 29:365.

McKennirey, John S. 1996. 'Labor in the International Economy.' *Canada-United States Law Journal*, 22:183.

Mearsheimer, John J. 1994. 'The False Promise of International Institutions.' *International Security*, 19:5.

Memorias: Encuentro Trinacional de Laboralistas Democráticos. 1998. Universidad Nacional Autónoma de México, Mexico City.

Middlebrook, Kevin. 1995. *The Paradox of Revolution: Labor, the State, and Authoritarianism in Mexico*. Johns Hopkins University Press.

Montgomery, David. 1996. 'Labor Rights and Human Rights: A Historical Perspective.' (in Lance Compa & Stephen Diamond, eds., *Human Rights, Labor Rights, and International Trade*. University of Pennsylvania Press).

Moody, Kim. 1997. *Workers in a Lean World*. Verso.

Muniz, Manuel Fuentes. 1995. 'The NAFTA Labor Side Accord in Mexico and its Repercussions for Workers.' *Connecticut Journal of International Law*, 10:379.

Selected Publications

Nunez, Osvaldo. 1996. 'Quebec's Perspective on Social Aspects and the Broadening of Free Trade in the Americas.' *Connecticut Journal of International Law*, 11:279.

Oliver, Ranko Shiraki. 2007. 'In the Twelve Years of NAFTA, the Treaty Gave to Me ... What, Exactly: An Assessment of Economic, Social, and Political Developments in Mexico since 1994 and Their Impact on Mexican Immigration into the United States.' *Harvard Latino Law Review*, 10:53.

Perez-Lopez, Jorge F. 1995. 'The Institutional Framework of the North American Agreement on Labor Cooperation.' *United States-Mexico Law Journal*, 3:133.

—— 1995. 'The Promotion of International Labor Standards and NAFTA: Retrospect and Prospects.' *Connecticut Journal of International Law*, 10:427.

Pier, Carol. 1998. 'Labor Rights in Chile and NAFTA Labor Standards: Questions of Compatibility on the Eve of Free Trade.' *Comparative Labor Law & Policy Journal*, 19:185.

Pomeroy, Laura Okin. 1996. 'The Labor Side Agreement Under the NAFTA: Analysis of its Failure to Include Strong Enforcement Provisions and Recommendations for Future Labor Agreements Negotiated with Developing Countries.' *George Washington Journal of International Law & Economics*, 29:769.

Public Citizen. 2014. NAFTA's 20-Year Legacy and the Fate of the Trans-Pacific Partnership. Public Citizen Global Trade Watch, Washington, DC.

Salzman, James. 1999–2000. 'Labor Rights, Globalization and Institutions: the Role and Influence of the Organization for Economic Cooperation and Development.' *Michigan Journal of International Law*, 21:769.

Schurtman, Monica. 2005. 'Los "Jonkeados" and the NAALC: The Autotrim/ Customtrim Case and its Implications for Submissions Under the NAFTA Labor Side Agreement.' *Arizona Journal of International and Comparative Law*, 22:291.

Scott, Robert E., Salas, Carlos and Campbell, Bruce. 2006. 'Revisiting NAFTA Still not working for North America's workers.' The Economic Policy Institute, Washington, DC, available at *http://www.epi.org/content.cfm/bp173*.

Segenberger, Werner and Wilkinson, Frank. 1995. 'Globalization and Labour Standards.' (in Jonathan Michie and John Grieve Smith, eds., *Managing the Global Economy*. Oxford University Press).

Shelton, Dinah. 1997. 'Compliance with International Human Rights Soft Law.' (in Edith Brown Weiss, ed., *International Compliance with Nonbinding Accords*. American Society of International Law).

Summers, Clyde. 1999. 'NAFTA's Labor Side Agreement and International Labor Standards,' *The Journal of Small and Emerging Business Law*, 3:173.

Torres, Blanca. 1996. 'Redes y Coaliciones en el Proceso de Negociacion y Aprobacion del Tratado de Libre Comercio de America del Norte.' (in Arturo Borja, Guadalupe Gonzalez & Brian J.R. Stevenson, eds., *Regionalismo y Poder en America: Los limites del neorrealismo* CIDE).

Trubek, David M., Jim Mosher, and Jeffrey S. Rothstein. 2000. 'Transnationalism in the Regulation of Labor Relations: International Regimes and Transnational Advocacy Networks.' *Law and Social Inquiry*, 25:1187.

US Chamber of Commerce. 2013. NAFTA Triumphant Assessing Two Decades in Trade, Growth, and Jobs. Washington, DC.

Villarreal, M. Angeles, and Ian F. Fergusson. 2013. "NAFTA at 20: Overview and Trade Effects," US Congressional Research Service, Washington, DC.Weiss, Marley S. 1998. 'International Treaties and Constitutional Systems of the United States, Mexico, and Canada.' *The Maryland Journal of International Law & Trade*, 22:185.

Williams, Heather. 1999. 'Mobile Capital and Transborder Labor Rights Mobilization.' *Politics and Society*, 27:139.

Williams, Louise D. 1996. 'Trade, Labor, Law and Development: Opportunities and Challenges for Mexican Labor Arising from the North American Free Trade Agreement.' *Brooklyn Journal of International Law*, 22:361.

Selected Publications

Selected Websites

http://www.naalc.org (Secretariat of the Commission for Labor Cooperation)
http://www.dol.gov/dol/ilab/ (US Department of Labor, Bureau of International Labor Affairs)
http://labour.hrdc-drhc.gc.ca/doc/lab-trav/ (Canada Office of Inter-American Labour Cooperation)
http://www.stps.gob.mx/ (Mexico Department of Labor and Social Prevision, Office of International Affairs)

Selected Websites

Index

The numbers refer to paragraphs.

When several paragraphs are dedicated to the same word, only the first paragraph is noted in the index with the indication 'and following ones' (*et seq.*).

Abascal Carranza, Carlos: 198, 202, 231, 233, 300
Accor: 509
Aerovías de México: 186 *et seq.*
AFA (*see* Association of Flight Attendants)
AFL–CIO: 67, 78, 82, 143, 190, 192, 210, 211, 257, 295, 381, 393–394, 428, 444, 449-450, 512, 527, 534, 544,
AFSC (*see* American Friends Service Committee)
Alberta: 118, 453, 467
American Friends Service Committee: 157
América Móvil: 491, 495
AMLO (*see* López Obrador, Andrés Manuel)
ANAD (*see Asociación Nacional de Abogados Democraticos*)
Angelica Corporation: 228–229
Apple industry (Washington state): 274 *et seq.*, 383, 425 *et seq.*
Arbitral panel: 31, 53, 66, 100 *et seq.*, 252
Arbitration: 27, 32
Alabama: 345 *et seq.*
Arizona: 345 *et seq.*, 352 *et seq.*
Asociación Nacional de Abogados Democraticos: 157, 162, 169, 345–346
ASPA (*see* Mexican Airline Pilots Union)
ASSA (*see* Flight Attendants Union)
Association of Flight Attendants (United States): 186 *et seq.*
Autotrim: 192 *et seq.*
Aviacsa Airlines: 235 *et seq.*
AWPA (*see* Migrant and Seasonal Agricultural Workers Protection Act (US))

Bahrain: 534 *et seq.*
BLE (*see* Brotherhood of Locomotive Engineers)
Boeing: 370
Breed Technologies (*see* Autotrim)
British Columbia: 40, 118–119, 496
Brennan Center: 317
Brotherhood of Locomotive Engineers: 447
Bush, George Herbert Walker: 1, 2, 6, 16
Bush, George Walker: 44, 46, 145

CAFTA-DR (*see* Free Trade Agreement (US–Central America Dominican Republic))
CANACINTRA: 174
Calderón Hinojosa, Felipe: 45, 234, 258–264
Canada (special provisions): 114 *et seq.*
Canadian Auto Workers: 444
Canadian Labour Congress: 10, 67, 257, 324, 377–378, 496, 511
Cámara Nacional del Autotransporte de Carga (Mexico): 352
CANACAR (*see Cámara Nacional del Autotransporte de Carga*)
Cárdenas, Cuauhtemoc: 3
Carnival and Fair Workers: 331 *et seq.*
Cases (*see* Submissions or Public Communications)
CAW (*see* Canadian Auto Workers)
CCE (Mexico): 385
CDM (*see Centro de Derechos de Mujeres*)
CDM (*see Centro de los Derechos del Migrante*)
Central Independiente de Obreros Agrícolas y Campesinos: 302, 304
Centro de Derechos de Mujeres (Honduras): 544, 546
Centro de los Derechos del Migrante (US):

331, 343
CFE (*see Comisión Federal de Electricidad*)
Change to Win: 444
Chao, Elaine: 198, 201, 202, 300
Charter of Rights and Freedoms (Canada): 35, 362
Chrysler: 443
Child labor: 14, 31, 34, 50, 64, 83, 93, 100–103, 105, 133, 177, 237 et seq., 484, 518, 521, 538 *et seq.*
Chinese Staff and Workers' Association: 298
Cintas: 224–225
CIOAC (*see Central Independiente de Obreros Agrícolas y Campesinos*)
CJM (*see* Coalition for Justice in the Maquiladoras)
CLC (*see* Canadian Labour Congress)
Clinton, Bill: 7, 8, 16, 392, 393, 404-405,
Clinton, Hillary Rodham: 223, 392
Coalition for Justice in the Maquiladoras: 157, 192
Coalition of Latin American Banana Unions (COLSIBA): 141
Coco Tex: 224 *et seq.*
COECE (Mexico): 385
COLSIBA (*see* Coalition of Latin American Banana Unions)
Columbia University law school: 192
Comisión Federal de Electricidad (Mexico): 257 *et seq.*
Commission for Labor Cooperation: 58 *et seq.*
Common Frontiers: 10
Communications Workers of America: 167–168, 266, 268, 382, 435
Complaints (*see* Public Communications or Submissions)
CONAPRED (*see* National Council on the Prevention of Discrimination (Mexico))
CONCAMIN (Mexico): 385
Confederación de Trabajadores de México: 67, 140, 181 *et seq.*, 210, 214, 233, 243, 280, 428, 450, 505, 507
Confédération des Syndicats Nationaux: 378
Continental/Euzkadi case: 492
Constitution (Canada, Mexico, United States): 34 *et seq.*, 163, 165, 166, 186, 264, 326, 345, 349, 350,
Cooperative activities: 30, 49, 59, 85, 116, 120 *et seq.*, 151, 205, 362, 370-372, 384, 438-439, 464, 465–466, 475, 522
Cooperative consultations: 86 *et seq.*
COPARMEX: 231, 233
Core labor standards: 29, 377, 482, 518
Corporatism (Mexico): 11, 43, 389, 469
Council for International Business (United States): 384
Council of Ministers (NAALC): 59 *et seq.*
Cross-Border Trucking: 352 *et seq.*
CSN (*see Confédération des Syndicats Nationaux*)
CSWA (*see* Chinese Staff and Workers' Association)
CTM (*see Confederación de Trabajadores de México*)
Culture (Canada policy): 23
Custom trim (*see* Autotrim)
CWA (*see* Communications Workers of America)

Daimler-Chrysler: 192
Declaration of Fundamental Principles and Rights at Work (ILO): 29, 370, 513, 518, 521
Democratic Revolutionary Party (*see Partido Revolucionario Democrático*)
Dominican Republic: 79, 83, 392, 477, 515, 526, 538 et seq.
Duro Bag: 210 *et seq.*

ECE (*see* Evaluation Committee of Experts)
Echlin (*see* ITAPSA)
Economic reforms (Mexico): 2, 3, 12
Economic sanctions (*see* Sanctions)
EFCO: 288
Energy (Mexico policy): 22
Environmental Protection Agency (US): 207
EPA (*see* Environmental Protection Agency)
Equipo Pueblo: 11
Espinosa, Patricia: 223
EU (*see* European Union)
European Union: 20, 24, 92, 141, 145, 418, 517
Evaluation Committee of Experts: 70, 90 *et seq.*, 170, 200, 252, 294, 310, 366, 386
Excellon: 496 *et seq.*

Executive Director (Secretariat): 60 *et seq.*

Farm Labor Organizing Committee: 306, 330, 445
Farmworker Justice Fund: 302
Fast-track negotiation authority: 392, 396, 411
FAT (*see Frente Auténtico del Trabajo*)
FDC (*see Frente Democrático Campesino*)
Federal Law to Prevent and Eliminate Discrimination (Mexico): 173–174, 261
Federal Motor Carrier Safety Administration (US): 352-353
Fisheries ministry union: 136, 162 et seq.
FJF (*see* Farmworker Justice Fund)
Flight Attendants Union (Mexico): 186 *et seq.*
FLOC (*see* Farm Labor Organizing Committee)
FMCSA (*see* Federal Motor Carrier Safety Administration)
Ford: 192, 443
Four-year review (of NAALC): 372 *et seq.*
Fox Quesada, Vicente: 44–46, 231, 233
Free Trade Agreement (Canada–Chile): 513, 521
Free Trade Agreement (Canada–Colombia): 513, 521
Free Trade Agreement (Canada–Costa Rica): 513, 521
Free Trade Agreement (Canada–Honduras): 514, 521
Free Trade Agreement (Canada–Jordan): 513, 521
Free Trade Agreement (Canada–Panama): 513, 521
Free Trade Agreement (Canada–Peru): 513, 521
Free Trade Agreement (US–Australia): 79, 515, 516
Free Trade Agreement (US–Bahrain): 75, 79, 84, 133, 515, 516, 526, 534 *et seq.*
Free Trade Agreement (US–Canada): 4, 10
Free Trade Agreement (US–Central America Dominican Republic): 75, 79, 83, 85, 392, 477, 515-516, 526, 527 *et seq.*, 538 *et seq.*, 544 *et seq.*
Free Trade Agreement (US–Chile): 78, 79, 483, 515, 516
Free Trade Agreement (US–Colombia): 79, 392, 515, 516
Free Trade Agreement (US–Jordan): 78–79, 92, 146, 515, 516, 518, 519
Free Trade Agreement (US–South Korea): 79, 515, 516
Free Trade Agreement (US–Morocco): 79, 515, 516
Free Trade Agreement (US–Oman): 79, 515, 516
Free Trade Agreement (US–Panama): 79, 515, 516
Free Trade Agreement (US–Peru): 79, 82, 84, 515, 516, 526, 531 et seq.
Free Trade Agreement (US–Singapore): 78-79, 84, 515, 516
Frente Auténtico del Trabajo: 11–12, 181, 275, 324, 389, 423-424, 427-428, 494,
Frente Democrático Campesino: 275, 427
Fruit of the Loom: 411
FTVO-CROC (*see* Progressive Union of Workers of the Textile Industry)

General Electric: 136, 147 *et seq.*, 423-424, 445
General Motors: 192, 379, 443GM (*see* General Motors)
Grúpo México: 244 *et seq.*, 260
Grupo Modelo: 494
Guatemala: 78, 85, 341, 487, 495, 515, 526, 527 *et seq.*

H-2A Visa Workers: 302 *et seq.*, 342
H-2B Visa Workers: 305, 317 *et seq.*, 331 *et seq.*, 342
Haitian Migrant Workers: 538 *et seq.*
Hallmark: 210
Han Young: 136, 175 *et seq.*, 436,
Harmonization: 14, 28, 381, 452, 457, 461, 469, 471
Harper, Stephen: 44, 47
Hispanic Alliance for Hispanic Health: 207
Hispanic Forum on a Safe and Healthy Environment: 207–208
Hoffman Plastic Compounds: 307 *et seq.*
Honduras: 314, 513, 514, 515, 517, 521, 526, 544 *et seq.*
Honeywell: 136, 147 *et seq.*, 424
HRW (*see* Human Rights Watch)
Human Rights Watch: 162, 169 *et seq.*, 380
Hyundai: 175–176, 436

Index

IBT (*see* Teamsters Union)
IFA (*see* International Framework Agreement)
ILO (*see* International Labor Organization)
ILRF (*see* International Labor Rights Forum)
Immigration and Naturalization Service (United States): 283 *et seq.*
IMSS (*see* Mexican Institute of Social Security)
Income security: 128
Independent advisors' report (four-year review): 372 *et seq.*
Industrial Commission of Arizona: 352 *et seq.*
Industrial Relations Research Association: 390
Informative session (Mexico): 75, 277
INS (*see* Immigration and Naturalization Service)
Intellectual property rights: 15, 20–21, 381
International Framework Agreement: 141
International Labor Organization: 29, 96, 98, 133, 163, 165, 231, 235, 253–254, 261, 325, 326, 329, 330, 364 *et seq.*, 384, 476, 478, 518 et seq., 536, 537,
International Labor Rights Forum (Formerly the International Labor Rights Fund): 157, 162, 169, 356, 379, 428
Investor–state provision (NAFTA): 21
IPR (*see* Intellectual property rights)
IRRA (*see* Industrial Relations Research Association)
ITAPSA: 136, 181 *et seq.*, 436

Japan: 19, 273, 392, 480, 517
Job losses: 10, 392 *et seq.*
Jurisdiction (labor law): 50 *et seq.*

Kodak: 411
Kuk Dong (*see* Mexmode)

Labor markets: 59, 66, 87, 125, 372
Labor Policy Association (United States): 287 *et seq.*
Labor law reform (Mexico): 134, 230 *et seq.*
Labor laws: 124, 126, 130
Labor principles: 9, 15, 28–29, 31, 50 *et seq.*, 74, 88–89, 92, 121, 130, 146, 230, 237, 259, 276, 302, 332, 346, 357, 364, 370, 381, 390, 439, 461, 474, 476,
Levi Strauss: 400, 411
LFPED (*see* Federal Law to Prevent and Eliminate Discrimination (Mexico))
Life Uniform: 228–229
Light and Power (*see* Luz y Fuerza)
López Obrador, Andrés Manuel: 45
Lozano, Javier: 261
LPA (*see* Labor Policy Association)
Luz y Fuerza (Light and Power – Mexico): 257 *et seq.*

MAI (*see* Multilateral Agreement on Investment)
Manitoba: 118
Maquiladoras: 42, 147, 157, 169 *et seq.*, 214, 424, 466,
Maquiladora Health and Safety Support Network: 201, 255
Markey Tex: 224 *et seq.*
Matamoros Garment: 144, 153, 213 *et seq.*
Mattel: 237, 238
Maxi-Switch: 136, 167–168
McDonald's: 356 *et seq.*
Memorandum of Understanding: 6, 202, 223, 283 *et seq.*
Mexican Airline Pilots Union: 235 *et seq.*
Mexican Institute of Social Security: 196, 197, 260
Mexmode: 213
Mexican National Union of Miners and Metal Workers: 247 *et seq.*, 496 *et seq.*, 504 *et seq.*
MHSSN (*see* Maquiladora Health and Safety Support Network)
Michelin/Uniroyal case: 493
Migrant and Seasonal Agricultural Workers Protection Act (US): 303, 317
Migrant workers: 24, 29, 46, 50, 53, 93, 123, 128, 131, 132, 141, 202, 203, 225, 237, 274 *et seq.*, 280 *et seq.*, 283 *et seq.*, 298 *et seq.*, 302 *et seq.*, 307 *et seq.*, 317 *et seq.*, 331 *et seq.*, 345 *et seq.*, 425 *et seq.*, 448, 474, 519, 521, 538 *et seq.*
Ministerial Agreement (*see* Ministerial Declaration)
Ministerial Declaration: 131, 172, 185, 191, 200–203, 204, 210 *et seq.*, 246, 305, 310, 323, 342–344, 489,
Monetary enforcement assessment: 108 *et seq.*
MOU (*see* Memorandum of Understanding)
Mount Olive Pickle Company: 306

MSAWPA (*see* Migrant and Seasonal Agricultural Workers Protection Act (US))
MSPA (*see* Migrant and Seasonal Agricultural Workers Protection Act (US))
Mulroney, Brian: 1, 4, 6, 10
Multilateral Agreement on Investment: 20

NAAEC (*see* North American Agreement on Environmental Cooperation)
NAID Center (*see* North American Integration and Development Center)
NAO (*see* National Administrative Office)
National Action Party (Mexico) (*see Partido Acción Nacional*)
National Administrative Office: 67 *et seq.*, 485
National Advisory Committees (to NAOs): 69, 371
National Contact Point: 85, 228, 485 *et seq.*, 523
National Council on the Prevention of Discrimination (Mexico): 173–174, 261
National Labor Relations Board (United States): 254, 269, 272 *et seq.*, 287 *et seq.*, 307 *et seq.*, 510
National Labor Relations Act: 303, 338, 371,
National Labor Relations Act, Section 8(a)(2) (United States): 287 *et seq.*
National Institute of Occupational Safety and Health: 199
National Mobilization Against Sweat Shops: 298
National Safety Council: 207
New York Workers' Compensation: 298 *et seq.*
NCP (*see* National Contact Point)
NGOs (*see* Non-governmental organizations)
Niemann Marcus: 210
NIOSH (*see* National Institute of Occupational Safety and Health)
NMASS (*see* National Mobilization Against Sweat Shops)
Non-governmental organizations: 8, 11–12, 30, 72, 75, 122, 157, 175, 192, 218, 272, 361, 376 *et seq.*, 436, 457, 464, 466, 471, 475, 484, 492, 498, 503,
North American Integration and Development Center: 403
North American Agreement on Environmental Cooperation: 9
North American OSH Working Group: 204 *et seq.*
North Carolina H-2A Workers: 302 *et seq.*
North Carolina Public Service Workers: 324 *et seq.*
Northwest Justice Project: 317
NSC (*see* National Safety Council)

Obama, Barack: 47, 81, 82, 84, 141, 145, 257, 336, 392,
Objectives (of NAALC): 49
Obligations (under NAALC): 53 *et seq.*
OCAW (*see* Oil, Chemical and Atomic Workers)
Occupational health and safety (*Autotrim* case): 192 *et seq.*
Occupational Safety and Health Administration (United States): 199
OECD (*see* Organization for Economic Cooperation and Development)
OECD Guidelines: 224, 228–229, 479 *et seq.*
Office of Trade Agreement Implementation (United States): 78, 79, 145, 230, 232, 236, 249, 252, 253, 319, 321,
Office of Trade and Labor Affairs (United States): 79 *et seq.*, 133, 143, 145, 153–154, 244–246, 253–254, 260, 265, 526, 528 *et seq.*, 531 *et seq.*, 534 *et seq.*, 538 *et seq.*, 544 *et seq.*
OIG (*see* US Department of Labor Office of the Inspector General)
Oil, Chemical and Atomic Workers: 272 *et seq.*
Ontario: 40, 118–119, 131, 222, 454
Organization for Economic Cooperation and Development: 20, 85, 142, 143, 224, 228–229, 384, 478, 479 *et seq.*
OTAI (*see* Office of Trade Agreement Implementation)
OTLA (*see* Office of Trade and Labor Affairs)

PACE (*see* Paper, Allied-Industrial, Chemical and Energy Workers International Union)
PAHO (*see* Pan American Health Organization)
PAN (*see Partido Acción Nacional*)
Pan American Health Organization: 207

Paper, Allied-Industrial, Chemical and Energy Workers International Union: 210 *et seq.*
Partido Acción Nacional: 44, 45, 233, 234
Partido Revolucionario Democrático: 45, 231, 233
Partido Revolucionario Institutional: 11, 12, 43, 47, 233, 368, 379, 382, 427, 456
Pasta de Conchos Copper Mine: 247 *et seq.*
Pearl Roundabout: 534 *et seq.*
Peña Nieto, Enrique: 47, 234
Pesca union (*see* Fisheries ministry union)
Peso devaluation (Mexico): 395, 404
Perez, Thomas E.: 342
Peru: 531 *et seq.*
PKC Group: 504 *et seq.*
Plant closings: 126, 266 *et seq.*, 397 *et seq.*, 408
Porteadores del Noroeste SA de CV: 352 *et seq.*
Preamble (NAALC): 6, 48
Principles (*see* Labor principles)
Pregnancy testing: 169 *et seq.*, 173, 174, 234, 240, 245, 379, 466, 546
PRD (*see Partido Revolucionario Democrático*)
PRI (*see Partido Revolucionario Institucional*)
Prince Edward Island: 118, 372
Progressive Union of Workers of the Textile Industry: 237 *et seq.*
Public communications: 71 *et seq.*, 80–85, 143, 386 *et seq.*, 486 *et seq.* (*see also* Submissions)
Public hearings (US, Canada NAOs): 75 *et seq.*, 84, 139, 148, 152, 154, 158, 164, 168, 170, 178, 184, 190, 194, 216, 244, 252, 277, 294, 360, 375, 384–385, 422, 436, 489 (*see also* Submissions)
Puebla (Tarrant and Matamoros Garment): 144, 213 *et seq.*
PUMA: 214, 218

Quebec: 40, 118, 356 *et seq.*, 378, 453
Solis, Hilda: 330

Rail unions: 446 *et seq.*
Red Mexicana ante el Libre Comercio: 11–12
Reich, Robert: 156
Research reports (Secretariat): 124 *et seq.*
Right-to-work laws (United States): 453
Rincón Gallardo, Gilberto: 173
RMALC (*see Red Mexicana ante el Libre Comercio*)
Rubie's: 237 *et seq.*
Rules of procedure (arbitral panels): 102 *et seq.*
Rules of procedure (ECEs): 97 *et seq.*
Rural Letter Carriers (Canada): 361 *et seq.*

Salinas, Carlos: 1, 2–4, 6
Sanctions: 8–9, 21, 31 *et seq.*, 53, 92, 101, 111-112, 138, 177, 193, 200, 227, 252, 294, 426, 439, 462–463
Sanyo: 273
Secretariat: 8–9, 60 *et seq.*, 68, 70, 91, 123, 124 *et seq.*, 172, 206, 223, 256, 267, 270, 310, 338, 366, 370, 371, 373, 384, 388, 390, 439
SEIU (*see* Service Employees International Union)
Service Employees International Union: 345–346, 350–351, 444
Sindicato de Telefonistas de la República Mexicana: 266 *et seq.*, 435
Sindicato Mexicano de Electricistas (Mexico): 257 *et seq.*
SME (*see Sindicato Mexicano de Electricistas*)
SNTMMSRM (*see* Mexican National Union of Miners and Metal Workers)
Solec: 272–273
Sony: 136, 157 *et seq.*
Sovereignty: 8–9, 22, 26, 28, 140, 187, 329, 365, 375, 385, 387, 459, 470, 473, 476
Sprint: 126, 135–137, 254, 266 *et seq.*, 384, 435
St Mary's Law School: 192
Standing (legal): 74, 146, 281
STIMAHCS: 183
STRM (*see Sindicato de Telefonistas de la República Mexicana*)
Submissions: 30, 71 *et seq.*, 89, 99, 133 *et seq.*, 367–368, 376, 380, 384–385, 386, 388–389, 439, 466, 468
Sugarcane: 538 *et seq.*
Sunbeam: 379
Supreme Court (Canada): 35

Supreme Court (Mexico): 161, 166, 236, 250, 264-265
Supreme Court (US): 44, 308 *et seq.*, 326, 345, 349
SUTSP (*see* Fisheries Ministry Union)

TAA (*see* Trade Adjustment Assistance)
TAESA (*see Transportes Aéreas Ejecutivos*)
Tarrant: 144, 153, 213 *et seq.*
Teamsters Union: 147, 275, 356, 424, 426 *et seq.*, 433, 444
TPP (*see* Trans-Pacific Partnership)
Trade Adjustment Assistance (United States): 407–409
Trade sanctions (*see* Sanctions)
Trade union density: 41–42
Trade union cross-border collaboration: 141, 176, 213, 419 *et seq.*, 440–441
Transportes Aéreas Ejecutivos: 189 *et seq.*
Trico Marine Services case: 510 *et seq.*

UAW (*see* United Auto Workers)
UE (*see* United Electrical Workers)
UFCW (*see* United Food and Commercial Workers)
UFW (*see* United Farm Workers)
Unión Nacional de Trabajadores: 231, 257, 275, 427, 495
UNITE-HERE: 224 *et seq.*
United Auto Workers: 56, 156, 382, 443
United Farm Workers: 275, 426 et seq.
United Steel Workers: 247 *et seq.*, 496
United Food and Commercial Workers: 444
United Electrical Workers: 143, 147, 151, 324, 326, 330, 389, 423 et seq., 445
UNT (*see Unión Nacional de Trabajadores*)
UPM Kymmene case: 508
USAS (*see* United Students Against Sweatshops)
USCIB (*see* Council for International Business)
US Department of Labor Office of the Inspector General: 61
US Labor Education in the Americas Project: 237
US LEAP (*see* US Labor Education in the Americas Project)
United Students Against Sweatshops: 144, 213 *et seq.*
USWA (*see* United Steel Workers)

Volkswagen: 141

Washington Office on Latin America: 230, 237
WOLA (*see* Washington Office on Latin America)
Women workers: 50, 93, 128, 133, 145, 169 *et seq.*, 214, 223, 226, 240, 245, 261, 263, 304, 324-325, 361, 397, 399, 400, 539, 544, 546
Worker Rights Consortium: 141, 144, 216
Workers' Compensation: 298 *et seq.*, 352 *et seq.*
WRC (*see* Worker Rights Consortium)

Yucatan – Markey Tex and Coco Tex: 224 *et seq.*

Zedillo, Ernesto: 186

Index

www.ingramcontent.com/pod-product-compliance
Lightning Source LLC
Chambersburg PA
CBHW071446230926
51846CB00001B/356
* 9 7 8 9 0 4 1 1 6 0 1 0 2 *